FIDEL CASTRO:
Birán to Cinco Palmas

FIDEL CASTRO:
Birán to Cinco Palmas

EUGENIO SUÁREZ PÉREZ
ACELA A. CANER ROMÁN

Translated by:
Angie Todd

EDITORIAL JOSÉ MARTÍ

Original title in Spanish: *Fidel Castro: De Birán a Cinco Palmas*
Editing: *Mayra Fernández Perón and Josefina Ezpeleta Laplace*
Design and Desktop Publishing: *Enrique Mayol Amador*

ISBN: 959-09-0231-6

INSTITUTO CUBANO DEL LIBRO
Editorial JOSÉ MARTÍ
Publicaciones en Lenguas Extranjeras
Calzada No. 259 e/ J e I, Vedado
Ciudad de La Habana, Cuba

CONTENTS

INTRODUCTION

Fidel Castro, the maximum leader of the Cuban Revolution, is known throughout the world for his rebellious spirit, his clear and profound thinking, his vibrant use of language, his immense culture, his absolute sincerity and his unlimited generosity and solidarity. As Ernesto "Che" Guevara said, Fidel is "a leader of world stature at a height seldom known to history."

Approaching the life and works of Fidel does not merely signify coming into contact with the most noble and revolutionary ideas and actions of the contemporary world, but also with moments in the history of Cuba and the Americas that, at times, would appear to have been taken from a fabulous adventure story: It is to know a man of principles, an exceptional man.

Fidel Castro: Birán to Cinco Palmas is a book of impassioned passages that brings us closer to the fertile life of the Cuban president and arouses our interest in further research on this man, as sensitive as he is a revolutionary. That is, in essence, the supreme objective of this work.

Fruit of meticulous bibliographical research and selection, this book compiles excerpts from interviews with the Commander in Chief of the Cuban Revolution and his closest comrades in study and in arms, which give the book an intimate and colloquial tone. Also included in its pages are excerpts from Fidel's letters, speeches, indictments, defenses and charges, together with press notes, research material by eminent academics, and testimonies from collaborators, workers and campesinos whom he helped in difficult circumstances.

All the documented memoirs in the book have been published and their references are to be found at the end of each chapter, so that interested readers can have access to the sources and further explore the distinct stages or facets of Fidel's life.

In order to promote understanding of the text and make it easier reading, short paragraphs have been inserted to connect the diverse material compiled.

On account of the book's particular characteristics and because we are not in the presence of a complete or completed work, the historical events narrated do not always appear in rigorous chronological order, although they have been organized with a certain time orientation.

In such a context, this book, which covers the first three decades of Fidel's life, begins with details of his birth on August 13, 1926, in Birán, an almost forgotten point in the geography of the former Oriente Province; moves through distinct facets related to his childhood and adolescence, studies and hazardous life as a revolutionary combatant; and concludes on December 5, 1956, the date of the reencounter with his brother Raúl in Cinco Palmas after the Alegría del Pío dispersal, where Fidel, optimistic and confident in the power of his ideas and Cuban dignity, confirmed that seven rifles were enough to win the Revolution.

So, enjoy your reading of these pages that lead us, in Fidel's hand, along the glorious route from Birán to Cinco Palmas.

THE EARLY YEARS

I WAS BORN A GUERRILLA

B irán, a farm located in the former province of Oriente, not far from the Bay of Nipe, was the geographic point where, in the summer of 1926, the family of Ángel Castro Argiz and Lina Ruz González was increased by the birth of their third son, whom they named Fidel Alejandro.

Many years later, as a prominent statesman, Fidel Alejandro Castro Ruz referred to his birth and life in that remote place, asserting he was born:

On August 13, 1926. If you want to know the time, I think it was around 2:00 in the morning. Maybe that had something to do with my guerrilla spirit, with my revolutionary activities. Nature and the time of my birth must have had some influence. There are other factors that should be taken into account now, right?—what kind of a day it was and whether or not Nature has anything to do with the lives of men. Anyway, I think I was born early in the morning—I think I was told that once. Therefore, I was born a guerrilla, because I was born at around 2:00 in the morning.[1]

My father was the son of an extremely poor farmer in Galicia. At the time of Cuba's last war of independence, which began in 1895, he was sent here as a Spanish soldier to fight. So here my father was, very young and drafted into military service as a soldier in the Spanish Army. When the war was over, he was shipped back to Spain, but it seems he'd taken a liking to Cuba. Along with many other immigrants, he left for Cuba in the early years of this [20th] century. Penniless and with no relatives here, he got himself a job.

Important investments were made in that period. U.S. citizens had seized the best land in Cuba and had started to destroy forests, build sugar mills and grow sugarcane, all of which involved big investments in those days. My father worked in one of the sugar mills.

... Later, he apparently got a group of workers together. He managed them and contracted the men to work for a U.S. firm. He set up a sort of small enterprise that, as far as I can remember, cleared land to plant sugarcane or felled trees to supply sugar mills with firewood. It's possible that, as the organizer of that enterprise with a group of men under him, he began to make a profit. In other words, my father was clearly a very active, enterprising person, and he had an instinctive sense of organization.[2]

My maternal grandparents were also very poor; they came from a very poor family. My grandfather hauled sugarcane in an ox cart. He, like my mother, was born in the western part of the country, in Pinar del Río Province. During the early years of the century he and the rest of the family moved to what used to be called Oriente Province, 1000 kilometers away from his home, in an ox cart, and settled there.

... Two of my mother's brothers also worked there as ox-cart drivers.[3]

... she [his mother] learned how to read and write when she was practically an adult.

... My mother was practically illiterate. She learned how to read and write all by herself. I don't remember her ever having a teacher other than herself. She never mentioned one. With great effort she tried to learn. I never heard of her ever having gone to school.[4]

... So like my mother, he [his father] also learned how to read and write all by himself, through sheer determination.[5]

NOT LANDOWNER STOCK

I was born into a landowning family, but not of landowner stock. What do I mean by that? My father was a Spanish campesino from a very humble family, who came to Cuba at the beginning of the century as a Spanish émigré.

He began to work in difficult conditions. He was an enterprising man, who made his mark and came to occupy a certain leadership position in early-century labors. He gradually accumulated money and set about acquiring land. In other words, he was successful in business and came to be the proprietor of a certain amount of land, around 1000 hectares if I remember correctly. That was not so hard in the early period of the Republic. Then he rented more land. And when I was born, it's true that I was born into the heart of what could be called a landowning family.

Now, on the other hand, my mother was a very humble campesino, very poor. For that reason the traditions of what we could call an oligarchy in the heart of my family did not exist. Nevertheless, objectively speaking, our social position at that moment was of a family that had relatively plentiful economic resources. It was an owner of land and had all the comforts—we could say—and the privileges enjoyed by a landowning family in our country.[6]

There was no bourgeois or feudal society in Birán. There weren't twenty or thirty landowners whose families would get together, always forming the same group. My father was an isolated landowner. Sometimes a friend would visit him, but we hardly ever visited anybody. My parents usually stayed home; they didn't go to visit other families. They worked all the time. So, the only people we saw were the ones who lived there. I used to go to the Haitians' quarters, to their huts, and sometimes I was scolded for it but only because I ate the dry corn they cooked. I got into trouble because I ate with them—for health, not social reasons. Nobody at home ever said, "Don't go near so-and-so." Never. They weren't class conscious; they didn't have a rich people's or landowners' mentality.[7]

... The school was a small, nondenominational school. About fifteen to twenty children went there. I was sent there because there wasn't any nursery school. I was the third oldest child in my family, and my nursery school was that school. They sent me there when I was very young. They didn't have anything else to do with me, so they sent me there with my older sister and brother.

I can't remember when I learned how to read and write. All I remember is that they used to put me in a small desk in the front row, where I could see the blackboard and listen to everything that was being said. So, it may be said that I learned in nursery school—which was the school. I think it was there that I learned reading, writing, and arithmetic. How old was I then? Probably four, or maybe five.

Religion wasn't taught in that school. You were taught the national anthem and told about the flag, the coat of arms and things like that. It was a public school.[8]

LIFE OF THE POOR

Even before being baptized I was sent to Santiago de Cuba. My teacher had led my family to believe that I was a very industrious student. She made them believe that I was smart and had a talent for learning. That was the real reason why they sent me to Santiago de Cuba when I was around five; I was taken from a world in which I lived without any material problems and taken to a city where I lived poorly and was hungry.[9]

. . . Thus I could say that I went hungry, that I was left virtually barefoot, that I had to stitch up my shoes when they broke.

I was in that situation for a year or so. It could be said that on that occasion I knew poverty.

Could that have had an influence on me? Really, I don't know, I can't be sure of that.[10]

I was poor because the teacher's family was poor. She was the only one earning any money. That was during the economic crisis of the thirties, around 1931 or 1932. The family consisted of two sisters and their father, and one of the sisters was the only one who had a job. Sometimes she wouldn't be paid or would be paid only after a long wait. During the great economic crisis of the early thirties, salaries often weren't paid and the people were very poor.

I went to Santiago de Cuba to live in a very small frame house that leaked like a sieve when it rained. The house is still there; it's still standing.

Aged just three, Fidel Alejandro clutches a book in his hands. One of the first photos to be taken of Ángel and Lina's little son.

During the school year, the teacher kept working in Birán, and her sister had to live on that salary. My family sent forty pesos for my board, an amount that had the same purchasing power as 300 or 400 pesos now. There were two of us, my older sister and me. In view of that situation of poverty, their not receiving salaries, and the fact that they wanted to save, not much money went for food. There were five people to be fed—later six, because my brother Ramón came too, a few months later.

We got a small container with a little rice, some beans, sweet potatoes, plantains, and things like that. The container arrived at noon, and it was shared first by five and then by six people, for lunch and dinner. I used to think I had a huge appetite; the food always seemed delicious. Actually, it was just that I was always hungry. It was a rough period.

Later, the teacher's sister married the Haitian consul in Santiago de Cuba. Since I happened to be there at the time and my wealthy godfather hadn't materialized and the baptism hadn't been performed—I was around five years old and, as they said, a "Jew" because I hadn't been baptized and didn't even know what it meant—a solution had to be found for the problem. I guess that this use of the term *Jew* is also linked to some religious prejudices that we can discuss later on. Anyway, finally I was baptized, and the Haitian consul became my godfather, because he'd married the teacher's sister, Belén, who was a good and noble person. She was a piano teacher, but she didn't have any work or students.[11]

… During the period I told you about, I was sent to Santiago de Cuba while still very young. I had many unmet needs and went through a lot of hardships. Around a year later, things started to improve somewhat. At one point, my parents became aware of the difficulties I was facing. They protested and even made me return to Birán. But, after the protests, the teacher's explanation, and the subsequent reconciliation, I was sent back to her house in Santiago de Cuba. The situation, of course, improved after the scandal. How much time did I spend there in all? At least two years.

In the beginning, I wasn't sent to school; my godmother gave me classes. Those classes consisted of having me study the addition, subtraction, multiplication and division tables that were printed on the cover of my notebook. I learned them by heart. I believe I learned them so well I've never forgotten them. Sometimes I can calculate almost as quickly as a computer.[12]

. . . Most of the people who have played a role in our history had mentors, outstanding teachers, or professors. Unfortunately, I've had to be my own mentor all my life. How grateful I would have been if somebody had taught me about politics, if somebody had taught me revolutionary ideas![13]

That's how it was. I had no textbook, only my notebook and some notes. And of course I learned arithmetic, reading, writing and taking notes. My spelling and handwriting must have improved a little. I think I spent around two years there just wasting my time. The only useful aspect was the experience of tough, difficult conditions, hardships, and sacrifices. I think I was the victim of exploitation, in view of the income that family got from what my parents paid them.[14]

I SHOULD HAVE BEEN A MUSICIAN

In one of his conversations with Frei Betto, evoking the days of his childhood, Fidel confessed to the eminent Brazilian friar:

I also remember the Three Wise Men. One of the beliefs that was inculcated in five-, six- and seven-year-olds was that of the Three Wise Men. . . . I must have been three or four the first time the Wise Men came. I can even remember the things they brought me: some apples, a toy car—things like that—and some candy.

January 6 was the Epiphany. We were told that the Three Wise Men, who'd traveled to pay homage to Christ when He was born, came every year to bring children presents.

I spent three Epiphanies with that family. Therefore, I must have been there at least two and a half years.

FREI BETTO: So the capitalist Santa Claus never became popular in Cuba?

FIDEL CASTRO: No, never. What we had were the Three Wise Men, who rode camels. Children wrote letters to the Three Wise Men: Caspar, Melchior and Balthazar. I can still remember my first letters. I wrote when I was five and asked them for everything—cars, trains, movie cameras, the works. I wrote long letters to the Three Wise Men on January 5, we looked for grass, and I put it under my bed with some water. The disappointments came later.

FREI BETTO: What's that about the grass?

FIDEL CASTRO: Since the Three Wise Men rode camels, you had to provide them with some grass and water, which you put under your bed.

FREI BETTO: All mixed up?

FIDEL CASTRO: Either mixed up or the grass and water next to each other.

FREI BETTO: How interesting! I didn't know that.

FIDEL CASTRO: You had to provide food and water for the camels, especially if you wanted the Three Wise Men to bring you lots of presents, everything you'd asked them for in your letter.

FREI BETTO: And what did the Three Wise Men eat?

FIDEL CASTRO: Well, I don't know. Nobody remembered to leave food for the Three Wise Men. Maybe that's why they weren't very generous with me. The camels ate the grass and drank the water, but I got very few toys in exchange. I remember that my first present was a small cardboard trumpet; just the tip was made out of metal, something like aluminum. My first present was a small trumpet the size of a pencil.

For three consecutive years, three times, I was given a trumpet; I should have become a musician. After all—The second year, the Three Wise Men brought me a trumpet that was half aluminum and half cardboard. The third time, it was a trumpet with three small keys, made completely of aluminum.[15]

MY FIRST REBELLION

Once I started attending school the education was systematic, but the most important thing was the material and environmental improvement; for the first time I had teachers, classes, friends to play with, and many other activities that I'd lacked when I was a single student studying arithmetic from the cover of a notebook. That new situation lasted up until I launched my first act of rebellion, when I was still very young.[16]

When Frei Betto asked him about the reasons that impelled him to take this decision, the leader of the Cuban Revolution replied:

I was tired of the whole situation. At the teacher's house, I'd be spanked every so often, and if I didn't behave perfectly, they threatened to send me to boarding school. Then one day I realized that I'd be better off in boarding school than in that house.[17]

Those people had had a French education. They spoke perfect French. I guess that's how they got to know the consul. I don't remember exactly how it was they'd gotten a French education. I don't know if they'd been to France or had attended a school in Haiti. They knew how to speak French and had perfect manners. Of course, I was taught those manners when I was very young. Among other things, you weren't supposed to ask for anything. The very poor children used to have a penny to buy a *rayado* or *granizado,* which is what they called snow-cones, but I couldn't ask them for anything; that was forbidden, according to the rules of French education. If I asked another boy to give me some, the children, with the selfishness characteristics of that age and the desperate poverty in which they lived—they knew the rules I had to follow—used to say, "You're begging! I'm going to tell on you!"

That family had its code, and I'm not criticizing it. You had to do this and that and the other thing. You were subjected to a lot of discipline. You had to speak in an educated way. You couldn't raise your voice. Naturally, you couldn't use any improper language. When they threatened to send me to boarding school, I was already tired and had become aware of what had happened before. I even realized that I'd been starving and that I hadn't been treated fairly. I haven't told you everything in full detail, because I don't want to make this an autobiography; I just want to touch on subjects you're interested in. So one day when I got to school, I deliberately started to break all the rules and regulations. In what amounted to a conscious act of rebellion aimed at having them send me to boarding school, I raised my voice and said all the words I'd been forbidden to use. That's the story of my first—though not my last— rebellion, which took place when I was in the first grade. I must have been seven at most; my age could be verified.[18]

A VIOLENT CONFRONTATION

In the conversation with Frei Betto, Fidel confided they sent him to boarding school:

Yes, and I began to be happy. For me, boarding school meant freedom.

FREI BETTO: How long were you at La Salle boarding school?

FIDEL CASTRO: Nearly four years. I was there for the second half of the first grade, second grade and third grade. Because of my good grades,

I was promoted to the fifth grade straight from the third grade, so I made up for one of the years I'd lost.[19]

However, although the organization of the teaching wasn't bad, serious conflicts arose and Fidel made his second rebellion. He referred to the La Salle School:

. . . Those people hadn't had the training that the Jesuits had. Moreover, they used really reprehensible methods at times. Some teachers or authorities at the school hit the students every so often. My conflict there was over that, because of an incident with another student. It was a small quarrel typical of students of that age. I had the opportunity to see how violence is used against students in what would now be called bad teaching methods. That was the first time the brother monitor in charge of the students hit me with a fair amount of violence. He slapped both sides of my face. It was a degrading and abusive thing. I was in the third grade, and I never forgot it. Later, when I was in the fifth grade, I was hit on the head twice. The last time I wouldn't put up with it, and it ended up in a violent personal confrontation between the monitor and me. After all that, I decided not to go back to that school.[20]

MY BATTLE TO STUDY

I began as a day student at the school, after Christmas vacation—and also after arguing a lot at home. I had to argue at home and demand that I be sent away to study. That's when I launched my battle to study. I had to struggle, because the people at my old school had told my parents that I'd behaved badly, and those arbitrary reports had influenced my family. I said I wouldn't accept not being allowed to study. I knew what the problem was and what was behind the conflict. It stemmed from an abusive, violent act, the physical punishment of a student. I think I had very clear ideas about the matter—the result of instinct; because of some notions of justice and dignity that I was acquiring; or perhaps because, when I was still quite young, I'd begun to see some incorrect, unfair things by which I was victimized. I began to acquire values. I was very aware of them, and I had to demand very firmly that I be sent away to study—perhaps not so much out of a love of study but rather because

I felt an injustice had been committed against me. And I was sent away to study; my mother supported me. I convinced her first, and then she convinced my father. They sent me to Santiago de Cuba again, but as a day student. . . .

Summer came and they left me there because my older sister was there studying. A black teacher from Santiago de Cuba came to tutor my sister. She was very well trained. Her name was Professor Danger. She became interested in me. Since I had nothing else to do during my vacation, I went to class with my sister, who was preparing for high school. I answered all the questions in all the subjects the teacher taught, and this made her genuinely interested in me. I wasn't old enough to enter high school, so she began to draw up a study plan for both before and during the first year of high school at the same time. Then, when I got old enough, I could take the exams. She was the first person I ever met who encouraged me; who set a goal, an objective, for me; and who motivated me. She got me interested in studying when I was that young. I think you can stimulate children at that age with a specific objective. How old was I? Ten or maybe eleven.[21]

When I was in the fifth grade, then, I went to live in the home of a businessman's family. I couldn't say they were bad people, but they weren't my family; they couldn't have the same interest, and they applied some strict even arbitrary—rules. For example, they didn't take into account the fact that I'd had problems in my other school, as I've already explained, and that I'd transferred to a more rigorous school. They didn't consider the psychological factors involved in the adaptation to a new, more demanding school and new teachers. They wanted me to get the highest grades; they demanded it. If I didn't get the highest grades, I didn't get that week's ten cents for going to the movies, five cents to buy an ice cream after the movies and five cents on Thursday for buying some comic books. I remember that clearly. There were some comic books that came from Argentina, a weekly called *El Gorrión* (The house sparrow). I read some novels there, too. *De tal palo, tal astilla* (Like father, like son) was one of them. Five cents. The normal weekly allowance was twenty-five cents. If you didn't get the highest grades, you didn't get the twenty-five cents. That measure was arbitrary and completely unfair, because they didn't take my new circumstances into account. It wasn't the right psychological approach for an eleven-year-old.[22]

... I decided to create a situation in which they had no alternative but to send me to school as a boarder. Thus, between the first and sixth grades, I had to wage three battles to solve three problems.

By the time I started to board in the sixth grade, I was getting excellent grades, and in the seventh grade I was among the top students in my class. I also gained a lot in other ways, because the world of sports and trips to the countryside and the mountains were within reach. I liked sports a lot—especially basketball, soccer and baseball.[23]

Now, certain factors contributed to develop a certain spirit of rebellion in me. We could say that I rebelled in the first place against the unjust conditions in the house of the family where I was sent at the age of five. In the very schools to which I was sent I also felt a rebellious impulse against certain injustices. We could say that during the period of my childhood, I felt the sensation of things that appeared to me unjust and that fomented a feeling of rebellion in me approximately three times. Those factors could have contributed to developing a relatively rebellious nature. That spirit of rebellion could also have manifested itself in later life.

My social relations as a boy, during school vacations, were with very poor children from the place where I lived.

I could say that in spite of my family's economic situation, in the country where I was born, I always mixed with the children of the poorest families, as there was no aristocratic tradition in my family. Third, that the process of my childhood and adolescence led me more than once to adopt an attitude of opposition and rebellion against things that I believed were unjust. Although we received the education that goes with those particular schools, our training also contained a preeminence of certain principles of rectitude.

Now, while a character, a spirit might have been developed in all that phase of my life, I did not acquire any political awareness. It was as a university student that I acquired the political awareness that helped me to interpret life, helped me to interpret the world, helped me to interpret society and helped me to interpret history. Principally when I came into contact with Marxist literature, which exercised an extraordinary influence

24

over me, and helped me to understand things that otherwise I never would have understood.

Thus I can state that I acquired my political awareness through study, through analysis, through observation, not through class origin. But I do not believe in any way that class origin is an insuperable factor, I believe that people's conscience can raise them above their class origins.[24]

WITH THE HAVANA JESUITS

Fidel recalled details of his student life, affirming:

At that school, on my own, I decided to go on to the Jesuits' school in Havana. I hadn't had any conflicts there; I was completely successful academically and in sports. I had no problems in the sixth or seventh grades or in the first and second year of high school, as I was there until the end of the year. I consciously decided to seek new horizons. I may have been influenced by the prestige of the other school in Havana, by its catalogues and buildings and the books written about it. I felt motivated to leave the school I was in and go to the other one. I made the decision and suggested it at home, and I was allowed to transfer to the other school.

, , , The Colegio de Belén. It belonged to the Havana Jesuits and was the best Jesuit school in the country—perhaps the best school in Cuba in general, because of its material base and facilities. It was a huge place, a center with great prestige, where the cream of the aristocracy and the Cuban bourgeoisie went.[25]

I joined the basketball team and some other teams in the sixteen-year-old age group. I began to take an active part in sports and became quite good in basketball, soccer, baseball and track and field—nearly everything—right from the start. When I arrived, I found a wide range of activities. My favorites were sports and Explorers. I maintained my old love of the mountains, camping, and things like that, which I continued to do on my own. There was an Explorers' group there. It seems that during our first excursions, the teachers decided I was good, and they promoted me, until one day they made me the head of the school's Explorers—the Explorers' general, as it was called.[26]

While at this school, I climbed the highest mountain in the west. We had a three-day holiday, and I organized a trip to Pinar del Río Province with three of my friends. The expedition lasted five days instead of three, because the mountain was in the north and I didn't know where it was exactly. We went out to look for it and to explore it. We took a train that went south, but the mountain was in the north. We began the trip at night and hiked for three days before reaching the mountain—Pan de Guajaibón, which was quite a difficult one to climb. We reached the top but got back to school two days after classes had started.[27]

Many years later, Fidel recounted some of his experiences as a pupil of the Jesuits, of whom he said:

. . . I am very grateful to them because they taught me some things that helped me in life, above all, to have a certain fortitude, a certain sense of honor, and specific ethical principles that—while at a far remove from the political and social ideas I might have now—the Spanish Jesuits inculcated in their pupils.

But I came out of there an athlete, an explorer, a mountain climber and entered the University of Havana as a political illiterate, without the fortune of a revolutionary preceptor, which would have been so useful to me in that part of my life.[28]

A GOOD STUDENT?

I had some duties at school, because students used to be assigned specific tasks. If you were in charge of a classroom or study hall, you had to turn out the lights and close the doors and windows. I was in charge of the main study hall where we stayed a while for a while after dinner before going to bed. During exam time, I had to be the last to leave. I used to stay there for two, three, or four hours, going over my notes. Even though it wasn't exactly right, it was allowed—perhaps because it didn't hurt anybody. During exam time I studied all the time—before and after lunch and during recess. I studied the textbooks to learn everything I was supposed to know but didn't about mathematics, physics, chemistry and biology. I'm self-taught in all those subjects; somehow I managed to understand them. I developed a capacity to unravel the mysteries of physics, geometry, mathematics, botany, and chemistry with textbooks alone. I usually got excellent grades, which were often higher than those obtained by the best students.[29]

. . . So the teachers came and gave their exams, which were usually tough. It seems that my specialty was those exams given by the state teachers. Often when the best students became confused and didn't answer correctly, I managed to get the highest grades in subjects that were considered difficult. I remember when I got the only high grade on a Cuban geography exam; it was ninety. Our school complained to the state high school teachers, pointing to the low marks and they replied, "The textbook the students used isn't very good." Then our teachers said, "Well, there's one student who used that same textbook and got a ninety." The thing is, I used a little imagination and made an effort to explain the answer. For me the exams were a question of honor.

In short I was very involved in sports, the Explorers, all kinds of outdoor activities, and cramming during that period, but I got good grades.

I also made a lot of friends among my fellow students. Without trying—and without even realizing it I became popular as a sports enthusiast, an athlete, an Explorer, a mountain climber, and also as an individual who in the end got good grades. Some political virtues may also have been apparent without my being aware of them.[30]

Was I a good student? No, I wasn't a good student, and I should start by saying that I cannot present myself before this generation as a good student. I went to classes, that's true, and as Professor Delio was telling you—much to his displeasure because he wanted me to have been a model in everything—the teacher was in the classroom and I was there physically, but my mind was elsewhere. I explained to him that I was seated there with the rest of them, the teacher was explaining something and I was thinking about goodness knows what: mountains, sports, or any other of those things that boys, and girls, think about sometimes.

So I became a last-minute student, the worst recommendation that could be given to anybody; now, I was a good last-minute student. In that, I think I could maybe compete with Ana Fidelia [Quirot, Cuban runner] in her last race when she won the World Championship, because the rest of them were ahead and finally, I devoted all my time to studying: recreation, lunch, evening meal, like a self-taught pupil.

I told Delio that I even studied mathematics, physics and science on my own account near the end of the year, when I finally obtained good grades, often above those of the best year students. That was my final effort. The Jesuit teachers applauded me strongly in the championships period, forgave me everything and criticized me at the end of the year, when they wrote home predicting that I would definitely fail the year.

I haven't forgotten a teacher of great character, he was an inspector, and it was him that called me up one time, along with a gentleman that represented me there, a representative of my father, and informed him right there that I was going to fail the year. Of the three years, I don't even remember if it was the second in that school. He voiced his complaints. I studied like I always did, and I recall that one day, leaving the dining room, that strict inspector said to me: "Do you know how many marks you scored in physics?" with a Spanish accent.

I acted dumb and said to myself: There's something going on here to explain why he came out with that question, but I knew I'd done well in the exam, so I said: "No." He said: "One hundred!" The best pupil scored 90, the school's most brilliant student had scored 90 when he had to go to the state school for the exams or the teachers from the state schools went there for the exams.

They didn't manage to inculcate the habit of studying every day in me and, as I said, they consented to everything in relation to sports medals, they treated me better than the Cuban team. Criticism was left to the end. They didn't teach me the habit of really studying every day.[31]

In other aspects school life turned out well for me in terms of sports, explorations, excursions, all those things. I had good relations with the other boys, excellent relations, which I realized on the last day, really by the way they responded when they gave me the high school leaving certificate at the school.

I never imagined that I had so many friends in the school. I think that was the result of the kind of relations I had with the others, without practicing politics or far less; but when I went up to University, what did I know about politics?

What had I brought from school, what had I maybe brought from my home, what had I brought? A profound sense of justice, a specific ethic that was acquired over time. Those ethics must inevitably have Christian precepts, those that you learn in one way or another, those that you learn fighting against injustice from a very early age, fighting against abuses from a very early age, combined with a sense of equality in my relations with everybody from a very early age and, moreover, indisputably derived from a rebellious temperament or character—however you want to describe it. I reacted, I never resigned myself to abuse and things being imposed by force.[32]

I KNEW VERY LITTLE ABOUT POLITICS

I should say that when I went up to University, I knew very little about politics. What did I know about politics in that period? The most I remember is that I had a brother, or a half-brother, who was nominated as a representative for the Authentic Party, there in Oriente Province. I remember that at that time, there were forty-two representatives for Oriente, and that each party had its candidates. I was about fourteen years old, and I went about teaching people how to vote; there I was with some ballot slips touring the huts and houses of Birán, teaching people how to vote for Pedro Emilio Castro. I don't recall the exact number of candidates on the ballot slip, but I had to give an explanation to those people, who were almost all illiterate: the place, the party and everything, where they had to mark a cross.

But don't start thinking that I was a revolutionary at fourteen, or that I was a politician at fourteen and had chosen a specific political option; it was only that the candidate was my brother and he had offered me a horse if he won the elections. Really, it was a campaign—yes, yes, that was in 1939—what I did was hardly altruistic. But he talked to me, he was kind enough to take notice of me; boys always like to be taken notice of, to be taken into account, and he gave me that task which I carried out up until election day, when all my efforts came to nothing; the rural guard arrived and prevented everyone from voting.[33]

I REGRET NOT HAVING ALL MY LIFE
TO READ AND STUDY

I have read as many books as I could in my life and it pains me not having more time to read. I suffer when I see libraries, I suffer when I look over a list of the titles of all kinds of books, and I regret not having all my life to read and study.

I have read all kinds of literature.

My initial readings, those that most attracted me, were of history books: Cuban history, universal history and many biographies; I have read almost all the basic classical biographies. At school, at the high school leaving certificate, I came into contact with literature, basically with the classics of Spanish literature.

The Bible was not missing from my classical works, of course. Anyone who analyzes my terminology will find biblical vocabulary, because I studied for twelve years in religious schools, like La Salle Brothers and fundamentally with the Jesuits. I was at La Salle Brothers from first to fifth grade, and continued with the Jesuits from fifth grade until I obtained the high school leaving certificate. They put me very much in contact with Spanish literature above all, not so much with universal literature. It was later when I had the opportunity to read many works, and then when I was in prison. The most time I had for reading was during the close to two years when I was in prison from 1953 and 1955.

Let me say that I have always maintained an interest in Cuban history, for anything in relation to our independence fighters, in first place Martí, and everything on Martí's works.

The first books I really deeply immersed myself in were Martí's literature, Martí's writings; I don't think there's anything written by Martí—including his political declarations, his speeches, comprising two thick volumes of 2000 pages or more—that I didn't read either studying for the high school leaving certificate or at University. Then, the biographies of our patriots: Máximo Gómez, [Carlos Manuel de] Céspedes, [Ignacio] Agramonte and [Antonio] Maceo; I drank in all that literature, everything related to those figures! I could say that I obtained my first political training reading Cuban history, still as a student; but even after graduating, I always read a lot. I always liked and still like reading, and am fanatical about any literature that refers to our Wars of Independence, or to the figures of our fight for independence.[34]

DURING VACATIONS

Fidel recalls:
During my vacations I had to work. When I was an adolescent, my father used to take me to the office or have me work at the store. I had to spend part of my vacation doing that work, which wasn't at all voluntary—I had no alternative. I'll never forget the many poor people who came there—barefoot, ragged and hungry—looking for a chit so they could buy at the store.[35]

Lots of people in Birán have many memories of the times when Fidel returned to the land of his birth. Among them, a well-built man of exceptional height: Gilberto Suárez, better known as Llane, recounts:

On one occasion he was in the cockpit with a group of boys who almost always met there from the early hours to fight. When Mongo arrived he called me over: "Hey, you'd better put gloves on with Fidel." I told him: "Well, kid, I can see that the fights go on for a long time and I can't spend much time here; a little while, yes, but that's it, because Fidel always likes to prolong the fights." Mongo, who acted as Fidel's second, convinced me by telling me not to worry, that it was just going to be a quick bout, nothing more.

I put the gloves on, but he noticed I didn't tie them. He came over and said: "Tie your gloves," and I told him: "No, kid, I'm not going to, because when I want to take them off, I can do so, and when they're tied, that means a long time fighting."

I could see that Fidel was squaring up to have a good fight with me. We began to lock with each other. Somehow, he managed to catch me off guard and gave me a powerful blow. Then we started to go for each other until I connected with his head. Fidel would have been about fifteen and me, twenty.

Mongo quickly put Fidel in his corner and told him: "O.K. That's enough," and he replied straight off: "What's enough?" and with that

Fidel liked to explore and hunt while on vacation in Birán.

came back to me. It was then that I took off running, and everyone behind me, because at that time he went about with rifles and things like that and we thought he was going to kill us.

One day in the store, I heard someone climbing the stairs and when I looked, I saw it was Fidel and Lina. I immediately tried to hide, but the store-owner, a friend of Fidel's, called him over and said: "Hey, kid, what happened between you and Llane?"

"Don't tell me anything Bartolo, this black guy shows promise, he's got a fantastic punch, he gave me a blow here that still hurts," Fidel answered, resting his head on a block of ice that they'd brought to the store. Then he said: "I'm going to take him to Havana; I'm going to train him to really box there in Vedado."

That fight between Fidel and me was on a Thursday coming up to 4:30 P.M. Really, the fight took place because Mongo knew that if he didn't find a fighter, he'd have to put on the gloves again with Fidel, which he was constantly doing. Those were days when Fidel was on vacation in Birán.[36]

A journalist asked Llane about a baseball game when Fidel made a triple play.

"I didn't play in that challenge, but I remember it well, because a lot of us went to see the encounter. There was a tremendous hit, I think it was the Galician Iglesias who connected. Mongo's team was winning 1-0 in the ninth inning, no outs, when the rival team managed to fill the bases. Everything was ready for some sensational play: that man sounded a master hit, a fly that landed in the bushes, I think it was a *guásima* tree. In a split second Fidel came out of those bushes with the ball in his glove, threw in rapidly and the rest is easy to guess: triple play and victory for Birán.

On another occasion, Fidel demonstrated his qualities as a pitcher. My brother Felipe was the catcher in that game in which he pitched out fourteen strikers.[37]

FIDEL IS AN UNCUT DIAMOND. THE ARTIST HAS THE SPARK

From fifth grade in elementary school to the second year of high school, René Fernández Bárzaga and Fidel Castro Ruz shared the pleasant concerns of childhood and youth in the religious educational institution belonging to the Jesuit order, together with Balbino Pérez Suárez, the son of a prosperous businessman who owned the Puerto Padre El Encanto store. A firm friendship budded and developed between those adolescents, which has lasted for life.

Fidel, René and Balbino met four years ago in Las Tunas Province at a glass-bottling factory. Balbino showed the leader of the Revolution a photo capturing a trip to the country in which they appear with other classmates from the Santiago school.

Fidel, with lucid precision, set about identifying the members of the group, children in that period: Mastrapa, Prada, Martínez, René, Balbino, all of whom, with time, went their different ways. Fidel and his brother Raúl, both pupils at Dolores School, threw in their lot with the poor of the earth.[38]

René affirmed that Fidel was the precursor of mountaineering and camping in Dolores and in Santiago de Cuba, and showed us a photo with Fidel and other students wearing scout uniform.

"One of our first expeditions was in Puerto Boniato, then in El Cobre, El Caney... Fidel scaled the highest mountain, he was the first to make the ascent and the last to come down; sometimes the bus that took us to the countryside had to delay its return to Santiago by two to three hours because Fidel was still up in the mountains."

After a pause, Fernández Bárzaga relates:

"Out of the whole group, Fidel was the mountain climber par excellence. He thrilled with emotion and joy every time we had an expedition to a mountainous area."[39]

René and Balbino likewise highlighted Fidel's role in sports, even as a young boy. On various occasions he was declared best student athlete of the year, mainly in Belén. Once he won the 800-meter inter-school competitions; he demonstrated skill in basketball and practiced all sports: soccer, swimming and baseball.[40]

"Escapades? Those of our age and class background. Despite the discipline imposed by the Jesuits, they allowed us to get away with some fooling about because we were our daddies' sons, and daddy was a rich trader, landowner or politician and paid well for our education.

"There were exceptions in order to change our attitudes and Brother Salgueiro is recalled today with much affection, without forgetting that he came down hard on any indiscipline. Fidel, for example, recounted that he quickly became an expert in long division because instead of lines, Brother Salgueiro used to give out division sums with six figures in the dividend and three in the divisor as a general rule, and twenty sums for each punishment.

"The teacher in this story of ours was Spanish, short but with a fearsome character; he didn't swear out of respect for his habit, but when he got into a bad mood he fumed and was unashamed of it, but he was very noble. He was in charge of the boarding students.

"Salgueiro has lived in the Dominican Republic for many years, we have a letter from him here in which he evokes the days of Dolores School when we called him 'Twenty sums.' And there's a piece of story that Fidel has related of that episode: 'At the end of vacations one year we brought a parakeet from Birán for the father Prefect, who really liked those little creatures, and prepared a perch in a little garden outside the study room where Brother Salgueiro supervised us.'

"Taught by the boarders, the first thing the parakeet learnt to say was 'Salgueiro, twenty sums, twenty sums!' And it was always repeating 'Twenty sums!' Salgueiro didn't kill the bird because he was one of the Prefect. He ended up giving the parakeet to the San José home, where the nuns taught it to pray, and people speak wonders of it."[41]

Fidel distinguished himself in the Jesuit School in Havana, where he studied for his high school leaving certificate. A large number of references to the boy born in Birán appear in the Ecos de Belén *yearbooks published between 1942 and 1945.*

At the end of the account of the 1944-45 course, the Jesuit School yearbook contains a report on Fidel by Father Amado Llorente, which reads as follows:

Fidel Castro Ruz

Always distinguished himself in all subjects related to letters. Showing excellence and sociability he was a true athlete, defending the School flag with courage and pride. He has won the admiration and affection of everyone. He is to follow a Law Degree and we have no doubt that he will fill the book of his life with brilliant pages. Fidel is an uncut diamond. The artist has the spark.[42]

ENDNOTES

1. Frei Betto, *Fidel and Religion: Conversations with Frei Betto* (Sydney: Pathfinder Press, 1986), 71.

2. Ibid., 69.

3. Ibid., 77.

4. Ibid., 67.

5. Ibid., 68.

6. Centro de Estudios de Historia Militar de las FAR (FAR Military History Study Center), *Moncada: la acción* [Moncada: the Action], 2d edition, Vol. 2 (Havana: Editora Política, 1985), 3-4.

7. Frei Betto, op. cit., 109.

8. Ibid., 75.

9. Ibid., 79.

10. Centro de Estudios de Historia Militar de las FAR, op. cit., 4.

11. Frei Betto, op. cit., 79-80.

12. Ibid., 84.

13. Ibid., 111.

14. Ibid., 84.

15. Ibid., 84-85.

16. Ibid., 86.

17. Id.

18. Ibid., 86-87.

19. Ibid., 87.

20. Ibid., 90-91.

21. Ibid., 93.

22. Ibid., 92.

23. Ibid., 94.

24. Centro de Estudios de Historia Militar de las FAR, op. cit., 6-7.

25. Frei Betto, op. cit., 101.

26. Ibid., 102.

27. Ibid., 103.

28. Fidel Castro, "Una revolución solo puede ser hija de la cultura y las ideas" [A Revolution Can Only Be the Child of Culture and Ideas]. Speech given in the Aula Magna of the Central University of Venezuela, February 3, 1999 (Havana: Editora Política, 1999), 49.

29. Frei Betto, op. cit., 104-105.

30. Ibid., 105-106.

31. Fidel Castro, "Discurso pronunciado con motivo del inicio del curso escolar 1995-1996 en la enseñanza superior y sus 50 años de vida revolucionaria" [Speech Given to Mark the Beginning of the 1995-96 Academic Year in Higher Education and His Fifty Years of Revolutionary Life], *Granma* daily (September 8, 1995): 4.

32. Ibid.

33. Ibid., 3.

34. Tomás Borges, *Un grano de maíz* [A Grain of Corn] (Havana: Oficina de Publicaciones del Consejo de Estado, 1992), 265-266.

35. Frei Betto, op. cit., 114.

36. Reynaldo López Rodríguez, "El gigante que boxeó con Fidel" [The Giant Who Boxed with Fidel], *Ahora* newspaper (September 2, 1990).

37. Id.

38. Aldo Isidrón del Valle, "Viaje al mundo de los recuerdos" [Journey to the World of Memories], in *Antes del Moncada* [Before Moncada] (Havana: Editorial Pablo de la Torriente, 1989), 1.

39. Ibid., 2.

40. Ibid., 3.

41. Ibid., 7-8.

42. *Ecos de Belén,* Year VII, June 1945.

After gaining his baccalaureate, Fidel Castro Ruz presented this photo for his undergraduate file in the Faculty of Law at the University of Havana.

POLITICAL INITIATION

FIDEL AT UNIVERSITY

In 1945, Fidel enrolled in the Faculty of Law at the University of Havana. His vocation as a politician and revolutionary quickly revealed itself. There, right from the outset, he felt that a whole new world was opening up for him.

On the 50th anniversary of his entry into higher education, Fidel told a group of students:

Well, I shared the first few months at University with playing sports, because I wanted to keep them up, as well as initiating myself in political activities. But at that point it was a political involvement that didn't extend beyond the University, but remained as internal politics.

So, I put myself forward as a delegate within the anthropology course. It was a special course because one could help students in various ways, giving information about practice days and warnings of laboratory and exam days, because many students didn't attend the University as such; they were registered but didn't attend. I also organized the first-year nominations.

Naturally, there were some second- and third-year students who were trying to capture us so as to gain a majority because, at that time, delegates from the various courses elected the year delegate, and the year delegates elected the president of the Law Faculty. That's how it was.

I got involved in those activities in the first year; of course I had to share them with sports. It wasn't long before it became apparent that the time I had to devote to sports and political activities was irreconcilable. Without thinking twice I totally opted for political activities, organizing the nominations' slate, supporting it, seeking support among the students; we were working well together. We discovered that it was dominated by a political mafia, but our working methods produced results.

I remember that on election day, around 200 students turned out to vote. I received 181 votes and my adversary 33, and our party won all the course subjects and all the delegates in the first year, totally—in contrast to the last elections—it was a united vote; the majority won and elected me year delegate. It would seem that afterwards they elected me faculty treasurer. Really, when they elected me treasurer of the Faculty of Law, I didn't have and never had a single cent, so it was an honorary post, the treasurer of nothing. That was how the first year began.

I was already beginning to stand out, relatively speaking, people were starting to notice me and, at the same time, governmental disrepute was rapidly increasing and, as students, we came out against that government.

Chibás' rebellion with the Orthodoxy movement virtually coincided with that period, and culminated in a party called the Orthodoxy Cuban People's Party, in a response to the frustrations of the Grau government; and we had already demonstrated against the government. Those University leaders had positions, sinecures, responsibilities and everything in the government, and they had governmental resources.[1]

MY BATTLE GETS COMPLICATED

In that way my battle became more complicated in the second year, when the Faculty of Law became decisive in terms of the FEU [Federation of University Students] elections. So I did the same work in the second year—the course that came afterward, the first career year—I continued working on the second year and the first; we engaged in the same politics. But it should be said that in the second year, our adversaries couldn't produce a nomination slate, they didn't have the people to organize the slate, and that was a fact. And by employing a similar working method in the first year, we attained another crushing victory. We now had both year courses, and the largest ones in the Faculty of Law, and that's when governmental interest in maintaining the FEU at all costs came into play; first wanting to beat us and then, to intimidate us.

In that second year at the Faculty of Law, my adversaries at faculty level in the second elections—not all of whom were pro-government—had some strength, and thus there was a certain division of forces. The result could have turned out differently; but because there were five courses, one of those individuals in the fourth year, who had a vote, became decisive, and despite his weak character, was elected president of the faculty with a commitment to vote in the FEU against the government candidate. I think I acted somewhat precipitately and with great passion in terms of the faculty's in-fighting, because with a little more experience I'd have worked out some kind of election strategy and found somebody more capable and loyal among the internal adversaries, who were not as yet very defined in one position or another, but were necessarily pro-government students. So we had a split between the lower and higher years, and that split promoted an individual who had a solid commitment to vote against the government candidate in the FEU. That individual didn't fulfill his commitment to vote for the government opposition in the FEU, and so we were forced to remove him from office. We simply obtained a majority of four and got him out, because as four year delegates—first, second, third and fifth—we managed to agree on the issue of the FEU nomination.

So the Faculty of Law become the apple of discord and the decisive vote in the University.

It should be said that at that time and as a consequence of a frustrated revolution—as I have already explained—there was a set of so-called revolutionary factions, made much of by the media and generally accepted by a significant sector of public opinion, all because

41

of some antecedent, because they'd been involved with this or that. So there was a set of groups that started off being revolutionary, all of them in relation to the government, although with certain rivalries amongst themselves.

So there I was on my own in the University, absolutely on my own when, during the election process, I suddenly found myself confronting all that mob which dominated the University. They were determined not to lose the University: as I said, they controlled the rectorate, the university police, the street police, they controlled everything, and so they decided that the removal of the president was invalid. They used the simplistic argument that as the statutes didn't make any mention of removal, in spite of significant precedents to the contrary accepted by those same authorities, that was it. They decided in the rectorate that the removal of the Faculty of Law president wasn't valid and, of course, his was the vote that would decide whether the University would remain in the hands of the government supporters or if it would be in the hands of anti-government people. That was the story.

For me, that translated into an infinity of dangers, given that the atmosphere I observed in the University from the first year—although it was still sustainable and nobody bothered about us—was one of force, fear, pistols and arms. And the group dominating the University was closely linked to the government, had the full support of the government and all the government resources and weapons.

In what way do I think I might have precipitated myself a bit? Perhaps I should have delayed that fight or confrontation a bit longer, but I couldn't stand the attempts at intimidation and threats and went into open battle against all those forces, into an open fight, on my own. I have to say on my own because I didn't have any organization with which to confront all of that, I didn't have a party to give me support, so it was a rebellion against the attempt by those groups to dominate the University and to impose themselves on it by force.

... the physical pressure was very heavy, the threats were very heavy, the FEU elections were approaching and that was the point at which that mob prevented me from attending the University, I couldn't go back to the University.[2]

A BROWNING WITH FIFTEEN BULLETS

I've told friends about this more than once. I didn't only go to the beach to meditate, I even cried, at twenty years of age, not because they were preventing me from attending the University, but because I was going to University in any case. Nobody knew how many there were in that gang but they had all the authorities, everything. I decided to go back, but to go back armed. You could say that was the beginning of my peculiar armed struggle, because armed struggle in those circumstances was virtually impossible. I asked an older friend of mine with a certain anti-Machado and anti-Batista history to get me a weapon, and he found me a Browning with fifteen bullets. I felt super-armed with a Browning and fifteen bullets because I was a good shot overall, because of having lived in the country, where I used the guns that were in my house without anybody's permission, revolvers and every weapon around, and it so happened that I was a good shot.

Now, why did I cry? I cried because I thought I'd have to sacrifice myself in any case, because after the battle I'd been waging in the University with the support of the students, with the support of the faculty, almost total support—in terms of my year and the ones behind, as well as students from other faculties—how was I going to accept being prevented from returning? So I'd made my decision, I got hold of a gun, but it pained me deeply to think that maybe nobody would acknowledge the merit of my death, and that my very enemies would be the ones to write up a version of what happened. But I was determined to return and not only to return, but also to barter my life at a high price. We couldn't guess how many adversaries would have to pay together with me for that encounter, and I decided to return. Really, I never doubted that for a second.

What prevented me from dying that day? Well, as it turned out, this friend of mine had other friends and there were various people, various organizations and enough armed people all over the place—some of them valuable and valiant young men—so he took the initiative. He had very good relations with the students and said to me: "You can't sacrifice yourself like this." And he talked another seven or eight people into coming with me, people I didn't know and who I met for the first time on that day. They were excellent. I have known men, I've known combatants, but those were good, brave boys. So I didn't return alone.

Today I was asking about the two stairways, and that's where we met, at a cafeteria there—and there should still be one, even outside in another spot, but there's nothing now—the braggarts and the mob had concentrated there, outside and inside the Faculty of Law. I said to the others: "You three go in the front way, three of us will go up the stairs there, and another three this way," and we all arrived there suddenly, and frightening the fifteen to twenty of them. They didn't even stop to think about whether we could challenge such a power, such a force. So on that occasion nothing happened, all they did was to panic. I came to the University and continued coming to the University, but once again on my own. That was one day, another time I came on my own.

I had a gun, yes, sometimes I did; but then another problem arose: they had the university police, the street police, all the repressive bodies I mentioned before; they had the courts, they had the Emergency Court, and there was a law under which you could be arrested for carrying a weapon. So I came face to face with my third dilemma: I had to confront that armed mob and I couldn't use a gun, because if I used a gun they would pull me out of the game and have me imprisoned. Those courts were very rigorous and pulled anybody out of circulation on strict instructions from the government. So I had to continue the fight against that armed gang almost always unarmed, because I could only get a weapon on exceptional occasions. A gun, I didn't have anything else!, but mostly I was unarmed.

You could say I had to wage that whole battle around the University and the University's position in relation to the government without arms. That's why I said it was an armed struggle under very peculiar conditions, in which I only had my own skin on many occasions. And they got tired of making plans of one kind or another; chance, luck... There was one occasion when an entire anthropology class left the University and accompanied me home, because I was unarmed and they, the adversaries, were both organized and armed.[3]

ACADEMIC RECORD

I have a little academic record somewhere here—I don't know if it's worth very much, I'll have to search out the details—of the forty-seven subjects in which I was examined in a year and a bit. I enrolled in twenty as an independent student—studying on my own—and dedicated myself to my studies in the midst of other activities, but mainly studying, and in one year I passed twenty; in the following year I enrolled for thirty. It wasn't a mania for enrolling on courses, I needed to because I wanted to get four degrees: Law, Diplomatic Law, Administrative Law and then a doctorate in Social Science and Public Law. There were only three subjects missing for the doctorate, which I knew very well.

At that time I was thinking of taking a break to study and I wanted to study Political Economy, but for that I needed a scholarship. To get the scholarship I had to pass those fifty subjects, and I would have done it; but at that moment events accelerated in Cuba and I changed my plans, abandoned that idea and dedicated myself totally to the revolutionary struggle.

Don't take me as a model, I accept the honors you have given me as a gesture of generosity, friendship, and affection from all of you. I don't see myself as a model, and far less as a model student. But I have tried to be a good revolutionary, I have tried to be a good combatant, and if it should occur to any of you to imitate a case like mine, I ask you to imitate my few successes and save yourself from the many mistakes I probably made.[4]

I STARTED OFF AS A UTOPIAN COMMUNIST

In a conversation with Frei Betto, Fidel confided that he attained his Marxist-Leninist training at the University, through contact with revolutionary literature. He told the Brazilian religious leader:

There's a curious thing, however: as a result of studying capitalist political economy, I started drawing socialist conclusions and imagining a society whose economy would operate more rationally even before I discovered Marxist literature. I started off as a utopian communist. I didn't come in contact with revolutionary ideas, revolutionary theories, the *Communist Manifesto,* and the first works by Marx, Engels and Lenin until I was a junior in the university. To be quite frank the simplicity, clarity and direct manner in which our world and society are explained in the *Communist Manifesto* had a particularly great impact on me.

Naturally, before becoming a utopian or a Marxist communist, I was a follower of José Martí; I mustn't omit that. I've been a follower of Martí's ideas since I was in high school. Martí's ideas impressed all of us; we admired him. Also, I always wholeheartedly admired our people's heroic struggles for independence in the past century.

I've spoken to you about the Bible, but I could also tell you about our country's history, which is extremely interesting, filled with examples of courage, dignity and heroism. Just as the Church has its martyrs and heroes, so too the history of any country has its martyrs and heroes; it's almost part of a religion. Something very like veneration filled my heart when I listened to the history of General Antonio Maceo, the "bronze titan," who waged so many battles and performed so many feats; or when I was told about Ignacio Agramonte; or Máximo Gómez, that great Dominican internationalist and brilliant military commander who fought on the Cuban side from the beginning; or the innocent medical students who were shot in 1871 for having allegedly desecrated a Spaniard's grave. We heard about Martí and Carlos Manuel de Céspedes, the father of his country. So together with the biblical history we were talking about, there was another history that we considered sacred: our country's history, the history of our nation's heroes. I got that not so much from the other members of my family—because they didn't have the required educational level—as at school from books. Gradually, I came in contact with other models of people and behavior.

Before becoming a Marxist, I was a great admirer of our country's history and of Martí.[5]

CAYO CONFITES: I WASN'T GOING TO GET ARRESTED

Fidel was twenty when he joined the internationalist contingent being organized in Cuba to support the Dominican struggle against dictator Leónides Trujillo.

Cayo Confites, to the north of the eastern region, was the location of the revolutionary army camp composed of Cubans and exiled Dominicans, headed by Juan Rodríguez and Juan Bosch. However, the treason of unscrupulous politicians soon made itself felt. In the summer of 1947, press headlines read: "Cuban boats intercept anti-Trujillo fleet in the Bay of Nipe; crew of invading boats arrested. Combined army and naval forces order those besieged to hand over their arms. U.S. squadron on maneuvers off the Dominican Republic."

Recalling those incidents, Fidel told Colombian journalist Arturo Alape:

I don't want to talk about that expedition, of the errors its organizers committed, given that that's another subject, but the fact per se is that I was president of the Faculty of Law, an official student at the University of Havana.

To be a leader there you had to officially enroll.

Self-taught or independent students, as one category that could take subjects in different courses, didn't have the right to vote, but in that year 1947 I was finishing my third year in Law and still had some exams to take.

A lawsuit had been filed because those controlling the majority of the University and associated with the Grau government, were trying to maintain that control. In my faculty, the majority of the delegates had expelled the president who was closely associated with the government, and had elected me. The government-controlled university authorities did not want to recognize that decision. So I was vice president of the faculty and was subsequently elected faculty president. . . .

But I was also the president of the Pro-Dominican Democracy Committee at the University. And when the expedition to the Dominican Republic was organized, more or less at the end of the academic year in July, I considered it my first duty to enroll as a soldier in the expedition and did so, although I wasn't one of the expedition organizers. But I had a lot of connections with Dominican leaders, above all with Rodríguez, one of the main ones at that time, as well as many others who had been in exile.

The expedition brought together around 1200 men. Everything was very badly organized given that there were good people, both Dominicans and Cubans who felt for the Dominican cause, but because of recruiting in a rush, antisocial and lumpen elements joined, anybody and everybody. I enrolled in that expedition as a soldier.[6]

Nearly fifty years later, Fidel recounted some of the details of his battle in the University of Havana and the Cayo Confites episode to a large group of students:

By the end of the second year the battle was quite intense—that was 1945, 1946 and mid-1947—I had already been appointed president of the Pro-Dominican Democracy Committee, and president of the Pro-Puerto Rican Liberation Committee. There was a large anti-Trujillo movement in the University, as well one supporting Puerto Rican independence. Albizu Campos was there during that time and led some of the uprisings and organized important demonstrations.

Included in all that, I haven't mentioned the huge number of demonstrations organized outside the National Palace in the anti-government struggles. In some of those photos there I'm on the wall outside the Palace, making a speech against Grau outside his office; he wanted to meet with a representation of us, but we didn't want any contact at all. It was a protest at the death of a young man—I don't remember the exact circumstances—there were various cases like that.

But in the midst of those battles there were ups and downs; it was all very difficult as those people wanted more and more power. It was the period of Alemán, the infamous BAGA[7] and uncontrolled robbery. He had political ambitions and all those groups dominating the University joined up with Alemán, and used the noble Dominican cause as a banner of revolutionary politics.

It was around the time people believed the conditions for organizing a final battle against Trujillo had arrived. Apart from the Dominicans, it was really many of those people who organized the Cayo Confites expedition and it was Alemán, Minister of Education, who provided the funds. It was one of the worst organized things I've ever experienced:

48

They picked up loads of people off the streets of Havana without paying any attention to cultural conditions or knowledge. They went ahead and organized an artificial army of more than 1200 men.

Naturally, I could see what a battle against Trujillo would lead to and as I was president of the Pro-Dominican Democracy Committee, I didn't think too much about it, packed a suitcase and, without saying anything to anybody, went to Cayo Confites and joined up for that expedition.

But perhaps the most important aspect is the fact that I enrolled in something that included the overwhelming majority of my enemies; but the strangest thing was that they respected me. Because there is something that I learned, like a lesson, in all those years when I had to defy death unarmed many times and almost every day: that an enemy respects those who do not fear it. My gesture of going to fulfill my duty as a student inspired their respect. That's how it was.

It was while I was in Cayo Confites during the final stage—with Alemán as the financial czar supplying all the resources for the expedition—that Trujillo bought off Genovevo Pérez, who was chief of the army, and that is when open fighting broke out among various of those groups describing themselves as revolutionary. And many of them believed they were, honestly believed it, because they didn't know what a revolution was. Who really could have been or were revolutionary leaders or had revolutionary ideas? The communists, people who defended the workers, who had an ideology, who had a revolutionary theory and, in addition to that, what could the revolutionary theory be? For many of those groups the revolution consisted of punishing a henchman from the Machado period or the Batista period, who had committed crimes against the people. That was their concept of what it was to be a revolutionary.

So things were degenerating and that's when the Orfila massacre occurred. The group involved had the massive power of the police and repression, the works; when things escalated into a shoot-out in a house during an attempt to take out one of the enemy capos. They even killed the lady of the house, killed other people and the army had to be sent in to put an end to a battle that had gone on for four hours. We were in Cayo Confites.

A journalist made himself famous because he managed to get footage of the entire incident and it was published, giving rise to a huge scandal.

That incident gave Genovevo, as chief of the army, an opportunity to liquidate the Santo Domingo expedition. Logically, he saw in that expedition an adversary in terms of the country's internal politics, people who spelled danger to him in the case of being successful in that Santo Domingo fighting movement. That's what gave them the chance to take advantage of the situation and liquidate, imprison many of those capos. They took away all the commands they had in the mobile units, in the Enemy Activities Bureau, in the secret services, in the juridical sector, in the national police; took away all their commands, they lost them all.

So, when the invasion was frustrated—we were still set on going to the Dominican Republic with others who remained true to the cause— there were many desertions. I already had the idea of guerrilla struggle, I had been given a company of soldiers, even though it was chaotic: lack of organization, lack of efficiency, lack of everything. But I said, we have to go. So I almost initiated my guerrilla warfare period over there because, based on Cuban experiences and many other things that are too lengthy to go into here, and starting from the conviction that it was possible to fight against the army, I was already thinking of the possibility of guerrilla warfare in the mountains of the Dominican Republic. I'm talking of the year 1947.

When I came back I avoided capture, I couldn't resign myself to the idea of being captured—that's a long story as well—so I escaped and managed to salvage some weapons that were later lost because of a leak. Everybody in Havana believed that I'd been devoured by sharks in the Bay of Nipe; the specter of death appeared on the University stairway and everyone went about with long faces, because I was out of contact for days, until I arrived here in Havana.[8]

The Commander in Chief of the Cuban Revolution affirmed:

We spent a few months in Cayo Confites training for the expedition. I had been made lieutenant of a platoon. In the end contradictions between the civil government and the army in Cuba resulted in the expedition being called off. In the way that things happen, some people deserted in the face of danger and they made me chief of one of the expedition's companies. We left anyway, in an attempt to reach the Dominican Republic. The expedition was finally intercepted twenty-four hours before reaching the region, and everybody was arrested. They didn't arrest me because I jumped overboard; I wasn't going to get arrested, most of all as a question of honor, and the shame of that expedition ending up with its members arrested. So I dived into the Bay of Nipe, swam to the Saetía coast and made my way back.[9]

Many years later, Fidel returned to Cayo Saetía and recalled incidents from that historical episode with Lalo Guzmán, an old sailor and friend from his youth, who was the young expeditionary's guide when he reached land.

Lalo, a coastal pilot, hoarded that secret for twenty years. He never revealed the identity and patriotic mission of the young revolutionary who arrived on the doorstep of his modest home in the early hours of a day in 1947 after exhausting episodes, and said: "I need you."

That weary rookie insurgent in a wet uniform had traveled on foot between mangrove swamps and jagged rocks and woods, and fought his way through tracks and confines never penetrated by humans, with their craters of trapped water, turbid and burning. . . .[10]

ENROLLED AS AN INDEPENDENT STUDENT

On his return to the University of Havana, Fidel had to face new setbacks. He recalled:

But then, I had a problem, which was as follows: the expedition was to leave in June or July and last until beyond September. But I had to take some exams in September in certain subjects, and when I arrived it was no longer examination time. So I had to choose—another dilemma— between enrolling as an official student so as to carry on working in the FEU official institutions in the second year—I had to enroll again—or becoming an independent student. And that was a very important decision, because one thing I couldn't stand was that business of eternal students and eternal leaders, enrolling time and time again. I was very critical of that and couldn't fall into it myself. So I said: however strong the arguments, I'm simply going to enroll as an independent student.

After I enrolled in that capacity there was a noticeable contradiction in terms of the great support from the students, very noticeable! And my condition as an independent student, which meant I couldn't aspire to official positions in the organization. But I didn't hesitate and I'm happy and satisfied at having done what I did at that moment.[11]

THE DEMAJAGUA BELL

Comrades from Fidel's youth recall that the objective of the protest marches on the Presidential Palace during 1947 was to promote a situation of popular insurrection. The first one coincided with the burial of student Carlos Martínez on October 10, 1947, on the same day that Ramón Grau San Martín completed his third year as President of the Republic.

Martínez was killed when students at Havana's No.1 Institute demonstrated against a BAGA propaganda caravan. Exhortations by a group of students headed by Fidel, then in his third year of Law and twenty-one years of age, succeeded in rerouting the funeral cortege; instead of taking the shortest route to the cemetery, the students directed the funeral procession various blocks to the north and the funeral car passed in front of the Presidential Palace.

Four days later, on October 14, 1947, a student protest was organized outside the Palace, during which—standing on the remains of the old city wall—Fidel addressed the impassioned student body.

There was a similar purpose one month later, in November 1947, when Fidel managed to bring the Demajagua bell[12] to Havana from Manzanillo, something that the veterans of the independence war of the last [19th] century had denied President Grau. Fidel intended to use it to call the people to a huge mass demonstration on the University stairway and attack the first and corrupt Authentic government with the powerful incentive of sounding the symbolic bell.[13]

In early November 1947, Fidel, as vice president of the Faculty of Law Students Association at the University of Havana, together with a group of his faculty and FEU comrades, proposed to rescue that marvelous symbol of national dignity. Unscrupulous politicians were trying to get hold of the bell for their anti-popular and demagogic campaigns during Ramón Grau San Martín's corrupt presidency and, to this end, they were hypocritically trying to win over veteran groups from the independence wars, despite having created divisions within the groups and reneging on commitments made to their social organizations, all in the interests of their electoral campaign.

The background to Fidel's battle to recover the homeland's most precious heirloom had occurred a month previously, in the city of Manzanillo.

On October 6, 1947, Alejo Cossío del Pino, Minister of the Interior in the regime, arrived in Manzanillo. It was Sunday. The press described the meeting that had to be immediately organized in the city hall as "a scandalous spectacle." The Minister of the Interior was trying to make concrete the government initiative to transfer the Demajagua bell to Havana, to be used in what he called a "patriotic" political meeting to commemorate October 10 and Veterans' Day.

Previous contacts, bombastic declarations and promises to the veterans that the bell would be promptly returned seemed to have guaranteed its handing over with the Manzanillo City Hall's approval.

But César Montejo, a councilor in the Authentic Party itself, burst into the Municipal Chamber followed by a crowd of Manzanillo residents and led an energetic protest. They shouted: "Thieves, not the bell, no! They've taken everything else and now they want the bell as well! Where's the money earmarked for public works in Manzanillo? This is a government of pirates, don't let them take the Demajagua bell, we won't let them take it... because they would insult it!"

It was an energetic and just protest.

That incident had led to a flood of sentiment on the part of Manzanillo's population, alerted by progressive sectors in the locality, including local leaders of the People's Socialist Party and the nascent Orthodoxy Party.

Cossío del Pino had to leave immediately; he gave a press statement describing that dignified act "uncivilized" and those promoting it a "gang of loud-mouths," took a train to Bayamo and from there a plane back to Havana, defeated.[14]

Around that time, Fidel made contact with one of his comrade FEU leaders, Alfredo Guevara, then secretary of the Federation of University Students. He approached him in the café on L and 27th Streets, took him aside and detailed the plan to him.

With a group of university students, Fidel guards the Demajagua bell, symbol of the beginning of the Cuban independence wars.

Fidel's idea was that the FEU should take the situation into its hands without losing any time and that the students should bring the historic heirloom to Havana, place it at the top of the stairway and convene a huge mass meeting. This would come at a time of the great political upheaval characterizing those days, in the midst of a climate of condemnation of the government and internal contradictions, even between the president and the chief of the army. The Demajagua bell would be struck as it was to initiate the War of Independence and with the masses participating with patriotic fervor, they would march on the Presidential Palace to demand Grau's removal from office, and after the collapse of the regime, would establish a revolutionary government.

The FEU secretary warmly welcomed the bell initiative and the federation agreed that Fidel himself should travel to Manzanillo to ask the veterans, custodians of the bell, if it could be used in this way. Guevara proposed that Lionel Soto, student and vice president of the Faculty of Philosophy and leader of the People's Socialist Party in the University (who with Guevara—a secret member of the Socialist Youth—and other students, made up a united front) should accompany Fidel.

Fidel and Lionel flew to Manzanillo.

"I remember it was the first time I'd been on a plane," Lionel told us. They returned to Havana, in possession of the bell, on the central railroad.

The veterans and Manzanillo City Hall agreed to the FEU request proposed by Fidel, and the Municipal Chamber named Juvencio Guerrero, vice president of the City Hall, a cigar worker and a member of the Communist Party, to travel back with the students. The president of the Veterans Association and others also accompanied them.

They stopped in Bayamo and Matanzas, and a crowd of people was waiting for them at the station terminal in Havana.

While the FEU delegates were in Manzanillo, the students followed Fidel's directions for the reception and protection of the highly symbolic bell. . . .

Fidel's motto at all times was to rely on the masses for the bell's custody, independent of the armed student guard. But his followers lacked the organizational level or military capacity, and had no experience at all for such a situation facing forces as powerful and unscrupulous as those that nourished the BAGA.[15]

In this context Alfredo Guevara stated:

It was a fact that we weren't capable of looking after the bell, due to irresponsibility. And I can say now—although it might seem like hindsight and because Fidel is Fidel—that he was the only one with enough lucidity to see that, because the truth is that if we had maintained a mass guard and an armed guard twenty-four hours a day, that bell wouldn't have been taken, or would have been the object of an affray, and that wasn't the case. . . .

And how did they manage to steal the bell? Because up until 4:00 A.M. as Fidel said, the heirloom was heavily guarded by the student body. But at around that time, people started to get sleepy and the bell really did seem to be safe, behind something like bars... but without any doubt, after that time the guard dropped noticeably. Frankly we demonstrated we were no good. Fidel had insisted that we should keep the masses there, not just our armed people. He had a level of intuition even at that moment of how to do things, prefiguring the leader of the 26th of July Movement some years later.[16]

In the morning, when Fidel found out that the bell had disappeared, he angrily reproached his comrades for not following the ideas he had defended so passionately, including that of maintaining a mass guard and not just an armed one. From that minute he gave himself the task of finding the heirloom together with the FEU secretary.

First he went to Ovares' house and had a long talk with him trying to get a lead; leaving the house they passed a car in which Eufemio Fernández was riding with some other individuals. Everyone was armed to the teeth. Fidel talked him into getting out of the car and let him know in no uncertain terms that where he was, "in his world," was also where the stolen bell was. Eufemio roundly denied it, but Fidel was convinced that Eufemio was one of the direct authors of the robbery.

He had no doubt that the Demajagua symbol was hidden in the vicinity, probably in the house of "Tony" Santiago, leader of the Authentic Youth (nothing to do with the revolutionary of the same name and surname).

News of the stolen bell spread like wildfire. All the newspapers and radio stations widely reported it along with suppositions on where the heirloom could be and who could have stolen it. The students and newspapers affirmed that, just like the Capitolio diamond, the bell would turn up in the Presidential Palace, and so it did. Fidel immediately organized mass protests and led a march on Police headquarters, where the relevant charges were filed.[17]

Later evidence confirmed that Eufemio Fernández the gangster was indeed responsible for the theft of the bell.

Fidel energetically condemned the theft, described it as unheard of, an outrage to a heirloom of the Republic and expressed "our condemnation of and contempt for the authors of the deed." He added: "Those who have been saying that the university spirit is dead, are lying; we have also come to say to those who think that its conscience has been suffocated that they are lying."

He charged the government with the theft of the beautiful symbol, and with defrauding the people for failing to deliver the Authentic Party's promises. "Today all of that has collapsed and nothing but misery can be predicted for the coming years, faith has been lost, but woe betide those who killed the faith of the people, because the people could get angry!"

He continued: "Those of us for whom the deception was more terrible must proclaim that a youthful people can never say that they are beaten."

"In the face of the current crisis," he noted, "the student movement's position has to be an independent opposition, because we cannot allow ourselves to be mistaken for Machado's or Batista's men."

According to the press account of his words, Fidel concluded by proclaiming that the University was on a war footing alongside the people so as to avoid the government evil.[18]

On October 12, 1947, the government was forced to return the Demajagua bell to the city of Manzanillo.

A YOUNG MAN LIKE US

On the 76th anniversary of the shooting of eight medical students, one of Spanish colonialism's most horrific crimes, Fidel made a patriotic speech in Artemisa, a city east of Havana.

It was Juan Miguel Carvajal Moriyón, a young member of the Cuban People's Party (Orthodoxy), who suggested inviting Fidel to speak on that anniversary.

Juan Miguel received unanimous backing from his comrades at the Artemisa Institute to invite Fidel Castro to the event commemorating November 27, 1871[19] in 1947. He telephoned the FEU, found out how to locate Fidel and left for the capital. The pages of the newspapers of that period vibrated with charges and complaints from the population, accounts of outrages, attacks on the trade union movement, the economic crisis, and inter-gang warfare (the Orfila events were still being discussed).

The young student from what was also known as the Red Village located Fidel at a radio station where he was broadcasting his political commentaries. Juan Miguel explained the reason for his journey and Fidel remained pensive for a few seconds before responding:

"Thank you for your invitation; I have certain commitments, but I'll try to be there."

Juan Miguel confided his deep-felt satisfaction at that gesture from the young FEU leader in whom he perceived "maturity and strength of character, and a very clearly defined personality."

"I returned to Artemisa and communicated Fidel Castro's possible presence to my comrades on the association's executive, and commented that he was a distinctive leader, a young man like us, but who spoke another language. Life proved me right.

"I am making this observation to explain that with Fidel's presence at that event we broke with a tradition, as in previous ceremonies the Student Association Executive officially approached the FEU presidency at the University of Havana and requested the participation of a leader to speak at the event. On this occasion, we went directly to invite the speaker for November 27.

"Why? The question is an appropriate one. As I said at the beginning, for the sympathy we all felt toward Fidel. . . .

"Fidel's presence filled us with joy; we went to meet him; he talked with other young people from Artemisa and was the main speaker at our commemoration. . . . Using vivid examples, he denounced Grau's demagogy, vices and excesses, and spoke of the way to eradicate them, raising the vital role of youth in those necessary changes."

That night, so highly charged with premonition, Fidel came to know a valiant group of youthful patriots from Artemisa, radical and determined, who would accompany him in the historic Moncada attack.[20]

STRUGGLE FOR DEMOCRACY IN LATIN AMERICA

In 1948 a meeting of the Organization of American States (OAS) was planned in which the United States proposed to further consolidate its system of domination in Latin America. Colombia was to host the event.

Given this situation, Fidel conceived the idea of calling a meeting of Latin American students, based on anti-imperialist principles, to run in parallel with and in the same country as the OAS meeting. The leader of the Cuban Revolution recalled years later:

That was when I gave myself the task of trying to organize a Latin American students' congress in Colombia, to coincide with the famous OAS meeting, where goodness who knows how many reactionary agreements were going to be made. We managed to bring people together; I visited Venezuela, I visited Panama, and there was a lot of agitation in those places. Student contacts in Colombia put me in touch with Gaitán, who turned out to be an exceptional leader, with great mass support and who was unfortunately assassinated that April 9, an hour before meeting with us for the second time. We were getting ready to go and meet him when the Bogota explosion occurred.[21]

Without intending to, at a certain point I found myself at the center of that battle against the Grau government. That took place in 1948.

By that period I had also participated in and had become a member of the Puerto Rican pro-independence movement, as I had relations with Albizu Campos and his family and other Puerto Rican leaders. Given that I was president of the Pro-Dominican Democracy Committee, I was involved in the expedition to that country, although it didn't come to fruition. I actively participated in the Puerto Rican independence struggle, apart from political activities in Cuba, which were basically directed at criticism of and protests against the corrupt government that existed at that time. During that period we were already relating strongly to other Latin American causes, like the issue of the devolution of the Panama Canal to Panama. It was a period of student agitation in Panama, a period of agitation in Venezuela as well, as the defeat of the dictatorship had taken place, and Rómulo Gallegos had just been elected president of Venezuela. At that time there were already strong contradictions between Perón [of Argentina] and the United States. Thus we were in this movement that was confined to the following points: democracy in the Dominican Republic and the battle against Trujillo, Puerto Rican independence, the devolution of the Panama Canal, and the disappearance of the colonies still existing in Latin America. They were the four cardinal points, and this led us to establish certain contacts, let's say tactical ones, with the Peronists, who were also involved in their struggle against the United States and in their struggle over some of these issues, because at that time they too were reclaiming the Islas Malvinas [of Falkland Islands], then a British colony.[22]

During that time, given the OAS meeting in 1948—a meeting promoted by the United States to consolidate its system of domination here in Latin America—I came up with the idea of organizing a meeting of Latin American students in parallel with the OAS meeting and in the same place, to back these anti-imperialist principles and defend the points that I have already laid out: the battle against dictatorships in Latin America, not only in the Dominican Republic, but also in other countries involved in the struggle for democracy in Latin America. The idea of organizing the congress was mine and so I began to contact Panamanian students, who at that time had a very active position in the battle for the devolution of the Canal; also with the Venezuelans, I knew the positions and interests of the various countries. Thus I conceived the trip in this way: first to visit Venezuela, where a revolution had just taken place and there was a very revolutionary student attitude; then to visit Panama; and then on to Colombia. I was going to propose the idea in these universities, to ask for their cooperation. In their turn, the Argentines also committed themselves to mobilizing students in their country and it could be said that there was cooperation in that context with the Argentines, with the Peronists. Of course, we mobilized the resources for all that ourselves. We had very little money; exclusively for travel costs.[23]

Our idea was that the students should be organized and actively participate in the struggles of the nations I have already mentioned and against imperialism. We believed that an organization should exist, we even had the idea of creating a Latin American students' organization. I took all these steps and effectively, the congress was organized.[24]

A situation came up: I was the congress organizer and the role I was undertaking was accepted everywhere, but when the official FEU leaders in Cuba realized that the congress was a reality, they wanted to participate in an official capacity and send a representation that included Alfredo Guevara, at that time secretary of the organization and the FEU president. When this official FEU representation arrived, the issue of representation was posed in one of the first meetings; whether I could represent the Cuban university students or not. That was discussed in a plenary session; I spoke passionately, explained everything that I had done, how I had done it and why. I should say that the students backed me almost unanimously when I made my exposition a bit passionately, as was to be expected in that period and at that age. I was de facto presiding over that meeting. I said that I had no personal interest, that I was not pursuing honors of any kind, that what interested me was the struggle and the aim of that struggle, that what interested me was the congress and that I was prepared to renounce any position and honor, and that my only interest was the struggle and the congress going ahead. The students applauded loudly when I talked and supported the idea that I should continue in the role of event organizer.[25]

Fidel recalls:

Afterwards we flew to Panama, already with the support of the Venezuelan revolutionary students, virtually the entire university... In Panama we met with the student leaders. There had just been one of the many shoot-outs over protests against the U.S. occupation of the Canal and a Panamanian student had been injured, and was left disabled. He was like a symbol for all the students. I made contact and visited him.

The Panamanian students were very enthusiastic and very much supported the idea of a congress, they supported it and decided to send a delegation to Bogota. Now we had two important countries.[26]

The Colombian journalist Arturo Alape, who undertook a meticulous investigation into Fidel's visit to Panama during the congress preparations, related:

"I asked Álvaro Menéndez Franco, Panamanian poet and ardent journalist, to sift through his memory to recall the 1948 visit to his country of a Cuban student called Fidel Castro, en route to Bogota to participate in a Latin American Student Congress. The poet and journalist squeezed his memory as if it were an orange. He closed his eyes to retrace the steps of history."[27]

With the dialogue under way, Álvaro Menéndez replied:

"I remember him because there was a meeting of all the chapters of the Panama Students Federation in the former location of the National University of Panama, where the National Institute still functions. A great nationalist struggle had occurred from December 12 to 17, 1947, which led to many clashes with the old national guard, leaving a number of students wounded, one of them, Sebastián Tapias, paralyzed for life.

"And, taking advantage of that climate of struggle, that night at the end of March we called for a demonstration to confront a new aviation agreement that benefited the United States."[28]

"We explained the content of our struggle to the Cubans, what it was we were planning, how we were organizing a demonstration for the first few days of April in Lesseps Plaza, where the new legislative palace now functions, very close to the former Canal Zone."[29]

"What other activities did Fidel undertake during his stay in Panama?"

"I can confirm that a day or two later, Fidel went with Luis Carlos Noriega to Santo Tomás hospital, to visit Sebastián Tapias, the student who was wheelchair bound, due to a bullet that was never be extracted from his spine despite twenty operations, and who has remained paralyzed for life. . . . One other detail: Fidel came out of the Central Hotel with a wreath, which he laid at the bust of Panama's first president. A detail that I have never forgotten."

"What did the Fidel of that period look like physically?"

"Well, his height impressed me. He was an exceptionally tall man. He was slim, beardless. We saw him as an American student passing through the Canal."[30]

THE *BOGOTAZO:* MY DUTY WAS TO STAY ON

Thirty-three years after the events of April 9, 1948 in Santa Fe de Bogota, the leader of the Cuban Revolution granted an interview to journalist Arturo Alape on his recollections of the Bogotazo *(the Bogota uprising), a historical event that he experienced intensively together with the Colombian people. At that time, Fidel was barely twenty-one and just a student leader with a clear anti-imperialist position.*

Fidel recalls those days down to the finest details:

The following incident occurred when we were in Bogota, spending all our time in student meetings, organizing the congress and the meeting with Gaitán: There was a gala function in a theater over there. I don't remember the name, it was a very classical and attractive theater; I think the gala had to do with the governmental delegations participating in the OAS conference. Youthful to the end, a bit immature, we had printed a manifesto—I don't know if there are any left over there somewhere—a manifesto in which we stated all the congress slogans: the struggle for democracy in the Dominican Republic, the struggle for Puerto Rican independence, the Panama Canal, the disappearance of the colonies in Latin America, the devolution of the Malvinas to Argentina and the struggle for democracy. We took the pamphlets to the theater, to the gala function, and released them during the function. Technically, we might have been committing an infraction, I don't know, but we didn't do it with any intention of violating the law or much less, but to make propaganda for our congress. Afterwards, we were arrested.[31]

To tell the truth, maybe out of idealism, in the ardor of youth, we told the authorities over there who we were, what we were doing, about the congress, our aims in that congress, about Puerto Rico, the Panama Canal, what was in the pamphlet and the ideas behind the congress. To tell the truth, I think we had a bit of luck in the conversation with the detective authorities there; the fact is I even got the impression that someone with responsibility liked what we were saying. We had been persuasive with them. Maybe they realized that we weren't dangerous people, far from it, nor were we interfering in the country's internal problems. Perhaps because they liked some of the things we were saying, I don't know why, but the fact is that after that interrogation, they took our particulars and let us go. Perhaps we were running a greater risk than we imagined, but at that time we weren't aware of it. Simply; after the interrogation and all that, we went back to the hotel and tranquilly continued our activities.[32]

We had a meeting with Gaitán at 2:00 or 2:15 P.M. We had arranged it to continue talking about the congress and to firm up aspects related to the final part of the event, in which he was to participate.[33]

It was about 1:15, 1:30 or 1:20 P.M. when we left the hotel to go in that direction and stroll about until the time of the meeting, which, as I told you, was at 2:00 or 2:15 P.M. At approximately 1:00 P.M. we left on foot in the direction of Gaitán's office, and people began to appear running wildly in all directions. One, two, several at once, here and there, shouting: "They killed Gaitán!" "They killed Gaitán!" They were people on the streets, people from the town, rapidly circulating the news. "They killed Gaitán!" "They killed Gaitán!" Enraged people, indignant people, people reflecting a dramatic, tragic situation, affirming what had happened, news that began to scatter like dust. To such an extreme that after walking a couple of blocks further and reaching a park, we noticed at that moment that people were beginning to get violent. Even at that hour, around 1:30 P.M. people were committing acts of violence. Having gotten near Gaitán's office, we continued walking along 7th Avenue and the people had already broken into offices. I remember one detail just after we reached the park: I saw a man trying to smash up a typewriter that he had grabbed from somewhere, but that enraged man was having a terrible time breaking the machine with his hands, and I said to him: "Hey man, give it to me;" I helped him, took hold of the machine, tossed it into the air and let it fall. Seeing that desperate man, I couldn't think of anything else to do.

We went on walking, and acts of violence were also apparent on 7th Avenue. We were going in the direction of the park where the

Parliament building was located and the conference was meeting. We went by 7th Avenue, I think, and I saw people breaking show windows and smashing things. That was starting to worry me, because even at that time I had very clear and very precise ideas on the nature of revolution, what should happen in a revolution and what should not happen in a revolution. To tell the truth, I began to see displays of anarchy on 7th Avenue. People were breaking show windows. A state of great anger was apparent in the masses. In that always-crowded avenue, the multitude was devoting itself to breaking show windows, to breaking objects. I was worried; I began to feel concerned at the situation, because I could see the anarchic situation that was developing. I wondered what the leaders of the Liberal Party were doing, and whether anyone was going to organize things.

I continued walking along 7th Avenue—this would be between 1:30 and 1:45 P.M.—and we reached the corner of the plaza where the Parliament is located. There, somebody was on a balcony to the left, talking from a balcony, a few people gathered there, but more than anything, people dispersed all over the place in an attitude of absolutely spontaneous anger and violence. There were a few dozen indignant people in the park shouting in fury, and they began to break the lamps in the park, throwing stones at them, so you had to be careful not to get hit by flying stones or glass. I moved ahead and more or less reached the middle of the park. There was a line of recently polished up, very well dressed and well organized police in the Parliament doorways. As soon as those dozens or few hundred people who were breaking light bulbs and things approached the entries like a tornado, the police cordon broke; it looked like they were demoralized, and everyone stampeded into the Palace. I was in the middle of the park, stones flying in all directions. They entered the Parliament, which had about three or four floors. We didn't go right inside the Parliament, but stayed just outside the building, watching that eruption, because that was an eruption of the people. We were looking and the people went upstairs and from up there began to throw down chairs, began to throw down desks, began to throw down everything, you couldn't stand there because a deluge was raining down from above. And, as I said, a man was trying to make a speech

65

from a balcony in one corner close to the park, but nobody was paying any attention to him; it was an incredible spectacle.

We decided to go and make contact with the other two Cubans who weren't staying in the hotel: Enrique Ovares, and the other, one of our comrades of the Revolution, Alfredo Guevara, who was in a guest house not far from where we were. We went there to find them, see what they thought about the situation and to tell them what was going on. We reached the guesthouse, talked with them for a few minutes and at that point a great procession of people could be seen, a river of people approaching via a street more or less parallel with 7th Avenue. Some of them were armed, there were some rifles, others had sticks, iron bars, everybody had something, because people were gripping.sticks, iron bars, anything, in their hands. A great multitude could be seen in that street; as I said it looked like a procession along that long narrow street, probably thousands of people. When I saw that huge crowd, I didn't know where they were going—to a Police Division they said—I went and joined it. I incorporated myself into the front ranks of that crowd and marched in the direction of the Police Division. I saw that a revolution was underway and I decided to join it as one more man, just another man. Of course, I was convinced that the people were oppressed, that the people who were rebelling had a reason, that Gaitán's death was a crime, and I chose my side. To that point I had done nothing, until I saw the multitude passing in front of me, after having visited the two Cubans. When I saw the multitude of people marching, I joined them. One could say that that was the moment when I joined the multitude that had revolted. We reached the Police Division, the policemen were up there taking refuge with their guns trained, nobody knew what was going to happen. The crowd reached the entrance, the police cleared the entrance, and nobody fired a shot.[34]

I saw that the crowd was heading for the Division and I was among the first. They were training their guns, but they didn't fire. We turned the corner and the entrance was thirty meters away. The multitude, like an overflowing river, penetrated the building on all sides, retrieving weapons and things. There were police agents who had joined the crowd; you could see uniformed policemen in the crowd. That Division had a patio in the middle and two floors in the front part. I don't know how many arms there were, the few that were available were grabbed fast. Some police officers kept their weapons and joined the crowd. I went into the arms store, but I didn't see any guns, I really didn't see any guns. There were some teargas shotguns, with some long and dense bullets. And the only thing I could grab was one of those teargas shotguns. I started to fill my cartridge belt with those bullets; I loaded it with about twenty or thirty. I said to myself: "I don't have a gun, but at least I have something to fire with," a big double-barreled shotgun. And I thought: "I'm not dressed for a war." I found a cap without a visor, bam, and put on the cap without the visor. But, with all that, I had on my ordinary shoes, not appropriate for warfare and, moreover, I wasn't very happy with my shotgun. I went out into the patio, which was full of people, people registering everything; you have to imagine the picture, everybody running upstairs, downstairs, going here, there and everywhere, a mixture of civilians and policemen. Some of them were policemen who had allowed their weapons to be taken, others were armed and had joined the crowd. I climbed the stairs rapidly to the second floor and entered a room that turned out to be for police officers. There I was seeking clothing, apart from trying to see if any more arms came to light; I was putting on some boots, but they didn't fit me. An officer came in—I'll never forget that— and in the midst of that terrible chaos, he said to me: "Not my boots! Not my boots!" The boots didn't fit me and I said to him: "It's all right sir, keep your boots."

I went down to the patio to enlist myself in something, a squad or something, and saw a police officer who was organizing a squad. I didn't have any pretensions to be a chief or direct anything; I was going as a rookie soldier. I arrived with my teargas shotgun and my bullets and got into rank. The officer had a gun and he saw me loaded with those bullets and the shotgun and says: "But what's that, what are you doing with that?" I replied: "It's all I could find," and he asked me for the shotgun. It seemed that the man wasn't so keen on fighting, even though he was organizing a squad. He asked me for it and gave me his gun with twelve or fourteen bullets; he gave it to me. Of course when he gave me the gun loads of people hurled themselves at me, wanting to grab it, and I had a tough time keeping it. But I kept the gun and the fourteen bullets or so that the officer had. From that moment I was armed with a gun, but there was no organization there, only people leaving the Division without any order. In the same way as they had entered, the crowd was leaving without knowing where it was going; voices could be heard saying to the Palace, to who knows where. I left the Division and joined that crowd not knowing where it was going, without any direction. I was witnessing great disorder, great indiscipline, a complete lack of organization. We advanced about three blocks and ahead I saw about four or five soldiers imposing order at a crossroads. Given that there were so many people in uniform already with the crowd, I thought that those four or five soldiers were part of the crowd too and imposing order, so I went to help them restore order. I had already acquired my uniform, a visor-less cap that had turned into a beret and a police cape, that was my uniform.

So I helped the soldiers to impose order, saying like them: "Not this way, that way." At that point I believed they were soldiers who had revolted. Afterwards I realized that that was not the case, and that they were soldiers from the Presidential Guard, who were there with guns, not in a warlike attitude, but quelling that sea of people and trying to impose order. Initially I was confused and believed that they had revolted. Why were the soldiers imposing order? Because through the street where the crowd was passing, someone fired from some buildings belonging to a religious college. They fired from San Bartolomé School. I didn't know who was doing the shooting, I couldn't be sure. I was incredulous, I couldn't believe that they were firing from a convent; I was incredulous, just standing there on the corner. They were firing from the convent and I was just standing there, incredulous; finally I had to look after myself. It seemed like the soldiers had tried to divert... I don't really know what the soldiers' mission was. I don't really know if they didn't want the crowd to head for the Palace, or if it was the fact that that the shooting had started from within San Bartolomé School where they were diverting the crowd. But I helped them, believing that they were people who had rebelled and were organizing things. Because wherever I saw the possibility of someone who wanted to organize things, I tried to help.

In the midst of that shooting I situated myself on a corner. There, on that corner, I saw some students that I knew from the University, and who were with us. Students with loud hailers passed by in a car, carrying various corpses on top, they were agitating. It wasn't an organized agitation, but one of those things that happen spontaneously. We were about two or three blocks from 7th Avenue. At that point came the news that the students had taken the radio station and that they were under attack.[35]

Our situation was difficult because we were around ten to twelve unarmed men and just two with arms. We decided to support the students who were in the National Radio Station. The crowd had moved off in one direction or another when we heard the car telling us that the National Radio Station was under attack, and we decided to go there; to tell the truth, without really knowing exactly where it was; we were going to help the students. We kept to 7th Avenue and went north as if going to Monserrate Hermitage. I didn't know what time had elapsed since I joined the crowd, entered the Police Division, came out, helped those soldiers imposing order, the shooting from the convent, deciding to help the students and leaving. On 7th Avenue the crowd was already attacking everything in sight: buildings, businesses, already starting to sack those establishments. We were going via that street. Some people had gotten drunk; they arrived with a bottle of medium-colored rum like you Colombians have and said: "Bloody drink some of this!" Imagine, there I was with my gun and the other armed man and around fifteen unarmed men along the whole of that avenue. The situation was confused and nobody knew what was happening. Many policemen had rebelled; it was even reported that military detachments had rebelled.

At that point, the position of the Colombian army was unknown. Gaitán had sympathizers among the military, that was undisputed, but the confusion was significant. We advanced along 7th Avenue; I don't know how many blocks we had covered, six, seven, eight, ten or twelve; I'd have to retrace my steps along it to find out.

At that moment many buildings and offices were on fire. When we were walking along 7th Avenue, the crowd had already attacked all the establishments. In those circumstances we reached what I later realized was the Ministry of War. We reached it going in a northerly direction, I recall; it had a park on its right and another to the left. On reaching it, we saw a battalion of soldiers ahead, moving south. They were approaching with the German helmets they used at that time—I don't know what they use now—their guns, an entire battalion with tanks advancing. However, we didn't know who that army was with, if that army had rebelled or what that army was going to do. Seeing the battalion approaching, we took the precaution of falling back by some twenty meters, and barricaded ourselves behind some benches, waiting to discover if that battalion was friend or foe. As I said, there were about twelve students with me, and we had two guns. But the battalion took no notice of us and continued in military formation down the street. I think the tanks were behind the battalion, the soldiers in front and three tanks in the rear. They paid no attention to us and continued along 7th Avenue.

To comprehend what had happened you have to take the circumstances into account. A Police Division had been taken, the policemen had given way, many of them joining the people, there was great confusion, I had no information, we only knew that the radio station was under attack and we were going there with the students. We crossed the street and I remained in ignorance about the battalion, whether it was with the people or against the people, in rebellion or with the government, even though there wasn't really any government at that point. I crossed the street and we went to the other park facing the Ministry of War—without knowing it was the Ministry of War—which was a low-rise building, one or two floors at the most. There was a door and some bars, a fairly large number of soldiers, and then myself, gripped with a revolutionary fever as well and trying to get as many people as possible to join the revolutionary movement. I climbed onto a bench facing the Ministry of War and harangued the soldiers there to join the revolution. Everyone heard but nobody did anything and there was I with my gun haranguing from a park bench. I ended my harangue and followed the students headed there.

A bus was waiting at the edge of the park and I realized that that bus was going to the radio station; the students had commandeered it. So after giving my harangue, I went towards the bus that was leaving and we ran to catch it. The other armed comrade who was with me was left behind and I didn't see him again. I took the bus, thus leaving myself with a gun and a group of students, going to support those in the National Radio Station. I'm not sure how many blocks we traveled in the bus; it was around eight or ten. With all this I lost my wallet with a few pesos in it, as we didn't have any money to speak of. Somebody grabbed my wallet with the little it contained, took it off me. We went towards the radio station, and got off at the corner of an avenue, a street like a boulevard that led to the radio station. In real terms, we got off in the street, with just one gun, mine, to give support to the students in the National Radio Station. When we reached the avenue there was a tremendous burst of firing, we had barely arrived when I don't know how many guns began firing on us. We were able to barricade ourselves behind some benches and other objects and it was a miracle that we weren't all killed. We reached the corner again and our group of one armed and ten or twelve unarmed men continued. At that point we couldn't do anything to liberate the National Radio Station and decided to go to the University. We took the opposite direction to the hermitage. Goodness knows who was at the National Radio Station, maybe a whole company of soldiers; it was impossible to do anything so we went to the University, to see what was going on there. To see if there was any organization, if the students had organized a command post or established some leadership.

When we reached the University nothing had really been organized. News of actions and events was flying backwards and forwards, there were lots of people, and everyone was unarmed. There was a Police Division not far from the University, so we decided to go and take the Police Division so as to acquire some arms, given there were only me and my gun and a whole load of unarmed people. It was assumed that I was the one who had to take the Division, as I was the only one with a gun. We headed for the Police Division with a crowd of students; that was really suicidal. One had already been taken and we were thinking of taking another to arm all those people. Very luckily for us, when we arrived, the Police Division had already been taken. The men had rebelled. In other words, we went to take a Police Division with my gun and a few dozen students and when we arrived outside the Division it was taken and we were received in a friendly manner. Policemen and people were already mixed in the Division. When I arrived I introduced myself to the chief of the Division who turned out to be the chief of all the policemen that had rebelled. I introduced myself, told him immediately that I was a student, a Cuban, we were in a congress; in a few words I explained everything and the man made me his aide. At that point, at the second Division we intended to take, I became an aide.

The head of the rebel police was a rather tall man, not terribly but tall enough, I couldn't exactly describe him; he had the rank of commander or colonel, I don't remember. I became the aide to the head of the rebel police. He then decided to go to the Liberal Party office. This is an exact and rigorous account of the incredible things that happened that day. I climbed into the jeep with the chief of the rebel police who was heading for the Liberal Party headquarters. "What a relief!," I thought, as I was concerned at the lack of organization, the chaos, no sign anywhere of any element of leadership or organization, so I was happy to see the chief of the rebel police; I could see he was in contact with the Liberal Party. I knew that was where he was going and thought that things were beginning to get organized. I went with him in the jeep to the Liberal Party office; we arrived and entered. I believed at that point that I was helping to organize what was major chaos. We had traveled I don't know how many blocks. The streets belonged to nobody. There was great confusion and as I said, we had traveled at least twenty blocks. We reached the office and went in. We accompanied the chief to the door. He entered and I stayed outside; he talked to the Liberal leaders who were there, I don't know who they were. Then he returned in his jeep to the Division, which was close to the University. By this time, we had two jeeps.

We spent some time at the rebel Division and then decided to go back to the Liberal Party office, as dusk was beginning to fall. We left in two jeeps. He went in the front one and I was in the one behind. But in any case, both in the earlier trip and in this one there were crowds of people, as the group of unarmed students was still with me. They climbed in here and there and the two jeeps were full. In the second journey to the Liberal Party office I was in the front on the right, in the escort jeep. As I said, every time a car started up everyone around jumped in and everything happened very fast. Rush, rush over here, rush, rush over there, and a whole pile of people got in. Something unusual occurred on the second trip to the Liberal Party office, and I made a Quixotic gesture. It was already getting dark and the jeep in which the rebel police chief was traveling came to a halt, it had a mechanical problem and stopped; they were trying to restart it and it wouldn't budge. The police chief got out and remained standing and there was the other jeep full of people. I didn't like that, so I got out of the jeep and said: "You're an irresponsible bunch, the lot of you," and gave my seat to the police chief. I was left in the middle of the street with two or three other students, in the middle of the street without contact of any kind. I was on the sidewalk, standing by a large wall. That happened in a street parallel to no less than the Ministry of War, as I understood later. That was the second time I came upon the Ministry of War. A few seconds went by and a little door opened in the wall, and behind the door I could see an officer's cap and three or four guys, and various guns with bayonets. I said to the other students: "These are the enemies. Let's cross the street," and taking advantage of the darkness left by the headlights of a passing car, we crossed to the opposite sidewalk. We looked but really we didn't know who they were; I suspected they were enemies when the little door opened and we saw an officer's cap and four rifles with bayonets about six meters from us.

We crossed the street, suspecting they could be enemies, but with all the insecurity, they didn't fire. We continued along that street after crossing opposite the Ministry. Then we saw a man with a submachine gun and, not knowing whether he was friend or foe, approached him, and asked him who he was. He replied: "I'm from the Fifth Division of the Rebel Police," and we discovered that he was a friend, a friendly soldier. So I was at the Ministry of War twice, once haranguing in front of it and then at the side of it when I gave the jeep to the police chief. The officer and the men that appeared from the wall fired on us; they were evidently confused as well; they were on the lookout. We crossed, reached the opposite sidewalk, where I stopped the policeman from the Fifth Division. I couldn't say exactly where, but I have the impression that we crossed the avenue, took the street at an angle with it, turned right and met up with the rebel police officer on a corner. With that we decided to go to the Fifth Division and join them. I had lost contact with the police chief and decided to join what turned out to be the Fifth Division. Night had already fallen. Everything that I have related to you took place between 1:30 P.M. and 6:30 P.M. The entrance to the Fifth Division faces downhill; it is the one close to the hill and with the entrance on the other side. I went into to the Fifth Division and, as I did every-where, immediately identified myself, "I'm a Cuban student, and we are in a congress," and everywhere I was well received, immediately. So, we went in, I didn't even have a cent for coffee, I'd have you know. There was a large group of rebel policemen and civilians there, in total some 400 armed men organizing themselves.

I arrived; there was a large patio in the center, where people were organizing; I immediately joined the ranks and was organized there with the people. Rather than organizing units they were checking the number of men that were there. They assigned us different locations to defend the Division. I had the second floor. There was a dormitory there and I was defending the whole floor with other policeman. Every once in a while, every half-hour, three-quarters or hour they called us for inspection in the patio; afterwards, everyone to their posts. The confusion continued, nobody knew what was happening, and that confusion lasted almost to the next day.[36]

I observed that large force of 400-500 armed men, on the defensive in the garrison, and asked for a meeting with the garrison chief. There were various officers there and I said to him: "Historical experience demonstrates that a garrisoned force is a lost force." In the Cuban experience itself, any troop garrisoned during Cuba's armed struggles was a lost troop. I proposed that he get the force out on the streets and assign it an attacking mission, to take objectives against the government. I reasoned with him, argued with him and proposed that he send the troop out on the attack. I explained that it was a strong force which, on the attack, could carry out decisive actions but while it was inside it was a lost force. That was the proposal, it was discussed and he was good enough to listen to me, but did not take any decision and so I returned to my post. I think I pursued the idea more than once to put the force on the street at that point and deploy it to take the Palace, to take objectives; that a garrisoned revolutionary force was a lost force. I had some military ideas derived from studying the history of revolutionary situations, of the movements that arose in the French Revolution: the Storming of the Bastille, and when the quarters were mobilized and attacked; as well as of Cuba's own experience, and I could clearly see that it was absurd. What was going on? Were they waiting for an attack by the government forces? It was evident that the army had taken a position, had taken the side of the government and the police were there waiting for an army attack. We spent all night waiting for an army attack, all night.[37]

At that moment I thought of Cuba, of my family, of everyone and I felt a bit alone, because I was on my own in that Division with my rifle and the few bullets I had. I said to myself: "What am I doing here? I've lost contact with everyone, with the students, with the chief of police, I'm here in this rat-hole, this is a total mistake, it's crazy to be here waiting for an attack instead of going out on the attack with this force to engage in some decisive action." I spent some time thinking whether I should stay and why I should stay. Then I decided to stay. It would have been easy to hand over the rifle to one of the unarmed men. But at that time my thinking was internationalist and my reasoning went: "Well the people here are the same as the people of Cuba, the people are the same everywhere, this is an oppressed people, an exploited people." I had to persuade myself, and I argued: "The principal leader has been assassinated, this uprising is totally just, I'm going to die here, but I'll stay." I made the decision knowing that what was happening was a military disaster, that those people were lost, that I was on my own, that it was not the Cuban people, that it was the Colombian people. But I reasoned that people were the same everywhere, that their cause was just and that it was my duty to stay. And I stayed there all night until dawn waiting for the attack.[38]

As I have always had ideas of a military nature—basically the result of studying the history of warfare and so on—when I surveyed the terrain I saw that it was a lost cause there. Because the Division was in a skirt and there was a hill behind it, and beyond that, Monserrate Hill. I talked with the commander again and told him that if there was an attack on the fortress from above we were lost, and that we had to protect the heights behind the Division. I asked him for a patrol, and told him that if he gave me that mission I would protect the heights for him. He gave me a patrol—not a very large one, seven or eight men—the chief of police gave me a squad. I don't know if I'm going to recount all the anecdotes to you. So off I went with my patrol and took possession of the high ground between the Division and Monserrate Hill. My mission was really to take the heights, because I was expecting an attack. I spent the 10th patrolling the heights between Monserrate Hill and the Police Division.

Various things happened. I went on a little reconnoiter in a southerly direction to see if an enemy troop was coming from that side. I remember that at one point I saw a car turning the corner. I told the driver to stop; he didn't stop but continued without seeing me. So I ran and climbed a hillock on that bend to get a sight of him. After taking the curve, the guy heard a loud noise, rammed the car, jumped out. I told him to halt, shouting "Halt! Halt!" He didn't stop, but I didn't shoot him because I realized he was unarmed, but I thought he was a spy, I thought he was spying in the area.[39]

We were there all day. For what it's worth I fired some shots at the Ministry of War. I could see it from my position and fired around four or five shots at 3:00 or 4:00 P.M. Even at that time there was no sign of the army or troops. No enemy troops appeared anywhere on those heights during the whole time we were there.[40]

At about 4:00 in the afternoon we suddenly saw some men approaching from the Division with a submachine gun and lances. The men arrived, a patrol with a submachine gun, and I asked what was going on. They said that the Fifth Division was under attack. I exhorted them not to go, not to desert, that we should go there, that we couldn't abandon the people there. The men confronted us, pointing the submachine gun at us. I couldn't stop them, because while I was arguing with them, telling them not to go, to return to the Division, they suddenly confronted us and almost fired on us, almost killed us. I was trying to persuade them and they were in a complete panic, determined to go; they confronted us with the submachine gun and off they went.

I went back to the Division with my patrol, as they had said it was under attack. But when I got there it wasn't under attack, that was a lie. On the contrary, a Division patrol had gone out to a building—I think it was a church—where some snipers were holed up. The patrol went out to fight against those people holed up in a tower. I went with them, and we passed through some very poor streets. First of all we came across a series of brick, oven and roofing factories and I recall that a little boy came up to me; his father had been killed by a stray bullet and the distraught child was shrieking at me for help: "They've killed my daddy!

They've killed my daddy!" He was crying, a child of six or seven. The man was lying in the street, a civilian who had died. We went to the tower, the shooting there stopped and so we returned to the Division. I spent my second night in the Division, the night of April 10 to 11.

At dawn on April 11 there was much talk of an agreement, people began to talk of an agreement between the government and opposition forces. I remember that I had my rifle and also a sword, I had a saber. I don't know as well, I don't know where I got it. I had about nine bullets left and a saber, my police cape, my militia-type beret—a cap without a visor—and the sword.

The talking began, things relaxed and the whole troop was informed of an agreement reached with the government that would lead to peace. They were saying that the policemen should remain in the garrison, guns should be handed in, and civilians should return to their homes. Everybody had treated me very well since my arrival, I don't know, maybe with a certain admiration at seeing a Cuban there among them with a disposition to fight, that made a good impression. When we said goodbye in the morning, I wanted to take a heirloom of it all with me, the saber maybe, but they said no, not even that.

That was no agreement, it was a great betrayal, and in my opinion the people were betrayed. The people were told about an accord, but there was no accord. I handed in my rifle on April 11, at about midday. The other Cuban had turned up there, after experiencing a series of vicissitudes; it was a miracle that he hadn't been killed, he had headed for the same Division. Around midday, we were walking calmly back to the hotel, given that peace had been reached, a national agreement. However, on the way back to the hotel, shooting was still going on at many points. We saw many revolutionaries, who had found themselves isolated, being hunted down one by one, snipers who had been left isolated. They were in a tower and you could see the army pursuing the isolated snipers one by one, many combatants were killed. In my opinion the agreement reached had no just bases or guarantees for the people, and what really happened after it was reached, after the weapons were laid down, was that they began to hunt down revolutionaries all over the city.

On reaching the hotel, we realized that they were accusing us, the Cubans, when they said: "What are you doing here? Everybody's out there looking for you." They said: "Are you the Cubans?" We, the Cubans, had become famous by the time we reached the hotel. There were also Conservative Party members in the hotel and we were being sought as those responsible for everything. Without a cent, without any addresses; imagine our situation without a cent and without knowing a single address in Bogota. It was about 2:00 or 3:00 in the afternoon.

We left the hotel and could see snipers taking on the army, and headed for the guesthouse where Guevara and Ovares, president of the FEU, were staying. They had stayed at the guesthouse. The owners of the house received us well and promised to put us up there because of a 6:00 P.M. curfew. I arrived there burning with everything that I'd seen, I was a bit over-excited. First Gaitán's assassination, then all the fighting, the people's uprising, the whole tragedy that had occurred, the agreement and the betrayal. But, by chance, the owner of the guesthouse where the other two Cubans were staying and where it was agreed that the four of us would stay and get a meal and a bed, was a conservative. We hadn't said anything and had arrived there as unarmed civilians, but then the guy started to say awful things about Gaitán and the Liberals. My patience snapped and I committed that error just before the curfew, after 5:30 P.M. I told him that he was mistaken, that those people were oppressed, that they were fighters, that their cause was a just one, that they were fighting. I got carried away and contradicted the man, defending those he was attacking, and so he said that we couldn't stay there.

We were really immature to commit the mistake of getting into an argument with the owner of the house at 5:35 P.M. and then have the man tell us we had to go. To leave spelt death. We left the house and reached a hotel close to the center where many delegations were staying, the most important hotel, a white one close to the city center.[41]

It was five minutes to curfew when a vehicle belonging to one of the Argentines we had met while organizing the congress drove out. He was called Iglesias and was leaving in a diplomatic car, one of those that had been at the Pan-American Conference, and there we were, with the Cubans being sought everywhere.

We stopped Iglesias' car, told him about our situation and the curfew, and he said: "Get in!" So we got into the diplomatic car. He greeted us by saying: "What a mess you've gotten into! What a mess you've gotten into!" Those were his words of greeting: "What a mess! Get in and I'll take you to the Cuban Consulate." That was where he took us that night, to the consulate. There we were, enemies of the Cuban Government and he took us to the Cuban Consulate. Those are the paradoxes of history. It was the 6:00 P.M. curfew, everyone was armed to the teeth and checking all the cars. They said: "Diplomatic? Drive on! Diplomatic? Drive on!"

We reached the Cuban Consulate about 6:10 P.M. We were already famous at the Cuban Consulate, because everybody was looking for the Cubans and they received us very well. . . .

This happened on the 11th at night. Given the turn of events, the Cuban Government had sent a military aircraft, there were some military men there: commanders, captains and pilots. I think there were two planes, one that had gone to Colombia in search of some bulls for a bullfight, and another military aircraft that had flown in because of the turn of events, given that there was a Cuban delegation at the Pan-American Congress. . . . they arranged things and we returned to Cuba in the plane that had gone to look for the bulls, on April 12. The plane made a stopover in Barranquilla.

We returned with all the literature: the Peace Prayer, all the material that Gaitán had given us and we had kept, collecting it from the hotel before leaving. We reached Cuba at dusk after the stopover in Barranquilla.

Thus ended a whole succession of almost miraculous things that happened there. But above all, if we hadn't got into the Granada hotel at five minutes to six, we'd have been dead, because if they'd caught us there we would have been blamed for everything. The government was seeking to justify the lie that it was a communist plot hatched up by foreigners. If they had caught us they would have made mincemeat of us and blamed us for everything. The truth is that we had nothing to do with all that, and what we did was as youthful students, idealistic people, Quixotic people, joining the people's uprising.[42]

I'm going to tell you something; I already had revolutionary ideas—I'm not saying that they were as complete at that time as they are today—

theoretically my ideas were not as firmly founded as they were some years later. But I was already a fighter in that period, for Puerto Rican independence, Dominican democracy, for the fundamental Latin American causes. I was an anti-imperialist fighter, I was a fighter for Latin American unity, the unity of our peoples against U.S. oppression and domination. I had some of the rudiments of Marxism-Leninism, but it couldn't be said that during that period I was a Marxist-Leninist, far less a member of the Communist Party or even of the Communist Youth. . . . on April 9 I was a man with leftist ideas but, above all, democratic ideas, patriotic ideas, anti-imperialist ideas, popular ideas.

What was I in 1948? I'm going to say that I was almost a communist, but not yet a communist. I was what could be termed potentially close to a communist political concept, but in that period still highly influenced by the ideas of the French Revolution, especially the popular struggles, the tactics of the French Revolution, and particularly the military aspects of the issue.[43]

Imagine, at that time I was twenty-one and I believe what I did there was genuinely noble. For my part, I feel proud of what I did, first because my attitude was a responsive one in that I reacted with the same indignation as a Colombian at the news of Gaitán's death. I reacted with the same spirit as a Colombian in the face of a situation of injustice and oppression in that country. I reacted with resolve and selflessness and altruism. I think I reacted with a lot of commonsense as well in doing everything possible to help with the organization. I believe that the advice I offered at the Fifth Police Division couldn't have been bettered today, with the age and experience I have today. I think that the decision to stay on there—although I was on my own and everything that happened that night seemed to me to be a real tactical disaster—was a great proof of selflessness, a great proof of idealism, a great proof of the Quixotic in the finest sense of the word. I was loyal until the end when they told me during the afternoon of April 10 that the Division was being attacked and the policemen were deserting, and I went back to the Division with my patrol. In other words I would say that my conduct was blameless. I was disciplined, although aware that it was suicide to stay there. But, why did I stay there knowing it was suicide and that they were mistaken from the military point of view? It was out of a sense of honor, of idealism, of principle, morals; I stayed there that night while tanks went by every once in a while and they were expecting an attack every half-hour. I knew that everybody would have died in the event of an attack there, as it was a rat-trap. Despite totally disagreeing with the steps taken, in complete disagreement with what they were doing from the military point of view, I remained there. I was going to die anonymously there and nevertheless, I stayed. Personally, I am proud of that, because I acted responsibly, I acted with principles, I acted with correct ethics, I acted with dignity, I acted with honor, I acted with discipline and I acted with an incredible altruism given the things that went on there. Up until my final Quixotic act, which was to get into an argument with the owner of the guesthouse and which almost cost me my life; but I just couldn't remain silent in the face of that. Now I think: "I was twenty-one, perhaps with a little more experience I would have shut right up in front of that conservative, would have allowed him to come out with everything so as not to provoke a situation that we got out of by a pure miracle. If they had caught us, they would have blamed us for everything and I would not be here recounting the exact and factual truth of everything I saw and experienced on April 9. The people demonstrated an exceptional courage."[44]

FIDEL WAS ONE OF THE FIRST

The events took place in Havana, on March 11, 1949. It was a Friday and barely dusk when the U.S. squadron, moored in the bay, began to spew out waves of U.S. sailors who, within a few hours, had taken over the streets and flooded the bars, brothels and night spots of the capital with their alcoholic fumes.

Most of the members of the U.S. Navy who took part in the events belonged to the crew of the minesweeper *Rodman* which, with the aircraft carrier *Palau*, the minesweepers *Hobson* and *Jeffers* and the tug *Papago*, had arrived from the United States on the previous day, March 10.

As the finale to a scandalous binge played out along the whole of Prado Boulevard, totally drunken crew members approached the statue of the great revolutionary leader of the Cuban people (José Martí), situated in Central Park and, shouting and joking, began to climb all over it.

One of the savages, Richard Choinsgy—of a primate mentality and agility—managed to hoist himself onto the shoulders of the Martí statue, and utilized it as a public urinal. Sergeant Herbert David White and sailor George Jacobo Wargner were also among the most notorious offenders.

People's reaction was energetic and immediate. Dozens of citizens in the vicinity swiftly mobilized against the vandals, trying to settle things there and then. But the police arrived at the scene simultaneously, and instantly took the marines under their protection, laying into the angry public with their nightsticks.

It was obvious from the outset how police and government agents were going to react to the incidents provoked by that outrage against the Cuban hero's statue.

Meanwhile, popular anger was increasing and news of what had happened spread like wildfire through the warm Havana night.

By the time the marines got to the police station, hundreds of citizens were already crowding outside, demanding an exemplary punishment for the lunatic Yankees. Their blue-uniformed protectors had to form a police cordon to get them into the building. Given the tremendous tension in the crowd, fresh incidents broke out.

Bottles and glasses flew against the police station in protest and once again repression was unleashed against the people, with the police threatening them with sticks, rifle butts and shots fired into the air to make them disperse.

Many other clashes between the people on the one side and the imperialist marines and police on the other side occurred during that night of March 11, 1949.

However, the next day, surprise, surprise! Most organs of the so-called "serious press" didn't print a word about what had happened, and others blatantly underplayed the extent of the incidents by adopting an ambiguous and pacifying tone.[45]

The most politically aware sectors included the students and the University; the FEU was one of the first groups to spark the action that the people felt to be fitting.

Fulfilling instructions, the next morning, March 12, a large group of students gathered in the Plaza de Armas, opposite the former U.S. embassy.

Those who took part in the action recall that law student Fidel Castro, already characterized by his anti-imperialist position and his immediate readiness for action, was among the first to arrive. Fidel was among the first—when the group was still small—to hurl stones at the building, a symbol of U.S. arrogance and might, in protest at what had occurred the previous night.

Hundreds of people spontaneously joined the student group's resolute action.

The demonstrators were demanding that the guilty marines—who had been handed over to the U.S. authorities—should be given back to be tried in the Cuban courts, and that the U.S. flag should be removed until that hand over was effected.

Suddenly a number of police cars under the command of Colonel Caramés, chief of police, and Lieutenants Parra and Salas Cañizares burst into the area and brutally laid into the students and people gathered there with their nightsticks.

Students with contusions to the whole body included Baudilio Castellanos, who physically shielded fellow student and FEU leader Alfredo Guevara—still convalescent after an illness—, Fidel Castro, Lionel Soto and others.

Demonstrators there recall one incident when a well-built young man turned up in the middle of all that repression. Wearing a suit and looking like an office worker or a civil servant in some important place—maybe the U.S. embassy itself—he constantly repeated to journalists and the public in general: "These are not Cuban students. These are Communist agitators taking advantage of the situation to attack the United States."

The students immediately refuted the provocateur, loudly calling out their names and positions in the FEU, while Fidel took it on himself to confront that individual.[46]

Baudilio "Bilito" Castellanos, a law student injured in that confrontation, recalls:

"We took Obispo Street in the direction of the sea, where the embassy was located then, facing the Plaza de Armas, in the Horter building on Obispo and Oficios Streets. Hundreds of people were gathering there spontaneously: students, workers, and the people of the city.

"We began to look for stones. The only attack on the U.S. embassy during the neocolonial Republic that I've heard of was the one our generation mounted. Somebody, on Fidel's shoulders, wanted to tear off the shield on the embassy.

"At that point ambassador Butler came down, surrounded by his bodyguards, and began to apologize. But the people went on insulting him, nobody wanted to listen, and the people brought more stones. And the police started to arrive at the end of the street and the first to come into view was Lieutenant Salas Cañizares, who ordered the police to whip the crowd with the *'bicho de buey.'*[47]

"I tried to protect Alfredo Guevara, still convalescent from his illness, and they lashed my back with the whip. Riposting the attack, Fidel, who was at my side, took me to a First Aid post and demanded a medical certificate noting my injuries. When I lifted up my shirt, a photographer from *Bohemia* took a shot and subsequently published it in the magazine.

"Armed. with the medical certificate we went to the Ministry of the Interior and Fidel told the duty officer: 'We have come to charge the minister, as directly responsible for police actions, with criminal abuse.' Terrified, the officer begged him: 'Don't damage my reputation, sir, I have to keep my family on this small wage.' Fidel calmed him down and we went to the police station on Dragones and Zulueta and filed charges there."[48]

FIDEL ALEJANDRO: AN EXCEPTIONAL MAN

Ignacio Barbón Benítez, a modest man of the people, who worked alongside Fidel with Gildo Fleitas, René Rodríguez and other young people, recalls:
"At what point did I get to know the man who is now a universal political leader?"

A written testimonial replaces spoken words. He produces a small notebook of various pages. It is an unpublished article, and its title is: "Fidel Alejandro: An Exceptional Man." Any doubts are expelled in the first paragraph and later in the article.

"I want to contribute to a deeper understanding of the man whom I knew back in 1947-1948; he was a university student reading Law; and I was a black youth earning a few pesos as an aide in the legal office of Dr. Joaquín López Montes, on the second floor of 365 Empedrado Street. I had an elementary political education, but after meeting Fidel Alejandro and sharing his ideas, my political vocation took on a defined direction. I sympathized with the Orthodoxy (Party) and Chibás, its leader. In the Party slogan: 'Honor versus money,' I sensed something more than a theoretical program; it was a response to the clamor for popular justice, something that would change that climate of corruption that ruled in Cuba. A few meetings were enough for Fidel and me to develop an emotional, clean and long-lasting communication.

"When I say that that boy whom I knew around forty years ago is the same today: courageous, decisive, patriotic, altruistic, revolutionary and a friend, I am not exaggerating. I was also with him at political meetings, meetings at 109 Prado and for radio broadcasts.

"I remember that one day none of us: Fidel, Gildo, René Rodríguez and myself, had any money for lunch and, in a beautiful gesture, he (Fidel Alejandro) said to me: 'Barbón, go to the pawnshop (on San Rafael and Hospital, opposite Trillo park) and leave my watch in warranty there. Get some pesos.'

"And off I went. Vitorino, the pawnshop owner, valued the watch and offered me five pesos. I handed the money over to Fidel and a few minutes later, when we were on our way to the Único Market to have some lunch, we saw Isidro Sosa, a young man from Camagüey, a friend of Fidel's and a comrade at the University. He approached walking quickly, looking anxious. After the friendship ritual appropriate for all moments: greetings, shaking hands, he recounted his economic troubles, similar to ours, and told of his urgent need of a few pesos to solve some kind of domestic conflict, I don't know what. Fidel immediately put his hand in his pants pocket and asked Isidro: 'Is five pesos enough?'

"Gildo, René and me looked at each other. I asked Fidel: 'Hey man, what about our lunch?' He stood there pensively and serious, and said: 'Go and see Tinguao (Juan Martínez) and ask him to lend you some money on my behalf, and he and I can sort it out later.'"[149]

ONE VOTE AGAINST, FIDEL'S

By 1948 Fidel Castro was the Orthodoxy Party delegate for Oriente Province and likewise to the organization's National Assembly. But, in that same year, Millo Ochoa was aspiring to become governor for the eastern province, and in order to ensure his election he informed Chibás of his intention to form an alliance with other discredited political parties, but with a controlled source of votes, which would benefit his candidature. Eduardo Chibás was against coalitions, with good reason given the political conditions at that time in Cuba, and much less with political hacks with little or no influence among the masses.

Millo had assured Chibás that all the Orthodoxy delegates in Oriente Province were in agreement with the coalition, and he promised the Party leader and founder that he would only accept the coalition if the delegates voted unanimously in favor of it. If not, there would be no pact.

To this end the twenty-six Oriente Province delegates met under Chibás' presidency and in the presence of Millo Ochoa in the former's office in the López Serrano building in Havana. The issue was debated and then put to the vote; apparently all the delegates had raised their hands in approval, but Chibás asked if there were any votes against or abstentions. One delegate rose to his feet and asked to explain his vote against the pact: it was Doctor Fidel Castro Ruz. For close to an hour he spoke in favor of the Orthodoxy Party's independent line.

Two years later, on January 28, 1950, at the Orthodoxy Party National Assembly, a motion was passed that would become part of the so-called Orthodoxy doctrine, in which the line of the organization's total political independence was adopted, rejecting political alliances at any point in the movement's existence because such coalitions did not respond in any way to ideologies, and affirming that the Party was not bound to any other interest than the interest of the people.

That pact planned by Millo was never adopted and later, as president of the Orthodoxy Assembly in Oriente Province, he convened the delegates, leaving out Fidel Castro.

Fidel returned to the starting point with more impetus, hence his work among the masses in Havana's Cayo Hueso barrio and his subsequent election to the Havana provincial assembly, as an immediate step to his nomination as a representative, having continued the political process truncated by the events of March 10, 1952. [50]

POLITICAL STRUGGLE IN CAYO HUESO BARRIO

Adolfo Torres Romero, the barber on 823 Neptuno between Marqués González and Oquendo, had many clients among the Orthodoxy youth, both university students and people in the neighborhood. Fidel was one of those clients. At that time Adolfito was a person of weight in the densely populated barrio in terms of any pre-electoral regulatory adjustments, in his condition as Orthodoxy Party delegate, a modest but occasionally decisive position in the hierarchy for aiding and even guaranteeing electoral aspirations, given that each delegate controlled a considerable number of party members.

As was the case in other political organizations in the game of the so-called representative democracy, the Orthodoxy movement contained various tendencies among its ranks, and Adolfito had his, to which he had to respond. And his was not exactly the one espoused by Fidel, who came into the barrio from outside the established mechanisms.[51]

At that time Adolfito already had a very well organized force and was preparing for his re-election as a municipal assembly delegate for Chibás' Party.

"With that impulse for struggle, with that fighting spirit and innate sense of organization, Fidel approached me with an interest beyond that of the client-barber relationship. The barber's saloon was a meeting place for local Orthodoxy supporters in general. When he arrived there, Fidel became my client, and brought various friends; he was an assiduous visitor to the saloon and my home, because the barber's salon was installed in the living room of my house," Adolfito related.

According to the barber, that natural relationship between the youthful Orthodoxy member and a municipal delegate of the organization soon turned into a political battle.

"Overnight, I perceived Fidel as my strongest rival, and in fact he was," Adolfo Torres affirmed in his testimonial.

What had happened?

Fidel had cornered Adolfo Torres in Cayo Hueso barrio (consisting of thirty-nine blocks over a 26-hectare surface area), utilizing personal, direct persuasion and correspondence. With his friend and comrade Gildo Fleitas, and [Raúl de] Aguiar, another Moncada assailant who fell in action, Dr. Fidel Castro copied the register of Orthodoxy members in the barrio (with names and addresses) and sent them personal letters by mail, exhorting them to elect him as delegate in the first round of elections. The letters included a succinct program or projection of his future work. But moreover, he quickly visited all the tenements and numerous multi-family buildings and homes in the barrio to discover the needs of the huge neighborhood. Taking advantage of his profession as a lawyer, he also proposed solutions to conflicts that he came across on "ground visits," as we would say today.

That new way of working—very tough and combative—introduced by Fidel, gave him a real electoral strength. It was direct proselytizing with no intermediary, a crushing formula in terms of the traditional methods practiced by the political bailiffs who responded to Adolfito who, on the other hand, couldn't leave his work in the barber's saloon. His sedentary position prevented him from counteracting the young lawyer's dynamic activities.[52]

Things continued to advance and Fidel decided to aspire to nomination as a representative. Given that that policy had its own mechanisms, he had to make an impact on the assemblies. He wanted to be a delegate, he had to be a delegate, starting with Havana, and within a Havana barrio.

More than twenty years later Adolfito related: "He announced his wish to us: he proposed associations of force between us, in other words, with me; I clarified that we already had the barrio sewn up. We got on well, but that was the reality; we felt affection for him because he shared ideas with us, but we told him that he should go to another barrio and that we would help him if we could. But seemingly he had problems in other barrios and returned to Cayo Hueso, where he contacted Raúl de Aguiar, who did give him an entry in terms of his aspiration. When that came to my attention he had already perforated the barrio with those initiatives of his, visiting people, direct contact with the people in the neighborhood: that was the truth.

"Insofar as the letters he sent to the voters, I remember that there were two: one inviting them to cooperate with him, to vote for him, and the other thanking them for their cooperation.

"His drive in working among the masses was so great that we had to, I had to rapidly address the task of seeing how I could save my situation, otherwise I would be eliminated in the political struggle in Cayo Hueso barrio," the barber admitted.[53]

CAUGHT IN A HAIL OF BULLETS

Adolfito told us that in one of his Sunday radio broadcasts, Chibás made an exposé implicating Senator Rolando Masferrer, head of a terrorist group known as the Masferrer Tigers. The Sunday after that transmission, Masferrer would have the right to a space on the Orthodoxy leader's own program to refute the charges, which he was intending to use to gag Chibás, whose radio program was heard throughout Cuba, to the point that more than once movie screenings had to be halted so that the audience could listen to him through speakers attached to the projection room radio.

"That Sunday," Adolfito recalled, "there was a lot of excitement because the Orthodoxy masses were protesting against that restrictive measure. With Orthodoxy supporters from Cayo Hueso, Medina (Vedado), Marianao and other districts, we marched on the López Serrano building on L and 13, whose penthouse was occupied by Eddy Chibás and where he had his central office. We were thinking of accompanying him in an orderly march to the CMQ, there on L and 23 in the Radiocentro building. I remember Chibás climbed onto the roof of a car surrounded by the people; the people were angry, furious, because the police had arrived to prevent the march. The entire area was occupied by the police, Masferrer's people and even army elements; all of them well armed, unlike the people.

"I saw Fidel on that demonstration; he was indignant, protesting, walking from one side to the other. At that very moment the police started firing on us, on the people. They hit an Orthodoxy worker of Spanish origin called José Otero Bens, who died from his wounds. It was like seeing everything in a photograph. A stevedore whose surname was Segura was very close to Fidel. The situation was very delicate on account of the level of tension."[54]

Omar Borgess testifies that Fidel was indeed there, in the park facing the building, now the Camilo Cienfuegos clinic [currently the International Pigmentary Retinosis Center], in the epicenter of that hail of bullets. For him, the agent of repression who began the firing on demonstrators was Rafael Salas Cañizares, then head of the patrolmen with the ranking of lieutenant. Fidel Castro was so close to the firing line that the smoke irritated his eyes. A friend of both of them discovered the Masferrer Tigers waiting in a car, having identified Fidel, whom they viewed as an outright enemy, and he called Omar and informed him of the danger. Omar approached Fidel and said: "Get away country boy, Masferrer's people are going to shoot you. Those people want to shoot you." But he followed the rhythm of the crowd and took part in the protest. There is even a photo in which Fidel appears arguing with General Quirino Uría, chief of police, who was wearing battle dress.

His comrade insisted on getting him away; they had already wounded Otero Bens, and Chibás was calling for some sanity to avert a massacre.

Fidel left the area in open dispute with Omar; they took a bus and alighted on Línea and Paseo, from where they went on foot to the Fren Mar building on 2d and 3d Streets in Vedado, where Fidel was living at that time. His eyes were still irritated by the gunsmoke.[55]

A TREMENDOUSLY STIRRING SPEECH

"Almost forty years have gone by and I still conserve intact the emotion of that day, September 30, 1949. Fidel gave a tremendously stirring patriotic speech with a crystal-clear social emphasis; in which he gave a magnificent portrait of the sacrificial figure of Rafael Trejo, the university student leader who fell on September 30, 1930, during the historic revolutionary demonstration against President Gerardo Machado's dictatorship."

Ignacio Barbón Benítez looked at the old, unpublished photo, taken in the Radio Cadena Habana studio on San José and Belascoaín. He smiled and his face expressed various emotions.[56]

He went on to recount:

I remember that a few days before the radio meeting it was agreed to pay tribute to Trejo in a different way: by publicly denouncing the Prío government's excesses, by telling the people that the youth honored Trejo and his memory without any fear of reprisal by the army, police or hired gangs.

Fidel and I talked with Alejo Cossío del Pino, proprietor of the Radio Cadena Habana network, and he agreed to facilitate a broadcasting slot for the September 30 anniversary. It was, I repeat, something more than a speech. The program lasted half an hour (12:00-12:30 P.M.). With Cossío del Pino's approval, we began to promote the broadcast to friendly people

91

via press notes, phone calls and other actions. I did the opening part and Fidel read out a brilliant speech. He concluded with inviting people to go the university stairway. And the people responded. It was a tribute worthy of Trejo.[57]

ENDNOTES

1. Fidel Castro, "Discurso pronunciado con motivo del inicio del curso escolar 1995-1996 en la enseñanza superior y sus 50 años de vida revolucionaria," ed. cit., 4-5.
2. Ibid., 5.
3. Ibid., 5.
4. Ibid., 7.
5. Frei Betto, op. cit., 112-113.
6. Arturo Alape, "Fidel y el Bogotazo" [Fidel and the *Bogotazo*], in *Antes del Moncada,* ed. cit., 46-47.
7. The initials of a manipulative political bloc known as the Alemán, Grau and Alsina Bloc, headed by José Manuel Alemán, Minister of Education in the Grau government.
8. Fidel Castro, "Discurso pronunciado con motivo del inicio del curso escolar 1995-1996 en la enseñanza superior y sus 50 años de vida revolucionaria," ed. cit., 6.
9. Arturo Alape, "El Bogotazo: memoria del olvido" [The *Bogotazo:* Forgotten Memory], *Casa de las Américas* review (Havana, 1983): 639.
10. Aldo Isidrón del Valle, "Lalo, el guardafaro de Cayo Saetía: un hombre de palabra" [Lalo, the Cayo Saetía's Lighthouse Keeper: A Man of His Word], in *Antes del Moncada,* ed. cit., 48.
11. Fidel Castro, "Discurso pronunciado con motivo del inicio del curso escolar 1995-1996 en la enseñanza superior y sus 50 años de vida revolucionaria," ed. cit., 6.
12. Demajagua cane plantation bell, rung by Carlos Manuel de Céspedes on October 10, 1868 to announce to his slaves that he was freeing them in order to join the Cuban War of Independence. *Ed.*
13. Mario Mencía, *El grito del Moncada* [Moncada Cry], Vol. 2 (Havana: Editora Política, 1986), 379-380.
14. Marta Rojas, "Combate de Fidel por la reivindicación de la campana de Demajagua" [Fidel's Battle to Reclaim Demajagua Bell], in *Antes del Moncada,* ed. cit., 11-14.

15. Ibid., 16-17.

16. Ibid., 18.

17. Ibid., 18-20.

18. Ibid., 21-22.

19. When eight revolutionary medical students were executed in Havana. *Ed.*

20. Aldo Isidrón del Valle, "Noviembre 1947: Artemisa por primera vez" [November 1947: Artemisa for the First Time], in *Antes del Moncada,* ed. cit., 56-58.

21. Fidel Castro, "Discurso pronunciado con motivo del inicio del curso escolar 1995-1996 en la enseñanza superior y sus 50 años de vida revolucionaria," ed. cit., 6.

22. Arturo Alape, "El Bogotazo: memorias del olvido," ed. cit., 639-640.

23. Ibid., 640-641.

24. Ibid., 644.

25. Ibid., 644-645.

26. Arturo Alape, "Fidel en Panamá" [Fidel in Panama], in *Antes del Moncada,* ed. cit., 61.

27. Ibid., 60.

28. Id.

29. Ibid., 61.

30. Ibid., p.63.

31. Arturo Alape, "El Bogotazo: memorias del olvido," ed. cit., 648.

32. Ibid., 649.

33. Ibid., 651.

34. Ibid., 652-655.

35. Ibid., 655-657.

36. Ibid., 657-662.

37. Ibid., 663-664.

38. Ibid., 664-665.

39. Ibid., 665-666.

40. Ibid., 666.

41. Ibid., 666-669.

42. Ibid., 669-671.

43. Ibid., 671.

44. Ibid., 673-674.

45. Julio García Luis, "Afrenta de 'marines' a José Martí y la protesta que anunció futuras batallas" [U.S. Marines Affront to José Martí and the Protest Presaging Future Battles], in *Antes del Moncada,* ed. cit., 170-172.

46. Ibid., 174-175.

47. A kind of whiplash made of a bull's penis. *Ed.*

48. Pedro A. García, "Ultraje a la memoria de Martí" [Outrage to Martí's Memory], *Granma* daily (March 12, 1999): 9.

49. Aldo Isidrón del Valle, "Historia para una foto" [History for a Photo], in *Antes del Moncada,* ed. cit., 190-192.

50. Marta Rojas, "Adolfito, barbero de Fidel" [Adolfito, Fidel's Barber], in *Antes del Moncada,* ed. cit., 41-43. [On March 10, 1952, with the support of the U.S. Government, Fulgencio Batista perpetrated a coup d'état and created a social and political situation that could only be resolved by the Revolution. *Ed.]*

51. Ibid., 25.

52. Ibid., 26 and 31.

53. Ibid., 34.

54. Ibid., 35-36.

55. Ibid., 37.

56. Aldo Isidrón del Valle, "Historia para una foto," in *Antes del Moncada,* ed. cit., 187.

57. Ibid., 188 and 190.

A LAWYER CALLED FIDEL

WITH A REVOLUTIONARY OUTLOOK

In an interview with Frei Betto, the leader of the Cuban Revolution stated:

I graduated from the University in 1950, and I'd acquired a fully revolutionary outlook—not just in terms of ideas, but also in terms of purposes and how to implement them, how to apply it all to our country's conditions—in a very short period. I think that was very important.

When I enrolled in the university, I first became involved with an opposition party that was very critical of political corruption, embezzlement and fraud.

BETTO: The Orthodoxy Party?

CASTRO: Yes. Its official name was the Cuban People's Party, and it had broad mass support. Many well-meaning, honest people belonged to that party.[1]

After graduation, I wanted to take some graduate courses. I was aware that I needed more training before devoting myself fully to politics. I especially wanted to study political economy. I'd made a great effort at the university to pass the courses that would enable me to obtain degrees in law, diplomatic law, and social sciences, in order to get a scholarship. I was already living on my own; my family gave me some help during the first years, but when I was finishing college—I'd even gotten married—I couldn't think of continuing to receive help from my family. Even so I wanted to study, and the only way to do it was by getting a scholarship abroad. To get that scholarship, I had to get those three degrees. The scholarship was already within my reach. I had to take only two more courses out of the fifty I had to pass in two years. No other student in my class had done this, so there was no competition. But then impatience and my contact with reality forced me to act. I didn't have the three years I needed to continue my studies.[2]

Rather well equipped with the main ideas and with a revolutionary outlook, I then decided to put them into practice. Before the coup d'état on March 10, 1952, I already had a revolutionary outlook and even an idea of how to implement it. When I entered the university, I didn't have any revolutionary culture yet. Less than eight years passed between the development of that outlook and the triumph of the revolution in Cuba.[3]

Some people knew what I thought and some were already trying to block me. They called me a communist, because I explained everything to everybody rather candidly. But I wasn't preaching socialism as the immediate objective at that time. I spoke out against injustice, poverty, unemployment, high rent, the eviction of farmers, low wages, political corruption, and ruthless exploitation everywhere. This was a denunciation, a preaching, and a program—for which our people were much better prepared and where I had to start working in order to lead the people in a really revolutionary direction.

I noticed that even though it was strong and had influence among the workers, the Communist Party was isolated. I saw it as a potential ally. Of course, I couldn't have convinced a Communist Party member of the fact that my theories were right. I didn't even try to do that. What I did was to pursue those ideas after I already had a Marxist-Leninist outlook. I had a very good relationship with them. Almost all of the books I read were bought on credit at the Communist Party bookstore on Carlos III Street. I also had a very good relationship with Communist leaders at the university; we were allies in almost every struggle. But I would think, "There is a possibility to work with the large, potentially revolutionary masses." I was putting those ideas into practice even before Batista's coup on March 10, 1952.

BETTO: Did the members of the group that attacked the Moncada garrison belong to the left wing of the Orthodoxy Party?

CASTRO: They came from among the young people in that party whom I knew. I also knew what they thought. When the coup was staged, I started to organize them.

BETTO: Under what name?

CASTRO: I was organizing combat cells.

BETTO: Was that what they were called, "cells"?

CASTRO: I was setting up a military organization. I didn't have an independent revolutionary plan as yet, because that was in the first few months after the 1952 military coup. I'd had a long-term strategic plan since 1951, but it called for a preliminary political period.

Just after the coup I was proposing a revolutionary movement. I even had some political strength. The Orthodoxy Party was going to win the election. I knew that its leadership in almost all the provinces—all except Havana Province—was already in the hands of the landowners and the bourgeoisie, as was always the case. That party was virtually in the hands of the reactionary elements and electoral machines—except for Havana Province where a group of honest, prestigious politicians, intellectuals, and university professors prevailed. There was no machine, though some rich people were coming up and trying to take control of the party in the province, using the traditional methods of machines and money.

The party was quite strong in Havana. It had 80,000 members who'd joined spontaneously. That was a considerable number. It grew—especially after the death of its founder, a militant man with great influence among the masses who killed himself as the result of a controversy with a government minister. He'd charged the minister with having purchased property in Guatemala with embezzled funds, but he couldn't prove it. He fell into a trap, starting a controversy over that issue, for—even though corruption was rampant in the country—he couldn't provide any concrete evidence. He grew desperate and committed suicide. The party was virtually without leadership, but it had enormous strength.

I was already saying that that party was going to win the June 1952 presidential election. I also knew what was going to happen with that government: it would end up in frustration. However, I was already thinking of a preliminary political stage for preparing the movement and a second stage of seizing power in a revolutionary way. I think that one of the key things that Marxism taught me—and that I also knew intuitively—was that power had to be seized in order to make the revolution and that nothing could be accomplished through the traditional political methods that had been used up until then.

I was thinking of using certain positions as a platform from which to launch a revolutionary program—initially, in the form of legislative bills—that later came to be the Moncada program. It wasn't a socialist program yet, but it could win the support of large masses of the population, and it was the first step toward socialism in Cuba. I'd worked out the ideas of the Moncada program long before Batista's coup. I was already organizing a powerful base with poor shantytown dwellers in Havana and other poor sectors in the city and province. I also worked actively with Orthodoxy Party members.

Since I already was a lawyer, I had close contact with those sectors in an active, dynamic, energetic struggle, supported by the efforts of a small group of comrades. I didn't hold any leadership posts, but I had broad mass support in that party and a revolutionary outlook. When the coup took place everything changed. It became impossible to carry out that initial program, in which I'd even included the soldiers, as I considered them to be victims of exploitation—they were put to work on the private farms of magnates, the president, and the colonels. I could see all that, and I denounced it and even had some subtle influence among their ranks. At least they were interested in the denunciations. I planned to include the soldiers in that movement—soldiers, workers, farmers, students, teachers, professionals and the middle class—all in a broad program.[4]

I HAVE DEVOTED MUCH TIME TO HISTORY, GEOGRAPHY AND POLITICAL LITERATURE

For me, reading is one of my greatest pleasures and throughout my life I have read everything I could lay my hands on related to history, everything my agitated life has allowed me both when I was young and later. I read as a university student, in my pre revolutionary life, in my life during the Revolution, in my life in prison, in my life in exile and throughout these years of Revolution, robbing one, two, three and sometimes more hours from sleep or work. Of course I have read up on all kinds of matters, all kinds of writings, but I have always had a special predilection for historical works, and that's why I have been able to develop my own ideas and, on many occasions, question the way in which many events were related.[5]

After historical, comes political literature. I began to familiarize myself with political literature when I was studying at the university, especially when I was studying political economy, which I began in the first year at the Faculty of Law. It was capitalist political economy, but contained all the classics, the main schools of economy; we had references to those. Political economy studies continued in the second year as well, and then came labor legislation, which is when I started go more deeply into Marx, Engels and Lenin, the distinct schools, and I read their works extensively.

Curiously enough, it was studying capitalist political economy back then which converted me into a kind of socialist utopian, I made a critical assessment of all that economy and to me it seemed crazy, absurd, anarchic, chaotic. That's why socialist ideas are so deeply rooted in me, because I came to the conclusion—before reading Marx, Engels and Lenin, all those classics—that capitalism was madness and chaos, according to my own analysis, precisely from studying capitalist political economy. So I became what is now known as—because I didn't know then what I was, only later—a utopian socialist, and I began to elaborate theories as to how the economy should be organized.

The economy books in the Faculty of Law were voluminous and heavy, and the exams were difficult. Let me tell you that I obtained outstanding marks in that subject, in spite of them suspending many students and the exams being oral ones. I had thought a lot about it all, in spite of there not being much time available in the first years to study, as I was already involved in political activities and in sports. I was an athlete, a political activist and moreover, I wanted to study, I tried to study and I did study, but I didn't really have much time for studying in my first years at university.

Of course, as I began to develop my own ideas and make my own independent judgment on the entire existing economic system, then my mind, my spirit was totally inclined toward Marxist-Leninist ideas. That was the way, that was the open door, I would say, that I entered, because I became a fanatic—to put it one way—an impassioned sympathizer of the ideas of Marx, Engels and Lenin, and from that point I read a lot on political literature.

I have devoted a lot of time not just to history and geography, but also to political literature and definitely, universal literature. I'm always reading. For example, I have a large collection of books on Bolívar, I feel infinite admiration for Bolívar. I consider Bolívar to be the greatest character among the great figures of history, the man of difficulties, and the man who overcame all the obstacles, a really exceptional person.

I have read a lot about Hannibal the Carthaginian, his expeditions, his campaigns in Italy, his wars, his battles; everything related to Alexander the Great; on Julius Caesar, great historical figures and more modern great military figures like Napoleon, his military campaigns and all his history.

Among the great figures of history, I have my predilection, and that predilection is for Bolívar.

I haven't even mentioned Martí. Martí is a Bolívar of thought, and Bolívar was a political genius, a genius of warfare, a statesman, because he had the opportunities that Martí did not have to become a leading statesman. His idea of uniting that immense continent in the midst of such enormous difficulties is unprecedented; he not only contributed with his actions to the liberation of all those countries, but the mere effort of trying to unite them is such a fundamental idea, vital for all of Our America, for all our continent, for all people of Iberian descent—people of Spanish and Portuguese origin—that mix that started 500 years ago. Bolívar's philosophy and ideas have such transcendence!

But to define Martí, I would express it by saying that he was a Bolívar at the peak of political thought. Maybe I could be accused of sectarianism, but I don't recall anyone of the intellectual caliber of Martí.

Martí was fanatical about Bolívar, about his grandeur and his objectives. And, as I have read many books, I have a certain right to make a selection among persons that I have most affinity to in history.

It remains to say that I have read a great number of books on revolutions. I believe that I have read all the books that have been written on the French Revolution; I have read a great deal on the Bolshevik Revolution; an infinity of material on the Mexican Revolution; and I have likewise read a lot on the Chinese Revolution over all these years. Moreover, I have paid particular attention to literature on economics; I have read about economic problems but perhaps not to such an extent as historical problems.[6]

AN ATYPICAL COMMUNIST

Fidel recalls the tactic he followed at that time:

I was discreet, not as discreet as I should have been, because I would start to expound on the ideas of Marx and the class society to anyone I met, so that within a movement of a popular nature, whose slogan in the fight against corruption was "Honor versus money," and which I had joined shortly after going up to university, I was gaining fame as a communist. But, in the final years of my course, not a utopian communist, but this time a free-acting atypical Communist. I started from a realistic analysis of the situation in our country. It was the McCarthy era, and the virtually total isolation of the People's Socialist Party, as the Marxist Party of Cuba was called. However, in the movement that I had joined, which had already become the Cuban People's Party, there was a large number of people who, in my judgment, had a class instinct, but not a class awareness. It included campesinos, workers, professionals, middle-class people, good, honest and potentially revolutionary people. Its founder and leader, a man of great charisma, had dramatically killed himself a few months before the 1952 coup d'état. Our movement was nourished by the youthful ranks of that party.

I was a member of that political organization, which really was already falling—as happened with all of them—into the hands of wealthy people, and I knew exactly what was going to happen after the already inevitable electoral win. However, I had formulated certain ideas, by myself as well—as you can imagine anything can occur to a utopian—on everything that had to be done in Cuba and how to do it, in spite of the United States.

Those masses had to be led along a revolutionary road. Perhaps that was the merit of the tactic we followed.[7]

I DRAW UP A STRATEGY FOR THE FUTURE

The fundamental issue for me was my own political formation and acquiring a revolutionary awareness. I had the old idea of the war of independence, Martí's ideas, a great sympathy for Martí and his thinking, the wars of independence—on which I had read almost everything published—before I first came into contact with economic ideas, with the absurdities of capitalism and then I developed a utopian mentality, that of a utopian socialist rather than a scientific socialist. Everything was in chaos, everything was disorganized: excess here, unemployment there; food in excess here and hunger there. I began to become aware of the chaos that was capitalist society; that's where I started, reaching my own conclusion that the economy we were told about and were taught was absurd.

For that reason when I had the opportunity to read for the first time Marx's famous *Communist Manifesto,* it had a great impact on me, as well as some university texts that helped. The *Historia de la legislación obrera* [History of Labor Legislation], written by an individual who did not remain true to his history but wrote a good book; and Rosa's work [*sic*], and histories of political ideas. In other words certain professors' texts helped me to get to the point, until I set about acquiring an entire Marxist-Leninist library in the People's Socialist Party library—and on credit, because I didn't have money to pay anything. It was they who supplied me with the materials that I then devoted myself to feverishly reading.

The Orthodoxy Party was already founded and I was part of it from the beginning and prior to acquiring a socialist awareness. Then I became something like a leftist in the Orthodoxy Party.

Now, what was the key notion in everything that happened afterward? My conviction that the Communist Party was isolated and that, in the country's existing conditions, in the middle of the cold war and the volume of anticommunist prejudice abounding, it was not possible to make a revolution from the positions of the People's Socialist Party, although the Socialist Party wanted to do so. Imperialism and the reaction had isolated this party to the point that it was totally prevented from undertaking a revolution, and that was when I got to thinking of the ways, the roads and the possibilities of a revolution and how to go about it.

Given the state of ferment in the country and the strength gained among the masses by Chibás' movement, I found myself in a party that had great popular strength, certain attractive concepts in combating vice and political corruption, and ideas in the social context that were not as yet totally revolutionary. But, apart from in the capital of the Republic, the party was already falling into the hands of the landowners, because when a popular party emerged here its provincial directorates didn't take long to fall into the hands of landowners and the rich (a process that was already taking root in the Orthodoxy Party). And it was on the basis of that contradiction and the tragic death of its combative and tenacious leader, that I formulated the concept of how the Revolution had to be made within the conditions of our country.

Chibás' suicide left that party without a leader. It had to get to the elections and it had to win the elections in those conditions. However, with the great support left it by the death of Chibás himself, victory for the Cuban People's Party was inevitable in that election.[8]

Facing the possibility of revolution by that route and the inevitability of rapid frustration, I drew up a strategy for the future: to launch a revolutionary program and organize a popular uprising from within the government and from within Congress itself. And, from that moment, I had the whole concept; all the ideas put forward in *History Will Absolve Me,* what the measures should be, how to propose them, what to do. That was the first revolutionary concept that I was able to elaborate, let's say barely six years after going up to university that September. You could say that I took six years to acquire a revolutionary conscience and to draw up a revolutionary strategy.[9]

FIDEL ON "LA VOZ DEL AIRE"

Ignacio Barbón evokes the time when he worked very closely with Fidel:

I haven't forgotten that a few months after graduating from the university as a lawyer, Fidel began to work as a journalist-commentator on "La Voz del Aire" (Voices on Air) on 25th and G, Vedado. "Only the Orthodoxy Party can raise a combative tribune" was our slogan. Thus, the interminable sessions of political work for the electoral campaign were supplemented by the radio program, which was an impregnable position for denouncing Carlos Prío's corrupt government. But Fidel Alejandro the lawyer didn't slow down his rate of professional work. In 1950 he opened a legal office with Azpiazo and Resende.

According to public survey specialists, Fidel's broadcasts on "La Voz del Aire" had a formidable acceptance, principally in Havana. His charges against Prío and his politicking mafia were reiterated, as were death threats against Fidel. On more than one occasion we got warning calls from people who were friends: the paranoid Masferrer and his gangsters were roaming around in the vicinity of the radio station. Cheap thugs, nothing more.

It was said that that Masferrer lived to kill and killed to live, but he didn't dare to touch Fidel.

I will never forget that toward the end of the year Fidel set about composing a New Year greetings letter to program listeners, members of the PPC(O)[10] and friends who lived in all the municipalities of Havana Province. To confirm the effectiveness of the mail he proposed to send the first missives to our own homes. Gildo, René, Azpiazo and myself were the first to receive the New Year congratulations.

Gildo and René printed thousands of mimeographed letters.[11]

The text of the letters read:

December 1951

Comrade in ideas:

I am sending you these lines with my sincerest wishes for you and your esteemed family in this festive season.

Sad and recent memories have turned our festivities into mourning this Christmas, but new and heartening hopes are being born in the warmth of the first lights of the fortunate dawn that ignited the sacrifice.

For us, there is only one possible way of seeing in the New Year, by recalling Martí's last words that Christmas before the last freedom effort: For a suffering people there is no "other New Year than that made by the force of its fist in the ranks of its enemies."

With those words I remain yours sincerely,

Fidel Castro[12]

AZPIAZO-CASTRO-RESENDE LEGAL OFFICE

Fidel had just graduated as a Doctor in Law and in September 1950 he suggested to two of his university comrades, Jorge Azpiazo and Rafael Resende, that they should open a legal office together.

The majority of the legal bureaus, and the commercial ones, were located in Old Havana. That was the center of the country's economic activity and the young lawyers set up office in the Rosario building on 57 Tejadillo Street, first in apartment 204, then 303 and later in 206 in the same building, whose facade still bears a plaque to the effect.

The rental for that space was sixty pesos per month and had to be paid one month in advance.

Between the three of them they got together eighty pesos for José Álvarez, the owner of the building, promising to pay him the remainder soon. They acquired the place unfurnished and it opened because of Fidel's will. They loaned a chair and desk from the same proprietor; then they bought a typewriter in installments.[13]

Some years ago, journalist Marta Rojas,[14] accompanied by Dr. Azpiazo, visited apartment 206, 57 Tejadillo Street. On that occasion the reporter took some notes on the objects in the office and wrote this description:

The office contains furniture from the period in which it was set up. Here is Fidel's desk, a book cupboard, a typewriter, a small bookcase, a straw-stuffed sofa, two armchairs, a phosphorescent light, a bust of José Martí, some books and a box full of envelopes for printed letter heads stating: Azpiazo-Castro-Resende Legal Office: Civil, Criminal and Social Matters, Apartment 303, 57-59 Tejadillo, Havana. I took an envelope to copy and keep as a souvenir. I asked Dr. Azpiazo what else the room had contained. He replied: "Paintings, one of Martí; as everybody knows,

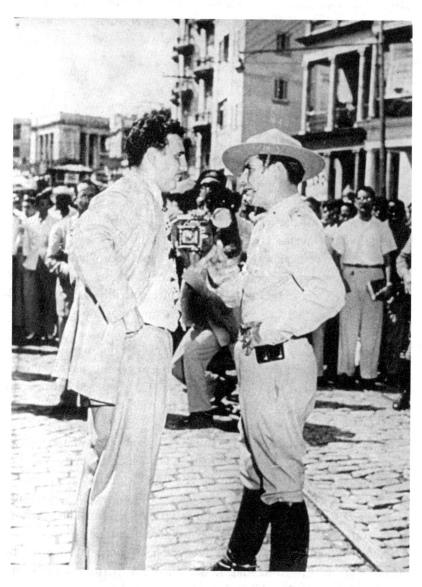

Fidel Castro argues with an army officer who is trying to stop a demonstration.

Fidel was always a follower of Martí. And a painting of Maceo and another of Ignacio Agramonte."

I noticed that one of the bookcases was empty. He told me that it had held the collection of Martí's works they acquired, but that many of the books were sent to Fidel in prison, when the penal authorities permitted the entry of certain items.[15]

FIDEL FINDS ANOTHER WAY TO SORT IT OUT

In 1950 Rubén López had a small carpentry workshop on the ground floor of the building on 18th and 23d (more exactly at the road fork ending on 21st Street) in Vedado, and the painter César Fonseca worked with him as an assistant. One of Fidel's sisters, Lidia Castro, lived in the vicinity, on 20th and 23d, and Fidel lived not very far away on 23d between 22d and 24th.[16]

Interviewed by a well-known journalist, Rubén López recalls:

I was introduced to Fidel, who was wearing a suit and tie, very correct. He said that he wanted me to make him some furniture for the office he had just opened in Old Havana. I replied in the affirmative. Azpiazo and Resende withdrew a bit and Fidel close a deal with me. He told me that there was no problem with the timber, that he had it. That day I became aware of Fidel's great powers of persuasion, because I didn't let clients give me the timber. Most people who contracted a job and brought the timber believed that the carpenter wouldn't use it all for the furniture they had ordered; I didn't allow that because of the slight on my personal honesty. However, I said yes to Fidel. He had convinced me. I said: "All right, I'll go and get your timber," thinking all the time that at the end of the day I would discount the value of the boards from what he paid me for the work. Then he said: "OK, go to the Gancedo Timber Yard and select the boards you need for the office furniture."

Rubén continued: The next morning Fidel returned to the workshop. He brought me a magazine specializing in furniture. "Look, this is what I picked, this is the bureau I want, with the armchair and the bookcase," he said. "Ah, that's all right," I replied.

I went with César Fonseca to Gancedo's and selected all the wood that we needed. We called the assistant to measure it, and after he'd done so, he told me how much it cost.

"That's to go on Dr. Fidel Castro's account," I told him.

The assistant didn't know him. "Who's Dr. Fidel Castro? As far as I know he doesn't have an account here in the timber yard, so I can't give you the timber."

"Well, kid, as I'm not taking it with me, I'm going to put it back where it was." "No, leave it here," he answered, and I left Gancedo's.

In the afternoon—Rubén continues relating—Fidel returned to the workshop to ask if I'd brought the timber; I told him that we'd gone to collect it but they wouldn't dispatch it to us. He placed a hand on my shoulder and asked me to go with him to the Gancedo Timber Yard. I got into his car, Fidel was driving, it was a black or very dark car; we got there; he went into the office and I stayed in the store. After a little while he came out and told me that we could go and get a van to transport the boards whenever we wanted. For his part, the administrator had ordered the assistant to cut the timber. Problem solved.[17]

Fidel paid us with interest. The fact is that I cannot repay him for what he did for us. It wasn't affordable in that period. This is what happened. I had that place on 18th Street, rented from a family who lived upstairs, but they sold the whole building to a man who worked as head of the Presidential Palace stenographers; it was during the Carlos Prío Socarrás government, and when the new owners occupied the property they threw us out.

The man who acquired the building warned both César Fonseca and myself that we had to get out in twenty-four or forty-eight hours. One afternoon I closed the workshop, or César stayed there, and I went home. When I returned the next morning, I found that things had been consummated. They had chucked the carpentry bench and everything that we had there into a passageway. César, who had arrived long before me, saw it all and immediately went to find Fidel at home.[18]

In minute detail, César Fonseca corroborated Rubén's account:

The owner had given us a matter of hours to leave the workshop, where I'd previously had a photo lab to develop aficionados' work. We had little time to solve the problem and went out to find alternative premises, but they were asking at least 500 pesos for the privilege of renting to us. I went to see Dr. Pérez Lamy, the Socialist Party lawyer, who was a criminal attorney, and so he sent us to Dr. Contreras, who attended to civil matters. He had told that time was very short, but to go and see him, and that's when we were thrown out. I'd talked to Fidel as well, and he had advised me not to leave the place. In that period, the time the proprietor had given us, I stayed in the workshop until very late, but I was cold and hungry and decided to go home to sleep. Very early the next morning, I arrived at the carpentry workshop and found that all our things were outside, in a passageway. I ran to Fidel's house; he was still asleep, they woke him up and he received me half dressed. I told him what had happened and he told me that we should wait until Gildo Fleitas arrived with the car. When he arrived we left for the workshop.

When we got to 18th I went upstairs to see the owner and told him that we were there with the lawyer representing us. Fidel gave an exposition of the rights we had. The man replied that we had no rights.

But the form in which the new proprietor had proceeded was totally unjust, and Fidel assured César: "We're going to sort this out."

The carpenters had to reoccupy the workshop and they did; Fidel himself helped to put the furniture and work tools back there. Afterwards he argued with the owner's son, a politician. César recalls that Fidel told him he was going to solve the matter legally, and the next step was to go to the police station and make a claim. Fonseca thought, logically, that those people had called out the patrol squad because cars arrived there within minutes. After Fidel dispatched them, we made the charges:

"I made a claim at the police station on the Malecón. Fidel went with me. Later, he came back to the workshop," César added.

"I spotted one of those patrollers," Rubén López related. The car stopped and Fidel told the police: "This matter is already solved, there's no problem," and the patrol squad followed at a distance.

"What I remember," Rubén continued, "was that Fidel told me that in law the prime issue is possession." "They threw your furniture out onto the street and put a padlock on the door and we took it off," he said. Everything happened in a trice. He was dressed in gray striped suit; it's as if I can see him now. I remember that he had told me he was in a hurry because he had to go and talk on a radio hour he had on G and 25th; at that time Fidel was exposing the corruption of Prío's government. César Fonseca explained that on that day Dr. Fidel Castro was involved in a campaign against a group of farm owners, friends of Prío, who were forming a society to set up a dairy consortium. So they were pressuring the campesinos who were unable to take what they milked to sell to the Dairy Company of Cuba (Concha No. 1). La Chata farm, property of then president Carlos Prío Socarrás, was included in this power circle and, for waging this battle on behalf of the campesinos—and others like them—Fidel had been threatened with death by gangster groups, including that of Jesús González Cartas, "The weird one." Fonseca recalls that a group of friends, including some people from La Pelusa, La Timba and La Corea barrios always accompanied him to the broadcasts on that radio slot.

The new proprietors of the building where the carpentry workshop was located were well aware that Fidel was exposing the Prío corruption. . . .

"As to the new proprietors," Rubén López told us, "I can tell you that they called me immediately to ask what I wanted. They were worried at the turn of events. We explained to them that we needed time to look for another place and had to complete some jobs we were doing, and they offered us money to move. They gave me much more than I had expected and we were able to set up another workshop at 417 Santa Felicia between Rosa Henríquez and Melones, Luyanó."

Rubén López asked us:

"In those years, what other lawyer do you think could have solved that case on behalf of a carpenter who didn't even have papers to protect him? Look, both César and I were communists, we were members almost from childhood, first in the Young Communist League and then in the People's Socialist Party; we didn't belong to the Orthodoxy, the party to which Fidel belonged at that time. And we had a communist lawyer, a good friend of mine, who always defended the workers, but he wouldn't have done what Fidel did, he would have gone through the normal legal channels of the court, an appeal, etc. until they were exhausted; but Fidel found another way to sort it out. We didn't have the money to pay him for what he did, it was worth more than all the furniture in Tejadillo put together; we never talked of payment or anything, neither César nor me."[19]

PROSECUTING LAWYER

"Someone, I don't remember who," Jorge Azpiazo told me, "had sought us out as lawyers in connection with some credits owed to the Gancedo S.A. Timber Yard, and it was in terms of that professional relationship that we acquired the timber for the Tejadillo legal office, likewise on credit. That excluded the sofa and some small armchairs in the reception area; we were given those by a lady living nearby, who was going to throw them out because she had bought a new three-piece suite for her living room.

"Gancedo S.A. had numerous unpaid accounts that, acting as their lawyers, we had to claim from those indebted clients. When we received the money we came out with a credit for the Tejadillo timber and furniture and also charged our fees. . . .

"Fidel himself directed the debt collection strategy. He sent an urgent communication to each debtor (carpenter) to come in person to the legal office. Gancedo's debtors would appear. In the interview with Dr. Fidel Castro they explained that they had not been able to settle their accounts because they were also owed money by the clients for whom they had undertaken carpentry work with timber bought on credit.

"Knowing that they were very poor people, Fidel Castro would tell the carpenters not to worry, that his client, Gancedo Timber Yard S.A., was not under any pressure and that the legal office would commit itself to collect monies from their clients, for which reason he asked the carpenters for the addresses of those persons who owed them money.

"The office immediately began to function as a representative for the carpenters and Fidel urged their debtors to settle the amounts due at the Tejadillo legal office. Each time a debtor paid up, Fidel phoned the carpenter to whom the money was owed to inform him; he would appear at the Tejadillo office and naturally, instruct Fidel Castro to hand over the amounts collected to his client Gancedo S.A. so as to liquidate the account with the timber yard. But Fidel would advise the carpenters not to do that, because—as he told them—Gancedo didn't need those twenty or thirty pesos. He then handed over the money collected to the carpenters."

Azpiazo told us that on one occasion he accompanied Fidel to the home of one of the indebted carpenters in Porvenir Street, Lawton.

"When we arrived," Azpiazo recounted, "the man wasn't there; his wife received us. There was terrible poverty in that house. The carpenter's wife was pregnant and had a little girl. The woman invited us to wait for her husband and kindly gave us each a cup of coffee in the midst of that massive poverty. She went to the kitchen to brew the coffee and while she was gone Fidel asked me to lend him five pesos. I gave it to him and he put it under a plate on the table. We drank the coffee and Fidel decided not to wait for the carpenter. He told the woman to inform her husband that he didn't have to worry about his debt to the Gancedo Timber Yard, and to come and see him at the Tejadillo legal office when he had time."

Azpiazo recalls that in that period Fidel often walked round with holes in the soles of his shoes and shared out the profits from the legal office in a communist way. They weren't large, but he distributed them equally. He also shared his time between his work as a lawyer and the revolutionary responsibilities he had assumed in his life: combating the corruption of the Prío Socorrás' regime and defending popular causes. He defended the red trade union against the sell-out yellow trade union in the Mercado Único, and also defended people in La Pelusa, La Timba and La Corea barrios in the vicinity of what is now Revolution Square, who were about to be evicted from their humble homes without any guarantee of another. This lawsuit turned into a political movement, and Azpiazo also recalled that a group of girls and young boys from those barrios went out into the street with pots and collection boxes to beg, and with the money collected the neighbors hired a bus to go to a meeting where Fidel Castro was speaking in Santiago de Las Vegas municipality.

Shortly afterwards came the military coup of March 10 which finally evicted the great majority or perhaps everybody from those barrios. What happened to them is not known.

During that period, Fidel also defended campesinos threatened with eviction, and was the prosecuting lawyer in the trial of police agents under the command of Lieutenant Rafael Salas Cañizares and Commander Rafael Casals, both notorious killers, for the homicide of young Carlos Rodríguez, whom they clubbed to death on the street (Hospital and San Lázaro). The case was filed after the Batista coup, when the dictator appointed Salas Cañizares brigadier and his chief of police.[20]

I WILL ASSUME MY OWN DEFENSE

In the archives of the former Las Villas Provincial Court there is an old file containing a minute that states:

In the City of Santa Clara, December 14, 1950 constituted in a Public Hearing, the First Section of the Las Villas Court of Justice, with President Mr. Armando M. Rodríguez Valdés.

And magistrates Messrs. Mario F. Márquez Martínez and Arturo Rebollar Martínez, in my presence, appeared for this Emergency Trial No. 543 of 1950. For Inf. Section 7, Article 23, Decree Law 292 of 1934.

Appearing as plaintiff:

Capt. Manuel Pérez Borroto Marrero

As accused:

Fidel Castro Ruz or Ramiro Hernández Pérez and Enrique Benavides Santos or Enrique López García, as prescribed in the trial.

Whom, instructed in the rights granted them by Military Order No. 213 of 1900, in its Article 24, paragraph 4 of Military Order No. 109 of 1899, when asked if they confessed to being authors of the crime imputed to them, stated that they were not the authors, and that Dr. Benito A. Besada for Benavides, and Fidel Castro Ruz on his own behalf, wished to make statements. Accompanied by the stamps of Lawyer's Writ.

Judge Alfredo Carrión Fernández.[21]

The events that led up to the prosecution of Fidel and his comrade took place in Cienfuegos, one month previously, on November 12. In bold headlines, the local press ran the news: "Arrested and taken to the Santa Clara bivouac, FEU leaders Fidel Castro, aged twenty-four, of 3d and 2, Vedado, president of the Faculty of Social Sciences Student Association, and Enrique Benavides Santos, aged twenty-six, of

306 Manrique, in Havana, delegate for the Faculty of Law, who had come to participate in the protests organized by the students against the resolutions of Aureliano Sánchez Arango, Minister of Education, which led to a strike in the institutes."

The student action was banned by Lomberto Díaz, Minister of the Interior, who issued orders to the army, police and paid gangs to break up the demonstration.

The demonstrators, initially assembled in the Institute and then outside the City Hall, were brutally attacked by the public force, machetes in hand.

While those events were going on, the chief captain of the army and other soldiers arrested Fidel Castro and his comrade, charging them with inciting the Cienfuegos students and attempting to hold by any means the meeting banned by the governor. . . .[22]

Journalist Aldo Isidrón del Valle, who meticulously researched these historical events, informs us:

Minister Sánchez Arango was attempting to eliminate the gains won by the students in secondary education institutes for the 1950-1951 year. He brought in a resolution that was immediately energetically opposed by the students. And having imposed the measure, he stationed police at the entrance to each institution.

The atmosphere was hotting up as the days passed in the island's twenty-one institutes and the educational year, set for October 3, came closer. That day the Cienfuegos Association of Senior High School Students decided on a general strike and called on the rest of the student institutions in the country to support it.

The strike spread like a chain reaction, accompanied by demonstrations and street protests. The Matanzas Institute was closed, and that of Cárdenas occupied by the police. A supreme disciplinary committee was formed in Cienfuegos and René Morejón González, president of the Students Association, was sentenced to five months absence from the institute. The movement acquired a national dimension: secondary education was not only paralyzed in the universities but in the technical and professional colleges and the home schools.

Infuriated, Lomberto Díaz, Minister of the Interior, illegalized the student associations, persecuted their leaders, suppressed the right to meet and prohibited the organization of public assemblies. He was determined to crush the student body's unyielding resistance.

In this situation the FEU constituted a fighting committee to support the secondary students, and its leadership included Fidel, who immediately set up a plan of action:

- A lightning meeting in the University of Havana's Cadenas Plaza.
- A demonstration in the streets of the capital to the Martyrs' Monument at La Punta.
- A 72-hour suspension of teaching activities in the Alma Mater and a plan to extend the stoppage for an indefinite period if necessary.
- A representation of the Fighting Committee to attend public demonstrations organized by the secondary education sectors for the repeal of the measures imposed by Aureliano.[23]

The strike continued for forty days in that southern city, and pupils from the institute had thrown furniture and other effects into the streets. A supreme disciplinary council was once again functioning and ten students were expelled.

The student leadership in Cienfuegos agreed to mobilize the people for a demonstration outside the teaching center itself, for the afternoon of November 12, and sent an invitation to the FEU Fighting Committee. By this point they were condemning both Sánchez Arango's reactionary rulings and Lomberto Díaz' abuses, and the cowardice of a teaching faculty that made itself an accomplice of the regime's injustice and lent itself to sanctioning the rebelling students.

The bed of a truck was fitted out as a rostrum, amplifiers installed, and young pickets were agitating in the streets.

Captain Faustino Pérez Leiva, military chief of the plaza, seconded by likewise captain of the police section, Manuel Pérez Borroto, announced that the demonstration was banned. Its organizers were deliberating on what to do when the FEU delegation arrived. Headed by Fidel, it was composed of Enrique Benavides, Mauro Hernández, Francisco Valdés and Agustín Valdés.

They decided to visit Pérez Borroto to explain that the ban on the demonstration was illegal and that the students were exercising an inviolable constitutional right.

Fidel led the conversation at the residence of the chief of police; his arguments were irrefutable; the student group was within its right, it had the right to protest, to demand the repeal of abusive measures... And the captain repeated time and time again: "I know nothing about laws, I know nothing about educational problems. And I don't discuss orders. I fulfil them, whatever they are."

Fifteen minutes went by. There was no agreement and so they left.

Another organizers' meeting. The majority held the view that confrontations with the police should be avoided and the objective of holding the meeting achieved. The idea came up to occupy the City Hall and, with amplifiers angled toward the street, to talk to the people from there. Fidel felt that that was the most logical and positive course of action. His comments decided the agreement.

At 6:00 P.M. as planned, the Municipal Palace was occupied. The student commissions worked on readying the large council meeting room. Railroad and port workers cooperated by bringing in chairs to accommodate the public. Everything was prepared quickly to commence the meeting at 8:30 P.M. and the tension rose.

They were waiting for the arrival of the main speakers, especially the Havana University students.

The old clock on the San Carlos and Martí cathedral indicated 8:10 P.M.

People were impatient; meanwhile the mobilization crowded in front of the Municipal Chamber in Martí Park to back the students' just demands with their presence and to listen to the valiant voices of Fidel and the other FEU leaders.

Just after 8:15 P.M. the university delegation approached the City Hall. Suddenly their way was closed by a group of police officers under the command of Lieutenant Julián Negret Pineda. Fidel and Benavides were arrested and taken to the police unit next to the City Hall. They were charged with inciting the strike and promoting a public event not authorized by the government, as the charge card read. . . .[24]

Prío's henchmen unleashed all kinds of mistreatment on Fidel and Benavides, ranging from verbal abuse to kicks, and further abuse was only spared because of the mobilization of students and the masses, whose cries of protest shook the old building to its foundations.

From a window in the upper part of the cell, which they reached by climbing up on each other's shoulders in turn, Fidel and his comrade could observe what was happening outside.

In the street, the army and police were attacking youth right and left with machetes and truncheons. However, despite the combined pressure of both repressive forces, the meeting was going ahead in the City Hall. Leaders from the FEU talked to the people, denouncing the government maneuvers and informing them of the arrest of Fidel and Benavides. The objective that took Fidel and his comrade to Cienfuegos was to a large degree attained.

The protest against the excesses of the Prío regime was even more violent and its repercussions had an impact that wouldn't normally have occurred in a meeting.

The unequal fight between the people and Carlos Prío's henchmen continued for more than four hours. The streets were only finally deserted in the early hours of the morning. That was when two pairs of rural guards arrived at the cell where Fidel and Benavides were being held with orders to take them to an unknown location.

"We put up resistance," Benavides told us years later, "we were taken from the prison under force, handcuffed and kicked. They put us into a car, protected by another one, and we took off for an unknown destination. After about twenty minutes they stopped the cars in a place surrounded by shrub and tried to force us out. We fought against them, kicking, elbowing and punching.

"This struggle was going on when a car appeared in the distance signaling with its lights and stopped beside us a few seconds later. A man got out asking indignantly:

"'What's going on with these two boys? Answer me!' It was the president of the City Hall, who had followed us from Cienfuegos because he feared for our lives, and with that valiant attitude he frustrated the act of aggression."

Fidel and Benavides and their custodians reached Santa Clara at four in the morning, and were locked in a cell. Three hours later an angry crowd of students surrounded the provincial penitentiary. The climate of tension extended to the capital, Villa Clara. Thousands of voices chorused: "Set them free! Set them free! Aureliano, murderer, coward!"

The combative action of the student body, the popular mobilization, and an exposé by Orthodoxy leader Eduardo R. Chibás combined to force the Carlos Prío government into granting bail for the FEU leaders.[25]

On November 14, the day after his release, Fidel sent an open letter to the people of Cienfuegos, which *La Correspondencia* newspaper included in its pages. Here is an extract:

". . . We went to the institutes in Cienfuegos at the invitation of comrades from the Institute, to speak at a demonstration which, as everyone knew, was convened with all the legal requirements and whose only aim was a more than just protest at the education minister's despotic attitude toward the students, as horrifically revealed yesterday against teachers and professors in secondary education.

"For that reason it is shameful to see how many of those same teachers are groveling to serve the dictatorial minister, on the pretext that they have the necessary support to restore order and discipline in educational centers.

"Government hysteria created a crisis in Cienfuegos, with the Minister of the Interior's arbitrary, illegal and unjustified order to repress the student meeting.

"The reactionary order denied the students their ultimate right, their only means of defense against injustice and calumny; now they are also going to have to defend themselves against violence. This is a serious precedent making future public demonstrations—a basic right within any democratic regime—dependent on the capricious will of a Minister of the Interior, who could turn out to be, like this one, a politician without morals or scruples, a bastard son of the prevailing situation.

"And they will calmly say that it is to safeguard public order, because the cynical justification of petty tyrants is always the same. They do not safeguard any public or private order, nor do they respect standards or sentiments, but violate the constitution, make mincemeat of the most elemental of citizens' rights; they are the ones who disturb order, peace and justice.

"And will those who act in this way be in the right? And will that brazen captain—who does not deserve to be one—of the Cuban army who, in an insolent and cowardly manner labeled us outsiders and took us to the Emergency Court in handcuffs, be in the right?

"What scant intelligence and bad faith on the part of that small-minded captain to accuse invited speakers who had barely shaken off the dust of the road and begun to replace lost energy with the food that an amiable student—like everyone from Cienfuegos—gave us in his home, of being outsiders and instigators. How heroic! How courageous! What a brilliant strategy! The genius of Napoleon himself resuscitated! With that intelligence, his supreme patriotism and the outstanding services rendered to Cuba with our detention he could well be forgiven for ignoring that paragraph in the Constitution, which states that any Cuban may enter and remain in national territory, leave it, move from one place to another and change residence without needing a letter of security or any similar requisite.

"I would like to state in this newspaper that his arbitrary attitude did not frighten us. There is no merit in being the public hangman, only ignominy. The captain should rectify his ways in time and desist from sowing hatred among those who have to suffer his presence. We will meet again at the Emergency Court!"[26]

Enrique Benavides told the journalist that Fidel and he appeared before the Las Villas Court in early December 1950.

"We left by train for Santa Clara at midnight. Fidel hardly slept. He was reading Martí for hours and on that occasion, as in November when the Cienfuegos incident occurred, the only books he took with him were Martí's works. He was preparing his defense.

"We reached Santa Clara at 6:00 A.M. feeling tremendously cold. We were ill fed and worse clothed

"We went on foot from the railroad terminal to the house of Benito Besada, one of our comrades from university classes and the revolutionary struggle, who was starting up practice as a lawyer. He was to take on my defense; Fidel had other plans.

"On the way we drew up our strategy. Fidel proposed that I should ratify what he said before the court: 'Follow my instructions to the letter,' he repeated.

"To be truthful I had my doubts and I argued that he had little experience as a lawyer and that court problems in that period were resolved by ruses and political bargaining. We argued it out and reached the conclusion that Fidel would defend himself and Benito Besada would represent me.

"It should be clarified that Chibás and the Orthodoxy and Popular Socialist Parties had appointed lawyers for us; we thanked them for their offer, but kept to the agreed strategy."[27]

In relation to the events of December 14, 1950, Aldo Isidrón del Valle also interviewed Benito Besada, one of Fidel's comrades from Villa Clara in the years of higher education and resident in Havana.

". . . Fidel and Benavides arrived at my house on Martí and Luis Estévez in Santa Clara as day was breaking; they looked tired. We had breakfast and exchanged impressions on the situation they were both confronting and I got ready to go to the hearing so as to discover the trial details and define our defensive strategy.

"I did my exploratory work for part of the morning; I found out at the Secretariat that the district attorney would be Dr. Carrión. I went to see him and explained that I was defending two colleagues from the University, that I had little experience in the profession, (I had recently graduated) and needed his opinions on the case and, if possible, which aspects I could work on in the trial to gain my clients' acquittal.

"Carrión reviewed the case. He told me he couldn't anticipate anything: 'Everything depends on the trial's development,' he warned.

"It was already known that the charges being heard in that court were agitation, public disorder; Fidel and Benavides were accused of having promoted a series of street meetings and inciting the people against the civil and military authorities.

"I went back home, Fidel was still resting. I saw a book on his chest, Emil Zola's famous *J'Accuse!*

"I woke him up. I told him that I had gotten a favorable impression from the district attorney, but that wasn't necessarily a reason for optimism. Because in emergency trials there is no indictment, there are elements that are presented during the trial and the defense needs to be alert to this kind of situation."[28]

Benito Besada talked things over with Fidel Castro and Enrique Benavides. A surprise was awaiting the Villa Clara lawyer.

"Well, in that conversation Fidel suggested that I should represent Benavides and that he would defend himself in order to denounce a series of abuses suffered by the people. Fidel's face burned with indignation. He insisted that the result of the trial would depend on the way it went, statements from witnesses and what the two accused would expound. A negative sensation came into my mind.

"I thought that an impassioned statement by Fidel might complicate the situation, and for that reason I had prepared a defense that would give the court a way out for acquittal, but. . . ."

Fidel didn't say any more on the subject. They had lunch and at 12:45 P.M. arrived at the court, an old and robust building constructed at the beginning of the century. The university leader continued reading.

Presumably he was studying his self-defense and plea. Efforts to obtain a gown for him from the Lawyers College were underway.

The court corridors were overflowing with the public, mainly young students and revolutionaries and they greeted Fidel, expressing support in their gestures.

"When the hearing commenced," Besada related, "the first person to give evidence was Manuel Pérez Borroto, the Cienfuegos police captain, who acidly accused Fidel and Benavides. He affirmed that he had proof that they were responsible for the Cienfuegos incident.

"The captain didn't refer to the repeated excesses and abuse committed against the students and the people, and formulated charges filled with hate against my comrades, asking the court to sanction them.

"Witnesses appeared but there was no substantive evidence against Fidel and Benavides."

The list of witnesses having been exhausted, Dr. Rodríguez Valdés, president of the court, informed Fidel and his comrade that it was their turn to speak. Both men remained in the dock, and stated that an emergency trial did not offer sufficient guarantees or legal procedure to analyze the crimes attributed to them.

District Attorney Carrión intervened and the following dialogue immediately ensued between the accused and magistrate Rodríguez Valdés:

"Are you represented?"

"Yes," affirmed Benavides. "Dr. Besada will defend me."

"And you, Mr. Castro?"

"I will assume my own defense."

"Please acquire your lawyer's stamp and take your place on the rostrum."

Besada recalled that Fidel went outside the room. Arturo Valdés, an old court employee, was waiting with a gown for his use. Fidel returned dressed in the gown and, as a lawyer, took his place next to him. A total and tense silence reigned in the court. The bailiff called the witnesses. Carrión spoke first and then us. Fidel called Captain Manuel Pérez Borroto for the prosecution.

Fidel went onto the offensive from his first question to the arrogant officer:

"You represent the people very badly when you repress and stifle their legitimate rights," stated Fidel.

Arrogantly, Captain Pérez Borroto pressed on with his accusation, but his arguments steadily weakened under questioning from the university leader, who did not allude to Case 543 in particular, but to the situation in Cuba. He attacked the political system.

"After the cross-examination," Besada continued, "Dr. Rodríguez Valdés asked Carrión to present his summing up and, despite the very tense development of the trial given the way in which Fidel conducted his questioning of the captain, the district attorney called for all charges to be dropped against the accused for lack of evidence against them."

Nevertheless, when the presiding judge conceded the word to the defense, Fidel rose to his feet and slowly and energetically denounced the outrages of the regime.

"The characteristic of that self-defense," Besada observed, "was valiant Fidel's 'J'accuse!' He made a dramatic speech, passionately denouncing the Prío regime's corrupt politics: the lack of constitutional guarantees, the embezzlement of our wealth, assaults by gangs on trade unions and other evils suffered by Cuba.

"Fidel barely referred to the charges against him; he charged the Prío government. It was a valiant and honorable attack.

"Fidel's charges imparted an unexpected tension to the trial. The public present in the courtroom was visibly moved. Nobody had ever talked in those terms in the Villa Clara Court; there was no precedent and nobody thought that someone could speak in that way.

"The court also received the impact of Fidel's 'J'accuse!' It was something completely new, an event greeted by shock and admiration.

"The magistrates withdrew for half an hour to deliberate their verdict, not a usual situation in the Emergency Hearings, which generally announced their ruling immediately. They didn't immediately accept the district attorney's instruction. I believe that Fidel's 'J'accuse!' was an influential element there.

"The panorama of the trial had changed. When I assumed Benavides' defense I subscribed to Fidel's testimony, but in more moderate terms.

"While the court was out, Fidel and I talked and he asked me what I thought. 'Well kid,' I replied, 'I'm sure they're going to find you guilty,' and I wasn't so far off the mark because Vázquez Martínez, one of the magistrates, cast his particular vote for a sanction. 'Our fate doesn't matter Benny, these truths had to be told,' a serene and confident Fidel whispered to me."[29]

Shortly afterwards the judge ordered the accused to rise and announced his ruling of innocent. Fidel's 'J'accuse!' left no room for doubt; however, it took many years for justice to become a reality on Cuban soil.

FIDEL CHARGES PRÍO AND HIS CLIQUE

Pedro Trigo, a 26th of July Movement combatant, recalls:

We met Dr. Fidel Castro at a public meeting in Santiago de las Vegas, at the end of November 1951. At that meeting, a comrade had referred to the false incineration of bank notes by the Carlos Prío government, to which I responded that we didn't need to go that far, as we had an example of that government's corruption in our own municipality. There was wealthy man here in Santiago de las Vegas, Mendigutía, whose interests were championed by Carlos Prío. This man had raped an eight-year-old girl, so neither his influence nor his money could save him from prison. On assuming the presidency of the Republic, Carlos Prío immediately reprieved this man who, to express his gratitude, gave him a small farm of approximately 3360 hectares in El Globo district between Calabazar and Managua. Prío so much liked that farm that he immediately took to buying up neighboring farms, including Lage, Potrerillo de Menocal, Casas Viejas, Pancho Simón, and Paso Seco, converting the original small farm into an extension of some 73,200 hectares, which he named El Rocío. Juan Rodríguez, the campesino leader in the area, was one of those renting the land and evicted without any legal ruling.

When I'd finished speaking, a young, tall, strong and well-built man approached me and asked if everything I had just said was a definite fact, which I guaranteed. Then he introduced himself as Dr. Fidel Castro and asked me what I thought of getting together to get hard evidence against Prío and his clique and thus vindicate the memory of deceased Orthodoxy Party leader Eddy Chibás. It was Chibás who had been asked for evidence that his party had not been able to provide at that time, and Fidel explained that if we devoted ourselves to this, with the evidence to hand, Prío's government could be exposed in court and before public opinion.

The idea appealed to me and I said yes. We arranged to meet at 8:00 A.M. the next day at my house—at that time I lived opposite the Tejidos Capitalinos factory, on a small farm owned by my father-in-law, Gregorio Crespo Rodríguez.

Early next morning Fidel arrived at my house accompanied by two comrades, José Luis Tasende and Gildo Fleitas, who were later killed during the attack on the Moncada Garrison. After talking I took them to see El Rocío farm. We drew up our plans and commited ourselves with these comrades to look for information and evidence concerning this farm. Fidel had the idea—among other things—of having a kind of outing to it one day, getting onto the land with some women comrades and Martínez Tinguao for a picnic, with the intention of being discovered there. Some twenty minutes after entering the land, we were discovered by Tejera, the sergeant, who was responsible for looking after the farm. Alarmed, he asked us how we had dared to enter the president's farm, to which Fidel responded was he was referring to the president of the Senate or that of the Supreme Court? Tejera replied the farm belonging to Carlos Prío Socarrás, President of the Republic, and how did we dare to go in there. Although we already knew the sergeant, Fidel took advantage of his skills to ask him his name and to make him repeat that the farm belonged to Prío, the President of Cuba. Then he apologized, saying that we didn't know whom the farm belonged to and that we were just out for a good time. The sergeant told us to get off the land immediately.

Comrades José Luis Tasende, Gildo Fleitas and myself devoted ourselves to taking photos of regular soldiers undertaking tasks like stonewalling and tree grafts with the Pestonit company; as well as constructing barns and stables on the farm patio. On one occasion both Gildo Fleitas and Fidel filmed the farm and the activities being undertaken by soldiers there from a plane.

Fidel managed to find out from Carlos Pérez, who lived nearby, that those farms now combined under the name of El Rocío, were registered in the San Antonio de las Vegas court. As a lawyer, Fidel was easily able to confirm this, by obtaining the file number and the inscriptions. They were registered as being owned by the Acirema Real Estate Company, whose president was Carlos Prío himself.

We also talked with campesinos employed in El Rocío who were paid a daily wage of only $2.50, from which they had to pay $0.50 for lunch and $0.50 for transport, leaving them with a wage of $1.50 per day. Among those workers I remember one named Guillermo Luis, nicknamed Pijirigua, being a native of that town. We also talked with evicted tenant Juanito Rodríguez, thrown off his farm, as I stated previously.

Additionally, we took on the work of seeking information on La Chata and La Altura in Pinar del Río, as well as a farm belonging to José Eleuterio Pedraza in Santa Clara, which was continuously guarded and protected by the army.

Fidel subsequently denounced all these things before the Supreme Court and in the *Alerta* newspaper, challenging Prío and his clique to refute everything he had just charged. Obviously, nobody came forward to refute it, because they knew it was a fact and that all the evidence was there.[30]

On September 11, 1951, Fidel had published in *Alerta* his article "Más vale morir de pie" (Better to Die on Your Feet), on the murder of young Carlos Rodríguez, which was also an exposé of vice and abusive practices by the police force.

On January 28, 1952, likewise in *Alerta,* he wrote another titled: "Prío rebaja la función de nuestras fuerzas armadas" [Prío Reduces the Function of Our Armed Forces], in which he demonstrated how soldiers' labor was being utilized for the personal gain of politicians, even extending to agricultural work on the properties of the president of the Republic himself. "34 fincas compradas en una sola provincia" (Thirty-four Farms Bought up in Just One Province) was the headline of the subsequent investigation in *Alerta,* February 11, 1952, which exposed the sordid story of how Prío's unconstitutional promotion of a latifundium was linked to immoral extortion and complicity with a millionaire who had raped a young girl, a man he defended as a lawyer and subsequently reprieved as president, so that he could act as his front man in the acquisition of more and more rural properties.

Six days before the coup on March 4, *Alerta* published Fidel's evidence that the government was subsidizing gangster groups with state funds: "$18,000 mensuales dan a las pandillas en Palacio" [$18,000 per Month to Gangs in Palacio], with a subtitle reading: "Sostiene Prío la terrible maquinaria del crimen" [Prío Supporting the Terrible Crime Machine].[31]

ENDNOTES

1. Frei Betto, op. cit., 115.
2. Ibid., 115-116.
3. Ibid., 116.
4. Ibid., 119-121.
5. Tomás Borges, op. cit., 21-22.
6. Ibid., 266-269.
7. Fidel Castro, "Una Revolución solo puede ser hija de la cultura y las ideas," ed. cit., 49-50.
8. Fidel Castro, "Discurso pronunciado con motivo del inicio del curso escolar 1995-1996 en la enseñanza superior y sus 50 años de vida revolucionaria," ed. cit., 6.
9. Id.
10. Cuban People's Party (Orthodoxy). *Ed.*
11. Aldo Isidrón del Valle, "Historia para una foto," in *Antes del Moncada,* ed. cit., 192-193.
12. *Fidel Castro: "Fidel siempre fue Fidel" [Fidel Was Always Fidel], in Bohemia* magazine, no. 17, April 26, 1959, 149.
13. Marta Rojas, "Fidel defiende a carpinteros deudores, como abogado del acreedor" [Fidel Defends Indebted Carpenters, As a Lawyer of the Creditor], in *Antes del Moncada,* ed. cit., 196.
14. Marta Rojas participated as a reporter in the trial against Fidel Castro for the attack on the Moncada Garrison in 1953. *Ed.*
15. Marta Rojas, "Fidel defiende a carpinteros deudores," in *Antes del Moncada,* ed. cit., 197.
16. Ibid., 198.
17. Ibid., 198-200.

18. Ibid., 201-202.

19. Ibid., 202-204 and 207.

20. Ibid., 208-211.

21. Aldo Isidrón del Valle, "Patriótico ¡Yo acuso! de Fidel Castro" [Patriotic Fidel Castro's J'Accuse!], in *Antes del Moncada,* ed. cit., 212-213.

22. Ibid., 214-215.

23. Ibid., 215-216.

24. Ibid., 218-219.

25. Ibid., 223-224.

26. Ibid., 224-226.

27. Ibid., 226-227.

28. Ibid., 227.

29. Ibid., 228-231.

30. Centro de Estudios de Historia Militar de las FAR, *Moncada: antecedentes y preparativos* [Moncada: Antecedents and Preparation], 3d edition, Vol. 1 (Havana: Editora Política, 1985), 188-190.

31. Mario Mencía, *El grito del Moncada,* Vol. 1 (Havana: Editora Política, 1986), 31.

Fidel fought actively against the coup d'état.

BEFORE THE COUP D'ÉTAT

A COUP, NOT A REVOLUTION!

W*hen Fulgencio Batista took the Columbia Military Camp on March 10, 1952 and declared that his coup d'état was a genuine democratic revolution, there were only fifty-two days to go to the general elections in which the corrupt government of Carlos Prío Socarrás would undoubtedly have been defeated. On June 1, 1952, the people's votes were going to give the victory to the Orthodoxy candidates.*

Analyzing the details, Fidel Castro intuitively realized that General Batista was preparing a conspiracy against the national interest and attempted to make that exposé public. Journalist Mario Mencía relates:

With his fine perception of the essential aspects of our political life, a few weeks earlier vehemently anti-Prío lawyer Fidel Castro had also announced his intention to expose the Batista coup plan. In addition to information collected in various ways deduced from public rumors, his recent conversations with leaders of the *Paupista* youth,[1] whom he knew from his student days, strengthened his idea of the imminence of a coup d'état. One of them heatedly defended his Party's victory, when in reality it had absolutely no electoral chances, as well as the supposed philosophy of force and the need for a dictatorial government that would bring order to Cuba. Another one, aware of Fidel's perspicacious and tenacious investigative qualities, tried to sound him out to see if he had any evidence that Batista was planning a coup. Logic dictated that Batista had no alternative but to stage a coup.

Those conversations reaffirmed his suspicions. Rapidly, he spoke with [Roberto] Agramonte and asked if he could be allowed to use the party's national radio space to substantiate and make public the charge. But instead of granting it, he was told that he needed to corroborate those suspicions, obtain some proof from worthy sources. The proof was limited to consulting a group of civilian professors at the Higher College of War, who affirmed that all the rumors were false. According to them, Batista was not conspiring with any soldiers. Thus Fidel was refused airspace on "La hora ortodoxa" (The Orthodoxy Hour).[2]

What was Fidel's initial reaction when the coup occurred? The answer was given by the leader of the Cuban Revolution himself, when he confessed:

"I felt a tremendous anger at what had happened. But one of the things that most hurt me was not having made that exposé affirming the imminence of the coup. Agramonte denied me the Party radio hour. He said that there was no definite evidence that Batista was conspiring with soldiers on active duty. Really, that Orthodoxy leadership was totally incompetent."

It didn't matter that March 9 was a Sunday: on that day, like every day, Fidel had returned late at night to his little apartment on the second floor of No. 1511 27th Street, between 24 and 26, Vedado. He lived there with his wife and son. Two of his brothers-in-law and his brother Raúl, who was studying at the university, slept in a bedroom on the roof, reached by a stairway from the kitchen.

It was usual practice for Fidel to arrive late. In addition to his interminable political activity for the ongoing election campaign, in recent months he had immersed himself simultaneously in investigations and exposés of corruption, fraudulent businesses and Prío's links with gangster groups.[3]

René Rodríguez, one of his closest collaborators at that time, recalls:

Sometimes we didn't sleep, and when we went to bed it was because there was nothing else to do. While there was something to do, Fidel didn't go to bed. I left Fidel at 23d and went to my house in Lawton. I woke up around 8:30 A.M. Usually I would go back to Fidel's house between 9:00 and 10:00 A.M. when we didn't have anything to do early. That was the time that Fidel began to prepare his commentaries for the radio space on "La Voz del Aire" (Voices On Air), which started at 1:30 or 1:45 P.M. depending on when Pardo Llada's program finished.

When I woke up that morning, my household already knew about the coup d'état. I got dressed rapidly and went to see Fidel. He wasn't in the apartment. Mirta, his wife, told me that he'd gone out early to his sister Lidia's house. Lidia lived about four or five blocks from there, in one of the third-floor apartments of a building that makes a fork on 23d Street: No. 1352. I went over there and, logically, we started to talk about the coup, the collapse of all our plans and Fidel immediately began to try to obtain information. Straight away he sent me to the University and other places. I went to the University several times that day.

Although nobody knew where Fidel was and so nobody went to see him, René Fiallo from the Dominican Republic was there and talked with Fidel about the situation. René Fiallo was Prío's advisor, Prío's spokesman, he wrote his speeches; he was a friend of Fidel's sister Lidia. After the students met with Prío, Fidel sent me to find Álvaro Barba to find out the situation at the University, what he thought and what the students were going to do. Fidel was really annoyed when he heard that Masferrer had been at the University and reproached Barba. They talked for a long while until Barba left.

Fidel also sent me to Roberto Agramonte's house, on 4th between 5th and Calzada, nearby. Agramonte was meeting with a cohort of Orthodoxy members from his faction. There was a lot of confusion in his house. They talked a lot but didn't decide on anything concrete. He didn't send any message to Fidel, nothing. Agramonte was already discussing the idea of civil resistance. When I told Fidel about that a tremendous row ensued.

That day I devoted myself exclusively to seeking information. Fidel didn't go anywhere until that night, when he thought he should leave Lidia's house. He went to the Andino hotel, a guesthouse where he'd lived before, opposite the University, at 1128 San Lázaro on the corner of M. He slept there that night. Meanwhile I set myself to finding somewhere for the next day. I went to talk with Orthodoxy member Eva Jiménez, posed the situation to her and Eva set everything up so that we could move into her apartment, bought in some food and even told her servant not to come, that she wasn't going to work.

On March 11, I went to collect Fidel at 9:00 A.M. at the Andino hotel. He came downstairs wearing some dark glasses that he never used. We took the 28 bus at the corner. As we didn't have any change, Fidel wanted to pay the fare with a five-peso bill that Lidia had given him, but the conductor didn't have any change and a man riding on the back seat paid the sixteen cents for us. To get to Marianao, the 28 route covered the whole of 23d Street, so we passed both Lidia's house and Fidel's. Before crossing Almendares bridge, when the bus went past the Bureau of Investigations, Fidel commented: "That's going to turn into a nest of vultures." We got off at 46th and 21st, in Almendares, and continued on foot to Eva's house. Eva Jiménez lived in an interior apartment on the second floor of the Raquel building, which is on 42d Street, No. 1507 between 15th and 17th. There Fidel immediately sat down to write "Revolución no, zarpazo!" (Coup, Not Revolution!) at the table in a small room, like a little dining room beside the kitchen. He spent that day and the next writing and writing, one draft and another, by hand, because we didn't have a typewriter. He had sent me to get paper and his typewriter from his house, but when I got there, I found his brother-in-law Rafael Díaz-Balart with some Batista people and the police, and they wouldn't let me take anything from the apartment. You can imagine Fidel's reaction when I returned empty-handed and told him. In the end we had to copy it all out onto clean paper. Raúl was also in Eva's house that night.

When the document was finished, Fidel sent Eva, and I accompanied her, to ask Vasconcelos to publish it. Márquez Sterling and other high-ranking political figures were at the *Alerta* newspaper waiting to talk to Vasconcelos. He was already measuring up that situation. He explained to us that he had economic problems with the newspaper, that it wasn't his, that he still had to be paid, that he was well screwed and that everyone was in on the action, in opportunism and others in shit, because he had met with the leadership of the Orthodoxy Party, with Millo Ochoa, Agramonte and all those people, and could see that they were in the clouds and weren't proposing anything realistic. In short, Vasconcelos refused to publish "Revolución no, zarpazo!" but ended the conversation saying surprisingly: "Take care of Fidel, take care of that boy, because he's the great reserve that the Cuban people have." That was how he said goodbye to us. We went back and informed Fidel that his piece couldn't be published in *Alerta*. We relayed everything that Vasconcelos had explained, because Vasconcelos had praised Fidel more than once during the conversation; he said that with Fidel you could talk about anything, politics or any other theme, and related conversations he'd had with Fidel on Shakespeare's works. That was engraved on my mind.

The big problem to sort out first was still the circulation of that document printed. We didn't go to any other press agency because censorship was already established and Fidel was in a very tight corner, very tight. Then he sent me to make contact with Raúl de Aguiar, and Raúl de Aguiar found a comrade whom I believe was a publicist, who lived close to San Lázaro, above a pharmacy, on the fourth floor, and out of his friendship with Raúl, he mimeographed it there and then, right in his apartment. Two or three days had already gone by. Before that, we had got a linotypist at *Alerta* to mount it in lead, but we couldn't find any press willing to print it.

Ñico López and Raúl Castro worked on that mimeographed printing of "Revolución no, zarpazo!" When I went to collect the already printed job Ñico and Raúl were there in the mimeograph room. Ñico took away a large volume to distribute and I took another load to where Fidel was.

Well, on March 12, Fidel changed address again. Negotiations were made with Miguel Ángel Quevedo's sister so that he could go to her house. But at the last minute, after he was going, the plans changed. I stayed behind at Eva's apartment because we had a telephone there and we were waiting for a response from the contacts we had made. I stayed there and Eva and another woman from the Orthodoxy Party took Fidel. When Fidel came back in the morning, I found out that he had slept in the family home of the woman who accompanied Eva, who was also a friend of Quevedo's sister.

At that point, near the end of the week, he had already made contact with José Luis Tasende. Tasende was one of the few people who knew where we were. And little by little the atmosphere cleared. In response to a journalist, a statement by Salas Cañizares appeared in a morning paper, affirming that he was not going to take revenge against Fidel. With the publication of that news, there was a certain relief of tension, because there was great antagonism between Fidel and Salas, and with all the power that Salas had, we didn't know what could happen.

Fidel already had the idea of going to the cemetery on Sunday, March 16 to hand out the pamphlets. We remained in hiding in Eva's apartment until that day and left for the cemetery from there. We didn't enter by the main gate but by a side entrance, and approached with great caution. There was no patrol. We began to hand out the leaflets. At the end of the commemoration,[4] the police did arrive. But when the patrols arrived, after Fidel energetically spelt out the central party leaders' thesis of civil resistance, a large group of veteran women Orthodoxy members surrounded Fidel and virtually physically shielded him. The incident went no further. There were no blows or arrests and we were able to leave as we had come.[5]

I BECAME A PROFESSIONAL CADRE

Fidel recalls:

When the coup took place, everything changed. As a first step, I thought we'd have to go back to the previous constitutional stage. The military dictatorship would have to be defeated. I thought we'd have to recover the country's previous status and that everybody would join forces to wipe out Batista's infamous, reactionary coup. I started to organize ordinary militant members of the Orthodoxy youth group on my own, and I also contacted some of the leaders of that party. I did that on my own. Some of the leaders said they favored armed struggle. I was sure that we would have to overthrow Batista by force of arms in order to return to the previous stage, to the constitutional regime, and I was convinced that that was the objective of all the parties. I'd already worked out the first revolutionary strategy with a large mass movement that would initially be implemented through constitutional channels. I though that everybody would unite to overthrow Batista's regime—all the parties which had formed part of the government and all the opposition parties: everybody. I began to organize the first combatants, the first fighters—the first cells—within a few weeks. First, I tried to set up a small, mimeographed newspaper and some underground radio stations. Those were the first things. We had some run-ins with the police that served as useful experience later on. When it came time to apply that experience, we were extremely careful in choosing cadres and in protecting the security of the organization. That's when we became true conspirators and started organizing the first nuclei for what we thought would be a united struggle by all the parties and all the other forces. That's how I began in that party, where I met a lot of earnest young people. I looked for them in the poorest sectors in Artemisa and Havana, among the workers, with several comrades who supported me right from the beginning: Abel Santamaría, Jesús Montané, Ñico López, and some others—a very small group.

I became a professional cadre. At the beginning, that movement had one professional cadre—me. Up until just before the attack on the Moncada garrison, we had just one professional cadre—one. Abel joined me a few days before the attack, so there were two of us cadres during the last month.[6]

What had happened, among other things? When the March 10 coup occurred, the only people to have money, millions, resources of every type belonged to the defeated government, and they began to mobilize all those resources to buy arms and, of course, those people had a very strong hatred of me. To understand why, you only had to look in the *Alerta* newspaper to find the exposés I made in the weeks leading up to the March 10 coup, which received the honor of appearing on the front page of the largest-circulation newspaper in the country. That was in January and February. They attempted to blame me for the coup d'état, and this was before the publication of two further articles I was preparing. They were worse still, demoralizing, under the headline: "No hay que ir a Guatemala" (No Need to Go to Guatemala).

I based it on the fact that Chibás committed suicide because he had charged certain politicians with having farms in Guatemala and was unable to prove it, which made him the target of exceptional pressure, and he despaired and killed himself. I wrote: "No hay que ir a Guatemala," and began to give information on all the farms that those people had here and all their dirty businesses. My new profession as a lawyer allowed me to search through the property registers and elsewhere for all the written material, all the documentation that I presented as irrefutable proof, and which had a great impact.

So those people even attempted to blame me for the demoralization that had given rise to the coup d'état, an unfounded and irrational idea but a powerful one, and I found myself, on the one side, faced with a tremendous hatred, and jealousy in the University, I have to say. But to make it absolutely clear, never, never on the part of José Antonio [Echeverría], who was always a good comrade and a good friend. But the problem was that a revolution was going on and it seemed that there were people who wanted to snatch the Revolution from the University. Those things happened and it was in those conditions that we organized the 26th of July. Only when we perceived massive errors on the part of those who, given their resources, could promote a rebellion; the divisions between parties and organizations; and the incapacity for action; when there was absolutely no alternative, that was when we decided to initiate the struggle with the forces of the 26th of July [Movement].[7]

CAPACITY TO REACT IN THE FACE OF ADVERSITY

After March 10, Fidel's economic situation became critical:

Leaving 109 Prado one afternoon, his old car wasn't where he had parked it. Had it been stolen? No, the reality was otherwise but no less of a blow: the finance agency had appropriated it because he had failed to keep up with the monthly payments.

Gloomily, Fidel went to the little shop where he used to drink coffee. He just wanted a cup of coffee and a cigar. He hadn't lunched. He said so to the owner but also informed him that he had no money. And as he already owed five pesos, the man refused to extend his credit. Gloomier than ever, Fidel walked up Prado, turned into Colón and reached Zulueta. He observed the armed posts of the Presidential Palace and felt the enormous distance between the power of that regime he was fighting to bring down and his concrete situation in terms of achieving it. His face grew somber. Why did politicians with sufficient means refuse to facilitate him the resources to struggle? He only wanted guns to initiate the combat. Mechanically, reaching Central Park where the statue of Martí stood, he stopped to read the headlines of newspapers put on the ground to sell. Not even five cents in his pockets for a copy. Suddenly the sharp voice of the boy vendor brought him rudely down to earth by shouting: "Move on!" He moved on among the crowds of people busying themselves in their purchases in the large stores on Neptuno Street; passed by Galiano's luxury commercial center and continued on foot for various kilometers to the small room in the student lodgings where he was living with his family. This accumulation of situations made him feel bitter, but resolved and determined to move ahead. He lay down on the bed and fell asleep. At 5:00 P.M. he awoke. It had been like a nightmare. Once again his decisiveness, energy, capacity to react in the face of adversity returned, and he took to the streets to pursue his conspiratorial labor. Montané negotiated the return of the car. He and Abel assumed payment for the subsequent bills and the rental of a small apartment, as well as electricity and telephone bills.

"I was the Movement's first professional cadre," Fidel joked on recalling those times. "They even gave me something for food."[8]

DICTATORSHIP AGAIN, BUT THERE WILL BE OTHER MELLA'S, TREJO'S AND GUITERAS'[9]

On Sunday, March 16—as on the 16th of every month—a crowd of Orthodoxy members gathered at the graveside of Party founder Eduardo Chibás in Colón Cemetery. They were awaiting directions for the struggle, the order for combat. It was yet another disappointment. Millo Ochoa was in charge of reading the awaited Orthodoxy Party manifesto to the people of Cuba.[10]

Suddenly, in a corner of the crowd, shouts and applause focussed attention on a tall young man who, standing on a tomb, had shouted something. Only those closest to him heard his brief harangue but everyone would know it shortly afterwards. In a crumpled *guayabera,*[11] the energy of his voice transmitted through his right index finger, he had simply said: "If Batista climbed to power through force, he will have to be defeated by force!" Somebody asked who the young man was and another man beside him answered: "That's Fidel Castro."[12]

In those initial circumstances one question was obvious.

In the institutional political sphere the only ostensible force with some possibility of successfully mobilizing the masses to confront the recently installed dictatorship was the Orthodoxy Party. An organization with a large popular majority, the coup had been specifically directed against it.

The real anti-Orthodoxy intention of the coup was denounced on March 14 in a manifesto where the deed was described as "Revolución no, zarpazo!" A historical coincidence, for that same date and month sixty years previously saw the first edition of *Patria,* founded by José Martí as an organ of the patriotic émigré movement for promoting revolutionary ideas supporting Cuban and Puerto Rican freedom.[13]

Sixty years after Martí's words, on the same date in the same month, "Revolución no, zarpazo!" was a convincing moral condemnation of another opprobrious regime but, above all, was the first genuine declaration of a people's war against the Batista dictatorship. In its own time, it would be yet another demonstration of its author's political courage, of his historical awareness, of the coherence of his development within our history, of his capacity to react in adverse situations, of his confidence in the people, of his optimism in the future, and yet another solid proof of his profound conviction in the strength of principles to win and sustain the nation's freedom.[14]

Fidel stated in that historical document:

A coup, not a revolution! Not patriots, but the assassins of freedom, usurpers, retrogrades, adventurers thirsty for gold and power.

It was not a putsch against Prío, that weak-willed, indolent president; it was a putsch against the people, on the eve of elections whose result was known beforehand.

There was no order, but it was for the people to democratically decide, in a civilized manner and to elect their rulers by will and not by force.

Money would be staked on the imposed candidate, that is undeniable, but that would not alter the result, just as it failed to alter the squandering of the public treasury in favor of the candidate imposed by Batista in 1944.

The idea that Prío would attempt a coup d'état is totally false, absurd, ridiculous and infantile, a clumsy pretext; his impotence and incapacity to undertake such an enterprise was irrefutably demonstrated by the cowardice with which he allowed power to be taken from him.

There was suffering from a lack of government, but that had been endured for years awaiting the constitutional moment to conjure away evil. But you, Batista, who cowardly fled for four years and engaged in useless politicking for another three, have now reappeared with your belated, perturbing and poisonous remedy, disemboweling the Constitution just two months before that goal was achieved in the proper fashion. Everything you allege is a lie, a cynical justification, a dissimulation of vanity rather than patriotic decorum; ambition rather than ideals; appetite rather than civic grandeur.

Well it is a fine thing to bring down a government of embezzlers and murderers, and we were attempting to do that by the civil route with the support of public opinion and the help of the popular masses. What right do you have to replace by the use of bayonets those that yesterday robbed and killed without measure? It is not peace, but the seed of hatred that is sown in this way. It is not joy, it is the mourning and sadness that the nation feels in the face of the tragic panorama that can be glimpsed. There is nothing in the world as bitter as the spectacle of a people who go to bed free and wake up as slaves.

Once again the boots, once again Columbia [Military Camp] dictating laws, sacking and replacing ministers; once again the tanks growling threats in our streets; once again brute force dominating human reason.

We were not accustomed to living within the Constitution, but we lived for twelve years without great mishaps in spite of errors and absurdities. Superior states of civil cohabitation are not attained without great efforts. In a matter of hours, you, Batista, have just dashed that noble illusion of the people of Cuba.

All the wrongdoing Prío committed in three years, you spent eleven years committing. Thus your coup is unjustifiable, it is not based on any serious moral reasoning, or on any kind of social or political doctrine whatsoever. It finds its reason solely in the force of arms, and its justification in lies. Your majority resides in the army, never in the people. Your votes are guns, never the people's will; you can win a putsch with them, but never clean elections. Your assault on power lacks any principles that could legitimize it; laugh if you want, but in the long run principles are more powerful than cannons. Peoples are nourished and formed on principles, with principles they are nourished in the fight, for principles they die.

Do not term revolution that outrage, that disturbing and inopportune coup, that dirty stab you have just inflicted in the back of the Republic. Trujillo [then president of the Dominican Republic] was the first person to recognize your government, he knows who his friends are in the clique of dictators that is the scourge of the Americas, and that more than anything expresses the reactionary, militarist and criminal nature of your coup. Nobody has the remotest belief in the governmental success of your old and rotten clique; the thirst for power is too great, and brakes are almost nonexistent when there is no other Constitution or law than the will of a dictator and his hirelings.

I know in advance that your guarantee of life will be torture and the palmacristi.[15] Your people will kill even if you don't want that to happen, and you will consent tranquilly because you are totally in their debt. Despots are the masters of the people that they oppress, and the slaves of the force on which their oppression is sustained. Now lying and demagogic propaganda will be raining down in your favor from all mouthpieces, for good or for evil, and vile slander will rain down on your opponents; that is what Prío did as well and it was worth nothing in the mind of the people. But the truth that illuminates Cuba's destinies and guides the steps of our people in this difficult time, that truth you will not allow to be spoken, will be known to the whole world. It will run clandestinely from mouth to mouth among every man and woman, even though nobody will say it in public or write it in the press, and everyone will believe it and the seed of heroic rebellion will take root in everyone's hearts; it is the compass needle in every consciousness.

I do not know what will be the insane pleasure of the oppressors in the whip they will let fall like Cain on human backs, but I do know that there is an infinite joy in combating them, in powerfully raising ones hand and saying: I do not want to be a slave!

Cubans: Another dictatorship is upon us, but there will be other Mella's, Trejo's and Guiteras'. There is oppression in our homeland, but there will be freedom again one day. I call on Cubans of valor, the courageous members of the glorious Party of Chibás; these times are of sacrifice and struggle. If lives are lost nothing is lost; as to live in chains is to live submerged in affronts and opprobrium. To die for the homeland is to live.[16]

WHAT DIFFERENCE IS THERE BETWEEN A PRÍO AND A BATISTA?

As opposed to the party leaders who appealed to the Social and Constitutional Guarantees Court with the idea of demonstrating the regime's illegality, Fidel individualized responsibility in the highest echelons of those involved in the March 10 coup and made it a common criminal act. The dart was launched at a political objective, not a legal one; having discounted this second aspect, he was seeking some effect in the ambit of the first. On March 24 he arraigned Fulgencio Batista y Zaldívar in the Havana Emergency Courts for sedition, treason, rebellion and nocturnal attack. "On all these counts and others too many to enumerate, Mr. Fulgencio Batista y Zaldívar has committed crimes whose cumulative sanction is more than 100 years imprisonment," he emphasized in the proceedings against his rival who, in that very year, was just twice his age.[17]

Fidel devoted several days to contacting the principal leaders of his party. He was not in favor of reacting passively or defensively. Civil resistance in the form of refusing to pay taxes, staying away from recreational diversions, withdrawing capital from the banks and others did not strike him as a way of dislodging Batista from power. He proposed the acquisition of weapons and the formation of a combat force capable of initiating revolutionary war as part of a popular uprising. His plan did not meet with approval. From then on he dedicated himself to forming such a force to see if, once it was organized, they would facilitate the arms it needed.

"What difference is there?" Fidel headed the following exposé, published in the only printed edition of Pardo Llada's *La Palabra* newspaper on April 6, 1952, on the same Sunday that the students marched

141

to the Martí Fragua in what was the beginning of the Constitutional Oath Campaign. That edition of *La Palabra* was simply one tabloid sheet printed on both sides, the popular commentator's way of outwitting the closure of the short program of the same name that went out on air daily at 1:00 P.M. and 6:30 P.M. on the Cadena Oriental de Radio. The regime's reaction was automatic. The printer and two operatives were arrested and taken to La Cabaña fortress; various young people selling the broadsheet in the street were detained, and for the sixth time in one month Pardo Llada was charged with demagogy by the SIM[18] and detained for a number of hours.[19]

La Palabra newspaper would not have had a place in history but for the appearance in it of Fidel's second public attack on the dictatorship. The young lawyer affirmed:

The drove that assaulted the Palace, the Public Treasury and the *Gaceta Oficial* to govern this country in the style of Leónidas Trujillo, must have thought that this is the most miserable people in the world.

Defeated in advance at the ballot boxes, they assaulted power with a coup.

No preaching, no theory, no revolutionary program, no mass mobilizations preceded the coup. However, they decided to call the infamous putsch a "revolution," through which the PAU sergeants shared the public administration booty. But it would be unheard of for Batista to say that he had made a revolution to do away with speculation, crime, dirty dealings and to bring peace and tranquility to Cuban families.

What difference is there between a Prío who made off with forty millions and a Batista who made off with fifty? What difference is there between a Cabrera who enriched himself in army headquarters and a Pedraza who accumulated fifteen million?

What difference is there between a Prío who send Salas to beat up the people, caving in Carlos Rodríguez' brain, and a Batista who makes him chief of police?

What difference is there between a Prío who makes Sergeant Martín Pérez, charged with the murder of Madariaga, a lieutenant, and a Batista who makes him a commander?

What difference is there between a Prío who protects Captain Casillas and a Batista who upgrades him to commander?

Were not Carlos Rodríguez, Francisco Madariaga and Jesús Menéndez the sons of Cuban families?

What difference is there between a José Manuel Alemán, creator of the BAGA,[20] and an Anselmo Alliegro, Alemán's partner and a creator of Subparagraph K?[21] What difference is there between a Ricardo Artigas and a García Pedroso, between an Eduardo Suárez Rivas and an Alfredo Jacomino, between an Orlando Puente and an Andrés Morales del Castillo, between a Nicolás Castellanos and a Justo Luis del Pozo? Is there any difference between those characters and these? And the same fawners, the same hired pens, the same bootlickers that yesterday made panegyrics for Prío are now making them for Fulgencio Batista.

But our present situation is far lower and more insufferable: the former won through the ballot box, but the latter by cunning ambush; the former were going to be swept away in the elections, the latter have indefinitely suppressed them; the former infringed the Constitution, the latter have destroyed it for ever; the former imposed the Mordaza Decree[22] which merited the people's rejection and, at the stroke of a pen, the latter have closed all educational airspace and have placed a soldier with a bayonet at the door of every radio station so that those speaking via the press speak in favor of the government or talk in undertones.

Through a monstrous decree all lawsuits involving soldiers have passed into war jurisdiction.

The sellers out and the timorous affirm that there is freedom of the press and the spoken word: yes, to speak in favor of Batista or to judge him gently, but not to tell the truth and unmask him from head to toe. But the truth will be stated revolutionarily, in defiance of the repression.

The seed of heroic rebellion is growing in everybody's hearts. In the face of danger, heroism appears and germinates with the generous blood that is shed.

Down with those who want to separate the youth from sacrifice with their puerile and accommodating counsel! The frustrations of the past are of no concern to us.

Shame and opprobrium on the collaborators and traitors who, as they did yesterday, are now denying freedom to the homeland and decorum to its people!

Onward all upright Cubans, those of you who, at this difficult hour, wish to place yourselves under the flags of honor.[23]

ABEL SANTAMARÍA MEETS FIDEL CASTRO

On May 1, 1952 Fidel Castro and Abel Santamaría met for the first time. Santamaría headed a combative group that met on 25th and O Streets, in Vedado.

Jesus Montané Oropesa recalls that at midday on May 1, 1952 he had set out with Abel Santamaría for Colón Cemetery to take part in a ceremony in memory of Carlos Rodríguez, a worker who was killed in the protest against the Mordaza Decree emitted during Carlos Prío Socarrás' presidency.

There they met up with Fidel, who was also paying tribute to the fallen comrade. And Montané explained:

"We remembered how Fidel, as a lawyer, organized the private prosecution in that case, and succeeded in arraigning Casals and Salas Cañizares who had murdered the aforementioned comrade with impunity. Later, during the Batista dictatorship, both of them were renowned for their cruelty to imprisoned revolutionaries.

"After the ceremony, Abel, Fidel and myself stayed behind talking. An animated and amicable conversation soon developed on political events in the country. We agreed that something had to be done to combat Batista's dictatorial regime. We lamented the inertia of certain sectors of the so-called opposition, which were demonstrating an evident incapacity to challenge the dictatorship with a genuine fighting front. Such politicking and vacillation made action by the youth imperative. The leader who would organize the people en masse in their battle against the dictatorship could already be perceived in that conversation.

"Fidel talked to us about a doctor friend of his called Mario Muñoz, who practiced in Colón, Matanzas Province, and who was also a radio ham. Fidel was thinking of asking Muñoz to construct us two small plants for his underground operation in Havana.

"As the light brown Chevrolet car that Fidel used was, as always, out of service, Abel gave him his to visit his doctor friend the following Sunday.

We went to Colón and Fidel didn't need much time there to convince the comrade to put together the two underground radio plants as quickly as possible". [24]

Immediately after Fidel's first meeting with Abel at the cemetery, the combative group at 25th and O joined the incipient Movement that Fidel was beginning to organize. The humane and revolutionary quality of this group would become apparent over the course of time. Abel, Boris Luis [Santa Coloma] and Montané came to be part of its National Directorate, Abel as the movement's second in command. Haydée [Santamaría] and Melba [Hernández] were the only two women to participate in the actions of July 26, 1953. It was Raúl Gómez who drafted the manifesto in which the Moncada assailants expounded their reasons for taking that decisive step in our history.

When the 25th and O group linked up with Fidel, he had spent seven weeks in intensive activity. He came and went from 109 Prado, the national Orthodoxy Party headquarters, visited leaders, argued, talked with his party comrades, wrote, spent time with his friends exploring ideas; and in short, created the nucleus of a solid number of young people who identified from the outset with his way of confronting events. [25]

EL ACUSADOR [26]

Jesús Montané Oropesa recalls all the details:

"Abel, Gómez García (the Centennial Generation poet) and ourselves published an underground newspaper that came out every week and which was called *Son los Mismos* [All the Same]. I vividly remember that Fidel proposed that we edit another newspaper with the combative title of *El Acusador.* We admit that it was hard to abandon *Son los Mismos* and, the first week that we started to publish *El Acusador,* the components of editing two newspapers to come out on time had us completely exhausted. Readers can imagine the labor involved in writing the material, cutting the stencils and finally, turning and turning the handle of the old duplicating machine that had cost us the astronomical sum of seventy-five pesos.

145

That old duplicating machine was our efficient printer that assembled the first sentences condemning the regime and was seized by the police on August 16, 1952. Fidel was surprised at that "exhaustion" and that speaking with half a voice until Abel confessed that we were still publishing *Son los Mismos.*

For us in particular it was difficult to understand that we should concentrate our "literary" efforts on one newspaper.

For the first anniversary of Chibás' death on August 16, 1952, we prepared a special edition of *El Acusador* (our third number), running off 10,000 five-page copies, printed on both sides.

There were also two cartoons on the front page demonstrating how our knowledge of layout and typography was improving. The *El Acusador* journalists were the following comrades: Fidel Castro, who signed his articles with the name Alejandro and who was the political advisor; Raúl Gómez García, who used the pseudonym El Ciudadano (The Citizen) and was the editor; Abel as deputy editor and the body of writers comprising Juan M. Tinguao and me. He signed as Don Tin and I used the name Canino (Canine), for my column entitled "Mordant Comments."

Due to a police leak by a petty traitor to whom Fidel referred once on television, our workshop, located in a Vedado house, was raided and some of the 10,000 copies we had worked so hard on were confiscated. In that initial raid by the Batista Porra[27] on our nascent organization, Abel, Gómez García, Elda Pérez, Tinguao, Melba and the author of these memoirs were arrested.

Those copies of *El Acusador* were handed out in the morning in the vicinity of Havana Cathedral and in the afternoon at Colón Cemetery at the ceremony organized by the Orthodoxy Party in memory of its deceased leader Eduardo Chibás.

One year after the death of their leader, the Orthodoxy masses were in confusion due to the incapacity and weakness of their leaders; for that reason, in that special edition of *El Acusador,* Fidel sent the Orthodoxy members an impassioned message headed: "A Critical Account of the PPC."

In the final paragraph Fidel noted:

"Anyone with a traditional concept of politics could feel pessimistic at that tableau of truths. On the other hand, for those who have a blind faith in the masses, for those who believe in the irreducible power of great ideas, the indecisiveness of those leaders cannot be motive for slackening or discouragement, because such spaces will be quickly enough occupied by upstanding men emerging from the ranks."

Thus Fidel criticized those Orthodoxy leaders, veritable clay idols, unable to give any direction to the eager Cuban youth and at a far remove from fulfilling the historical role that Chibás' mandate had shown them. So it is not at all surprising that Fidel should place his faith in the invincible strength of the masses.[28]

During the period August 1952 to January 28, 1953, our organization grew in numbers and discipline.

A few dozen comrades from all over the Island, particularly from Artemisa, Guanajay, Havana and rural Havana, joined the group with patriotic enthusiasm.[29]

Melba Hernández Rodríguez del Rey, a Moncada heroine, recalls:

It was May 1, 1952 when I made my first contact with what whould become the beloved Moncada group. I had gone to an event in the cemetery, where I got to know Abel Santamaría. Abel invited me to his house to hear Fidel's ideas. I went that same night, but Fidel couldn't make it. I also met Haydée Santamaría.

Two or three days later, in the home of Haydée and Abel, I did meet Fidel. At that time many of us young people understood what our duty to the homeland was, but had not found a way to channel that duty. When Fidel spoke at that meeting I had the instant impression that he would be able to guide us, and that his plans could be carried out successfully.

From then, I made daily visits to Abel and Haydée's home. And, in addition to a total revolutionary identification, I developed a sentiment of profound sisterly friendship with Yeyé [Haydée].

I had studied Law, which was not a "productive" career for me. The few areas I covered didn't produce much profit, although they were in accordance with my principles. My "clients" were exploited campesinos, a girl who swapped a brothel for jail, dismissed workers. I still remember a case I took on defending workers from Ómnibus Aliados.[30]

Right after Fidel's graduation, and with the aim of collecting funds for the 26th of July Movement, we were going to take up the case of Eugenio

Sosa, the owner of a rice plantation in Matanzas who, as we found out later, had interests in the *Diario de la Marina* daily. The more we got into the facts, the less we liked the work. When we knew all the details we decided to defend the campesinos that Sosa was accusing, rather than him. And thus renounce the chance of obtaining funds. Fidel was like that, from the beginning he remained faithful to the purity of our Movement.[31]

So, the first joint activity that Abel, Fidel and Montané carried out, days after that meeting at Carlos Rodríguez' grave, was part of a plan set in motion to attain those ends. With his old brown Chevrolet out of action, Fidel rang Montané at General Motors and put the problem to him, and the need to go to Matanzas Province as soon as possible. Abel offered him his car and the three of them left Havana in it on Sunday, May 4.

With the passion that characterized him, throughout the journey Fidel outlined the projects that were buzzing in his brain. *Son los Mismos* had enthused him, but what about a more combative title, like *El Acusador?* And the print run would have to be increased, so that it could reach the comrades in Cayo Hueso, Marianao, Santiago de la Vegas, Güines, Calabazar, Madruga, Artemisa and other places... Every opportunity had to be taken to increase the combative spirit... Everyone who was really determined to fight in the manner that circumstances dictated should be brought together... The revolutionary agitator that existed in Fidel, developed as a student leader during his time at the university and afterwards as an Orthodoxy member, understood the mobilizing effect of live speeches, having seen it in Chibás. At that time he ascribed a special practical value to tribunes, to the microphone. Many things needed to be said, many things needed to be denounced, many people had to be caught by those words. *El Acusador* would not be sufficient. They had to use radio. What did it matter if the stations wouldn't lend them airspace? They had to make efforts to find their own means. Characteristically, Fidel always thought on a grand scale, without vacillating between the goal and the starting point, however great the distance might be. Resources depended on effort, dedication, and tenacity in attaining objectives. Overcoming obstacles was purely a source of satisfaction...

Abel stopped the car outside a house with a wide doorway on the corner of Diago and Estrada Palma in Colón, 190 kilometers east of Havana. A physician by the surname of Muñoz lived and had his consulting rooms there. Mario Muñoz Monroy was fifteen years older than Abel and Fidel. He was two and a half months away from his fortieth birthday. Fifteen months later he would be one of only four assailants of the Moncada Garrison who were older than that when they fell.[32]

CUBA HAS ONLY ONE WAY FORWARD

By the first anniversary of Chibás' death, many things had happened in a very short space of time: Prío no longer headed the government, the June 1 elections had not taken place, and the dictator Batista was drowning the country in bloodshed.

The revolutionary group headed by Fidel had prepared a special edition of *El Acusador,* running to 10,000 copies, to be distributed that day by various comrades assigned to the task.

In spite of the fundamental reasons given in the first edition of *El Acusador,* its index finger did not only point to the ranks of the coup's perpetrators and the shameful renegades who went over to their side. It fulfilled the same role of condemning Batista and his hirelings as *Son los Mismos,* but at the same time, was directed against the weaknesses in the Orthodoxy Party leadership, charging it with being incapable of guiding the people. Thus the two central themes of *El Acusador* had Fidel's particular stamp.

In the third and last number of August 16, 1952, those characteristics were succinctly placed in two editorials both signed with the pseudonym Alejandro. In "Yo acuso" (J'Accuse) he attacked Batista. In "Recuento crítico" [Critical Account] he railed against the inept and Byzantine Orthodoxy leadership.

The tone of "Yo acuso," with as much or more mordacity than *Son los Mismos,* surpassed it in its breadth of knowledge and arguments on the essence and history of the dictator. In it Fidel affirmed:

"Fulgencio Batista, the dogs that daily lick your wounds will never be able to conceal the fetid odors coming from them. Your life, your past, your present, your lies will irretrievably result in your loss. "It is said that you aspire to glory. Without any doubt, Machado will have a hard fight on his hands to defend the sad glory you aspire to take away from him. Everything that you have uttered is lies, refined cynicism, and perfidious hypocrisy. You talk of peace and you are the civil war, the bloody chaos, the abysmal hatred and the fratricide among Cubans that will take many years to erase. You talk of your humble origins and you live in palaces, surrounded by luxuries, replete with millions and waited on by hundreds of servants.

"You are not the soldiers' friend that you claim to be, you merely want to convert them into the stepping stones of your ambitions, into hangmen and Cains, bringing down on them the hatred of the people and thus forcing them to take your side in an ignoble cause: your thirst for power and for gold, in which they assume the risks and labors and you take charge of the millions. You talk of dirty business and your whole fortune has been made in a dirty way. You talk of respect for human life and your born-again henchmen have mown down a hundred valiant lives. You talk of nepotism and crown your family with sinecures and privileges. You talk of gangsterism when you have set up the most infamous gunmen.

"You talk of elections and who could believe you...? You, who blocked the labors of Miguel Mariano[33] and destroyed him...? You, who won the 1940 elections through rigged rules and the force of bayonets."

The following passage of "Yo acuso" is highly significant and prompts meditation. Simply because of the anonymity of the pseudonym? Could there be a more complex reason? It is a fact that Fidel's Marxist background dated back to his university days, but he eluded any such identity with an ironclad self-control extending to his use of language. From that period onward, he was shaping a revolutionary project that pointed toward socialism but, with rigorous Martí-style tactics, he avoided communist affiliations or any revelation of his strategic intentions. He was aware that in that environment and at that time, "they have to be hidden in order to be achieved," given that "proclaiming them for what they are would give rise to too many difficulties in reaching the desired end based on them."[34] But on this occasion, he did not use his careful language in a public document and pointed the finger at the basic, long-term enemy. It would be the first and last time that this occurred prior to the triumph of the Revolution. It is when he states:

"You talk of work and there are more unemployed people than ever. You talk of progress and align yourself with the powerful Cuban and foreign interests. You talk, finally, of the homeland, but you are a loyal running dog of imperialism, and the fawning servant of all the ambassadors."

On the other hand, in critically locating Batista "on the side of the powerful Cuban and foreign interests," he was not only attacking imperialism but also defining his own opposition to Cuban capitalists, in an evident class distinction.

And Fidel ends:

"Facing you, Cuba has only one way forward: sacrifice and immolation for the sake of its beloved liberties.

"For the misfortune she is suffering, for the misery that is hurting her, for the blood that flows... JE T'ACCUSE... YOU RUINOUS DICTATOR!!

"And when history is written it will doubtless refer to you. But it will speak of you as one speaks of plagues and epidemics, as one speaks of Attila's horse... for the devastating tracks you will have left behind on your passing through this earth."[35]

THE TIME IS REVOLUTIONARY, NOT POLITICAL

In "Recuento crítico" the credentials move in another direction. Other values come to the fore that have become a proverbial part of Fidel's character with the passing of time. In the first place, his strict critical and self-critical awareness of errors, which leads him to list some of the acute weaknesses undermining Chibás' followers and incapacitating them. He moves on to attack the indiscipline and irresponsibility of the Orthodoxy Party leadership in plain language, and charges its leaders with distancing themselves from the masses.

The masses, the masses, he reiterates time and time again; his constant obsession, the essential motive for his actions. He talks of the "shock and indignation of the masses." He argues that it is "the turn of the great masses." He notes that "the vast mass of the PPC is on its feet," and reiterates what was then and has always been another of his ethical-practical standards: "Faith in the masses," unfailingly linked to another constant expression of Fidel's action and political thought: a firm belief in "the irresistible force of great ideas."

In his own language, which never gives way to any hint of indiscretion, he employs Leninist tools in terms of analysis and prediction to indicate the change of historical time which would affect and transcend the Party and expose its leadership, incapable of rising to the moment, as an anachronism. At the same time he anticipates the emergence of a new vanguard that will lead the people and that has to be built—again the Leninist line—on the base of genuine merit. The last paragraph of his account is classic in all senses. By making politics equivalent to electoral politicking as it was understood in that environment, he convincingly proclaims:

"The time is revolutionary, not political."[36]

And Fidel argues his assessment in this article:

Over and above the uproar of the cowards, mediocre individuals and the poor in spirit, it is necessary to make a brief but bold and constructive judgment of the Orthodoxy movement in the wake of the death of its great leader Eduardo Chibás.

The formidable final attack delivered by the champion of the Orthodoxy Party bequeathed the Party a huge wealth of popular emotion that placed it at the very gates of power. Everything was done; it only needed to know how to retain the ground gained.

The first question every upstanding Orthodoxy member has to ask himself or herself is this: Have we aggrandized the moral and revolutionary legacy left us by Chibás... or, on the contrary, have we misappropriated part of that wealth...?

Anyone who believes that everything that has been done to date has been done well, that we have nothing to reproach ourselves with, is very easy on his or her own conscience.

Those sterile fights that followed Chibás death, those monumental scandals for motives that were not at all ideological, but purely selfish

152

and personal in flavor, still resound like bitter hammer blows on our consciousness.

That totally disastrous procedure of taking Byzantine quarrels before a public platform was a grave symptom of indiscipline and irresponsibility. Unexpectedly March 10 arrived. One would have hoped that such an extremely grave event would have eradicated such petty feuds and sterile personality battles in the Party from the roots. But was that totally the case...?

To the shock and indignation of the Party masses, stupid quarrels were once again rife. The folly of those responsible was not to notice that the press doorway was too narrow to attack the regime, but on the other hand amply wide enough to attack the Orthodoxy Party itself. Batista has been loaned too many services by that kind of conduct.

Nobody will be scandalized that such a necessary account has been made today, the turn of the great masses who have suffered that misconduct in bitter silence, and at such an opportune moment as the day to answer to Chibás at his grave.

That vast mass of the PPC is on its feet, more determined than ever. At these moments of sacrifice one asks: Where are those who had aspirations... those that wanted to be the first to fill the posts of honor in assemblies and on executives, those who toured municipalities and set trends, those who demanded a place on the podium at large demonstrations, and who, these days, are not touring municipalities, nor mobilizing in the street, nor demanding honorary positions in the front of combat...?

People with a traditional conception of politics could well feel pessimistic given this depiction of the truth. But, for those who have a blind faith in the masses, those who believe in the unfailing force of great ideas, the leaderships' indecision is no motive for weakening or discouragement, because that kind of vacuum is soon filled by upstanding men from the ranks.

The time is revolutionary, not political. Politics is the consecration of opportunism for those who have the means and resources. Revolution opens the way to genuine merit, to those who have valor and sincere ideals, to those baring their chests and taking the standard in their hands. A revolutionary Party needs a youthful revolutionary leadership of popular origin to save Cuba.[37]

FIDEL GOES BACK TO UNIVERSITY

Pedro Miret was in the fourth year of a Surveying degree in the spare-time study plan and was working in the Aqueduct and Sewers Department of the Ministry of Public Works to pay for his studies and subsidize a scant family income. Closely linked to Léster Rodríguez, Abelardo Crespo Arias and Raúl Castro, Pedro Miret lived in a modest boarding house for students on Neptuno and Hospital, near the University. After March 10 he devoted himself completely to voluntary military training at the University, and thus was unable to complete his studies.

He knew Fidel when the latter was reading Law and was occasionally part of a group composed of Alfredo Guevara, Baudilio Castellanos, Mario García Incháustegui, Léster Rodríguez and other like-minded comrades during the student period prior to March 10, many of whom later played outstanding roles within the revolutionary movement.

Immediately afterwards, Miret began to devote his time to training anybody linked to and expressing an intention to fight against the dictatorship. He taught how to load, unload and accurately aim with the few weapons that he was constantly repairing in one of the basements in the FEU office or other parts of the University.

Miret realized that the group led by Fidel was the most serious of all those identified as insurrectionary. Fidel talked to him and they drew up a plan for training his men and the possible training of others at the University whom they perceived as having the necessary qualities. Afterwards, Fidel sent Ñico López to complement in practice what was agreed with Miret.

It is interesting to note that Fidel sent Ñico López—and José Luis Tasende and Ernesto Tizol later—to coordinate and control the military exercises, in spite of his long-term relationship with Miret. The reason lies in the extreme secrecy and discretion with which the developing movement was managed.

Nonetheless, Fidel's political dynamism, greatly augmented by the need to make a rapid and solid revolutionary response to the dictatorship, led him to evaluate the usefulness of his own presence at the University, the scenario of the major uprisings against the dictatorship at that time.

To that end, however, he acted with all the perspicacity of his conspiratorial talent. Out of the blue, on November 4, 1952, he presented himself at the University to enroll as a student in the recently initiated 1952-1953 academic year. In that way he could outwit any police search, as his position as a student justified his free access to the University precinct.

Thus, two years after having completed three university courses in one go, Fidel Alejandro Castro Ruz once again became an official student at the University of Havana, in the Faculty of Philosophy and Literature. This time he evidently wasn't going to totally dedicate himself to study as he had done in the 1949-1950 course when he took his final examinations and passed thirty-two subjects in just twelve months.[38] He had another distinct and superior objective to meet.[39]

Armando Hart's testimony is illustrative when he speaks of the first time that he had personal dealings with Fidel and was impressed by his personality:

In the Orthodoxy Party office at 109 Prado, a group of young people was discussing what kind of person should assume the leadership or command of the Revolution. On that occasion, Fidel defended the idea that completely new leaders would emerge, distinct in every way from those who were involved in political life at that point.

In the burning argument, unleashed in the old Prado lodge, I was one of the few in that group of young people—I cannot exactly say that they were all really young, because some of them had very old ideas—who fully agreed with Fidel.

I left 109 Prado with Fidel. We walked through various streets of Havana, him with his arm on my shoulder, as he used to do a lot—and he was still pressing the subject with me. I was surprised when he showed interest in the fact that I was visiting the FEU offices with a group of comrades to learn weapons' handling. I wondered how he knew that.

After the attack on the Moncada Garrison I learnt that Pedro Miret, the FEU representative responsible for organizing that activity, was one of the participants in that heroic action. From that time I noticed that, through Miret, Fidel knew many of those who went to the FEU offices with insurrectional intentions.[40]

IN FOUR DAYS I WILL COLLECT THAT MONEY

At the end of December 1952, just seven months before the Moncada attack, some thirty workers employed on the Ácana farm in Matanzas Province had gone six months without receiving any wages whatsoever. A dispute between the owners and a tenant farmer at the farm—a logical manifestation of the regime of land holding and exploitation— meant that the Ácana workers were not paid their due wages over that lengthy period, in spite of having nothing to do with the dispute.

Everything they did came to nothing. Many claims were made to the authorities and there were many arguments with their respective employers.

On December 27 the agricultural workers at the farm received a surprise visit from Dr. Fidel Castro, who identified himself as "a Havana lawyer who has come to help you to solve your problem and try and make them pay you what you are owed."

The total debt was more than 5000 pesos and, as the campesinos said, "we were afraid that it (Fidel's visit) was a maneuver by the owners and a tenant farmer." The young lawyer convinced them of his just motives and the campesinos placed their confidence in him. However, some of them weren't convinced that it wasn't a ruse until Fidel's approaches proved successful.[41]

Paulino Perdomo Ramos, who at that time headed one of the groups of agricultural workers at the Ácana farm, told a group of journalists:

And that day, as I was telling you, Fidel arrived. Well, he arrived like you, by surprise, without anyone expecting him and asked: "Which one of you is Paulino Perdomo?"

Some comrades told him who I was and where I was, which was up there, and he came up to me and said: "Look, Paulino, I've come here from Havana. I am Fidel Castro, a lawyer, and I've come to collect the money that you are owed here on the farm. If you give me authority... If not..."

I cut him off at that point and said: "Look kid, I'm surprised that a young lawyer from Havana should come here like this without us sending for you, selflessly as you say." I used the familiar you because I was an older person and at that time he was still just a boy. "That sounds odd to me. To me it smacks of a maneuver by the owners, so that we give you the authority, and then we'll never get paid!"

Then he replied, serenely: "Look, it isn't like that. What I want is for you to find me somewhere to bring the workers together... I was there in the trade union office and they refused me a place, I was in the municipality and they didn't want me there either."

The truth is that he had already been making efforts about the place but none of those people wanted to help him, you know? The trade union was in the hands of the *Mujalistas*,[42] you know? That was in the year 1952.

I looked at him, thought for a while and then said to him: "Well, my house is a bit small (I'd only laid the floor the day before, because it was earthen) but we could have it there."

We went there and with those things that he has, the agility, being an active person, he himself got ready the few bits and pieces we had, and I told the old lady to make "a drop of coffee."

Well, all that was very active on his part, in a simple and natural way, very impressive in his way of acting.[43]

He told us: "I give you my word of honor that if you give me the authority, within four days, I will collect that money off them." So then I said to him: "Listen lawyer, this business of word of honor might have great value for you, but for us, well, it doesn't have that value, because in many cases we don't know what word of honor means. The problem is that we've already had that beaten into us, we don't even believe in word of honor..."

And he came back and ratified what he was saying. So I said to him: "Look, anyway, speaking personally, I'll give you the authority. Now the comrades have the word and can say, you know?" But the comrades said: "No, Paulino, what you're doing is good; we'll accept it if you think it's a good idea..."

When the comrades said that, he took out a piece of paper, sat down at a little table and wrote out that minute, the authority, and we signed it. That was on December 27 of that year, 1952, at around 5:00 P.M. After he said: "Not tomorrow, but the day after tomorrow, more or less at this time, you're going to receive a telegram here in which I'll tell you how the case is going." And then he left for Havana.[44]

He drove around in an old jalopy... it even had a door missing... Well, lo and behold, on the third day, the mail messenger appeared with the telegram... It said: "Case going well, Fidel."[45]

Look, I'm going to carry on with the story... I took the telegram and left for the comrades' houses and told them: "Listen, I think we're going to win the battle. Look at this: the man's keeping to his word. He says things are going well." Well, I'm telling you now, at around 10:00 P.M. on the 31st, all of us were getting paid, receiving the checks each one of us was owed.[46]

He came to pay us himself. Well, the person that handed over the checks was comrade Gildo Fleitas, who as you know was here running part of the farm, right? But anyway, the payment was made with Fidel present. There's one thing: given that the workers were divided—like I told you some were working for the owners and others for the tenant farmer—Fidel himself went and found the Sabanilla group and the Cidra one; he found the tenant farmer and one of the owners and so, after everything was sorted out, or at least when everyone came to an agreement, the money was paid.

I remember that on that occasion he came with a kind of fair young man, a bit short, you know?, but we didn't know who he was: we didn't go into that, because then, who would have thought that seven months later Fidel would attack the Moncada Garrison there in Santiago de Cuba? That was the last thing that anyone would have thought of... I'm telling you that even then I talked with him about my doubts. I told him about my doubts then and there and that I thought that his presence here could have been a maneuver by those farm people.[47]

I also remember that when they paid us, after the last check was handed over, Fidel said a few words there... But first let me tell you that, when we saw what he'd done, all of us wanted to show our thanks, like you do, right? We wanted to give him at least two pesos from each of us for the gasoline, but he wouldn't even accept that. He had told us he wasn't going to charge anything for his efforts, but anyway, we agreed to do that; to put up two pesos each for gasoline, but he didn't want to accept anything!

And well, it was at the end when he said a few words... Ah, but hang on, I'd forgotten this: I remember that when he was doing that minute—and of course I didn't know his political position or anything like that—I went up to him and said: "Your attitude seems like ours, like that of the communists: an unselfish attitude."

And he told me, looking at me trustingly: "If my program triumphs some day it will be the same as the communists'; nationalization..."[48]

I should tell you that there was one thing I really liked, that I was in agreement with and that made me trust him, and that was when he was about to write the authority, that minute, and I said to Fidel: "Look, we're going to do things like you say... but under these conditions: in the minutes you have to put that, after the four-day period, if you haven't collected the money, then we can de-authorize you with that same minute and take away the authority we're giving you." I had to say that then because it seemed to me to be a maneuver.

That's why I said it. And he said in a very trusting way: "Yes, I agree. I'm going to do as you say." And Fidel wrote it as I said. That made me trust him although, truthfully, I wasn't at all convinced that we were going to get paid that day. And well, you know that we did, that we got paid.[49]

When they asked Santiago Anisio Ruiz, a former agricultural worker at the Ácana farm, about what remained most strongly in his mind about that episode, he replied:

The first thing was the unselfish attitude of Fidel, who we'd never seen hair or hide of before. What he did, as I already said, was something that made an impression... There's another thing that I'd forgotten; it is his memory! You know, when he saw us all in Paulino's house, he asked us our names and surnames and afterwards, on the day we got our pay, he was saying our names as we went past him. Hey, that's incredible! Someone would be there waiting, and he was saying to us: "You're So-and-so," and to another "And you're what's his name!" I don't think there are many people with a memory like that! There were more than thirty of us, and he more or less said everybody's names and surnames.

We noticed that and said: "How did he manage that, when he didn't even have us written down on a piece of paper or anything?"

Afterwards he said that what we needed was a contingent, from Oriente Province, of 500-600 men... Ah, now I remember as well: he said that if he got to be somebody one day, he was going to make an

Agrarian Reform... But well, imagine, at that time, when I was illiterate as well—I learned to read and write in '61 through the Literacy Campaign—who would have thought that that would come to be, that he was talking seriously?[50]

THE JOSÉ MARTÍ CENTENNIAL YOUTH

The year 1953 opened with a definitive crisis within the Orthodoxy Party leadership. Its national leadership council split on Tuesday, January 13 in an attempt to agree the line of a non-pact with the other political parties. From that point, the Party was divided into three irreconcilable factions, after a tumultuous meeting that ended in blows. That incident further discontented the young Orthodoxy revolutionaries. Polarizing that sentiment, the voice of Fidel was heard: "Let's go. These politicians can't be counted on to make a revolution.[51]

Armando Torres Santryll, recalling those days, relates:

By January 1953 and the centennial anniversary of Martí's birth, one could see a stronger cohesion among the youth—both within and outside the University—who attended those meetings. Around then the FEU convened a meeting attended by Fidel on behalf of the Orthodoxy Youth; Flavio Bravo, who spoke on behalf of the Socialist Youth; Léster Rodríguez on behalf of the pro-Martí Youth; Quino Peláez, who was FEU president; and us, representing the Authentic Youth. Once again, Fidel advocated unity among all the juvenile forces and posed the need to pay a tribute to Martí, one that should be made by the youth. And once more he affirmed that it was going to be and had to be the revolutionary youth who would fight on the basis of Martí's thought, and that the José Martí centennial youth would emerge from them.

So the march of the torches was organized to pay tribute to José Martí. During that parade—and this is a personal appreciation—we noted that Fidel was structuring an effective movement of real strength.[52]

Those men headed by Fidel included many that would be involved in the attack on the Santiago de Cuba and Bayamo garrisons on July 26, 1953. History would grant them an honorable name: the Centennial Generation.

THE MARCH OF THE TORCHES

During the night of January 27, while the official event sponsored by the regime was taking place outside the Capitolio, lines of students and the people were constantly arriving at the University precinct, forming a huge and boisterous throng. The Cadenas Plaza and the monumental stairway were packed. A distant view revealed the fantastic perspective of thousands of fiery-tongued snakes beginning to glide towards Infanta and San Lázaro Streets at 11:30 P.M. Each demonstrator carried a torch on high.

Various cars with movie and television news crews advanced to get footage of the parade, which was headed by a giant flag held by female university students and those from secondary education. Behind them was the full FEU executive.

The river of flames moved down San Lázaro to Espada Street. The contingent that had just come from the closing event of the pro-Martí Youth Congress joined the march. The pro-Martí Women's Organization contributed another solid block.[53]

Aida Pelayo, president of the pro-Martí Women's Civil Front affirms in a written testimony:

But the sensation of the night was a column of 500 youths, in immaculate ranks, marching behind Fidel. One could see that they were well trained from the display of discipline and cohesion that they presented. The voices of these youth rang out clearly among the shouted choruses of "Revolution! Revolution!" It was a thundering torrent that made a great demonstration even more spectacular.[54]

I WAS NOT UNDERGROUND

In an interview with Tomás Borgess, Fidel Castro confided to the eminent intellectual Nicaraguan:

Batista underestimated us, he was concerned about other leaders, other political organizations that had millions of pesos, that had arms, and discounted us, which greatly helped in carrying out all the work in absolute legality before the attack on the Moncada Garrison; everything in the most absolute legality, I was not underground! I was extremely pleased about that, because I have always found it very hard to be underground, as I am discovered on account of my stature. I could dye my hair and do anything else, but my experiences in working underground were always a failure, because I was immediately discovered. So I could only operate within a framework of legality.[55]

On January 15 [1953], in a protest demonstration at the profanation of the bust of Julio Antonio Mella facing the University stairway, students twice took to the streets in energetic marches, and were attacked by police gunfire. Student Rubén Batista was gravely injured on one of those demonstrations. After one month of agony he died on February 13. Fidel was on the mass demonstration into which his burial was transformed on February 14.

The enraged crowd shouted out their hatred of the dictatorship after the burial, on the return march from the cemetery to the University. En route, the residence of Batista supporter Margarita de la Cotera was stoned and damaged, as well as a car circulating with a September 4 banner, a symbol of the regime.

That same day saw the filing of a public disorder case in Room 5 of the Havana Hearings against Fidel and Orthodoxy fighter Aida Pelayo, president of the pro-Martí Women's Civic Front, who were charged with responsibility for those incidents. The trial, listed for June 10, never took place. On June 5 it became without effect through the Amnesty Decree-law 885 of 1953.[56]

THE GOVERNMENT HAS THE WORD

Eight days before the incidents in the wake of Rubén Batista's interment, *Bohemia* magazine published a defiant article written against the government for the destruction of various death masks—including that of Eduardo Chibás—statuettes of Martí and other works of art in the studio of sculptor Manuel Fidalgo.

The misdeed, committed by police agents, arose the simple fact that at the foot of the statuettes, manufactured in large quantities in that Centennial Year, the sculptor had engraved Martí's words: "For Cuba that is suffering."[57]

162

The *Bohemia* exposé had the graphic support of four photographs confirming the acts. It was signed by Fidel Castro, with photos by Fernando Chenard. Five months later Chenard would be one of the men who gave his life in the events of July 26 in Santiago de Cuba. The author of the article being known, the charge against the dictatorship and the energetic tone in which it was written comes as no surprise today. However, one other aspect is outstanding: the leader of the movement's capacity for maneuver and the tactical utilization of any means of political struggle, depending on the particular situation at the time.

Around that time, in its own way and within a rigid circle of power, the government had celebrated—in a veritable tournament of court hypocrisy, luxurious toasts and ceremonies in the absence of the people—the anniversary of the birth of the Apostle [José Martí]. With dozens of foreign personalities visiting the country, the dictatorship was obliged to present a liberal front, including the press, at least during the festivities.

Given that the incident at Fidalgo's workshop took place precisely at that time, the special juncture was utilized by Fidel to hit out at the regime via the largest weekly press publication in the country. It was the first time that he had used the legal press since Batista's coup. His last piece published in the legal media prior to this one was an exposé of Prío, published by *Alerta* four days before the coup.[58]

In his memorable exposé Fidel stated:

Five days have gone by and at the time of writing this brief information the government has still not given any explanation of the El Calvario incident, nor has Fidalgo materialized.

On Friday, two days after the centennial anniversary of Martí's birth, a group of police showed up at 10:00 A.M. outside the eminent sculptor's workshop in El Calvario; there they commenced the destruction that continued afterwards in his studios two blocks up the road. As usual, they had absolutely no legal warrant; they have never used them.

It was not the agents that initiated the misdeed: it was Captain Oscar González from the 14th police station that gave the bad example. Taking a death mask of Eduardo Chibás, he threw it furiously to the ground; then, grabbing one of the Martí statues, he said that he was going to make Fidalgo eat it and then make him produce Batista statues.

That was an order: dozens of statues of Martí were seized and kicked to smithereens, the rest were loaded onto a garbage truck and thrown into a corner of the police station; the death masks of Chibás were pulverized with ignoble fury; every bust of patriots in the workshop was dashed to the ground or carted off to the police station as well; the head was torn off a statue of the Virgin of Charity, and others disappeared. Not one mold was left intact in order to prevent reproduction.

Thanks to Chenard, our valiant and daring collaborator in *Bohemia,* we have obtained irrefutable evidence, despite the military occupation of the workshop and the press being totally refused access to it.

Moreover, Fidalgo had a beautiful collection of famous hands, a natural copy of the hands of each figure. They included those of [Franklin D.] Roosevelt, Chibás, [Miguel] Coyula, Miguel A. Quevedo, Guido García Inclán, Judge Justiniani and other political and scientific figures from all over the world. A product of the sculptor's lifelong work, it was thought to be unique. At this point it is not known how many of the hands were left intact after the boxes containing them were thrown to the ground.

That same day, María Mantilla presented Batista with the shackles that had tortured Martí's ankles and a brilliant reception was prepared in the Auditorium for eminent academics who were visiting Martí's homeland that is not free.

Fidalgo's crime: to have put at the foot of his statues those words of the Maestro pronounced at a time similar to this: "For Cuba that is suffering..."

In this context, they will have to suppress the complete works of Martí, seize them from bookshops and libraries, because all his works, a plethora of love for his homeland and human decorum, stand as a perennial accusation of those men who are currently governing the people of Cuba against its sovereign will.

And let us hope that it is only what they have done against Fidalgo, destroying his work as an honored artist whose hands have only sculpted figures of illustrious figures; let us hope they have not destroyed his existence as well.

Fidalgo is not a sensationalist or a man of notoriety. At this time, Wednesday afternoon, his unexpected and unjustifiable absence is alarming Cuban citizens. We have been prudent up until now on this point, it is too serious to speculate on, but it is also too serious to lose time. We do not wish to prejudge, but the evidences are already pointed... The government has the word.[59]

ENDNOTES

1. *Paupista:* member of the squalid political grouping that supported Batista. Its name is derived from the initials of the Unitary Action Party (PAU).

2. Mario Mencía, op. cit., Vol. 1, 51-52.

3. Ibid., 141-146.

4. You can find information about this commemoration on page 137. *Ed.*

5. Mario Mencía, op. cit., Vol.1, 145-151.

6. Frei Betto, op. cit., 121.

7. Fidel Castro, "Discurso pronunciado con motivo del inicio del curso escolar 1995-1996 y sus 50 años de vida revolucionaria," ed. cit., 6-7.

8. Mario Mencía, op. cit., Vol. 2, 411-412.

9. Refers to Julio Antonio Mella (1903-29), Rafael Trejo (1910-30), and Antonio Guiteras (1906-35), revolutionary leaders whose example came to form part of the Cuban people's finest combative traditions. *Ed.*

10. Mario Mencía, op. cit., Vol. 1, 121-122.

11. Cuban pleated shirt. *Ed.*

12. Mario Mencía, op. cit., Vol. 1, 123.

13. Ibid., 127.

14. Ibid., 129.

15. Method of torture employed by the dictatorship against detained or imprisoned political opponents, which consisted of making them drink a large volume of castor oil, also known as palmacristi, which provoked acute diarrhea. *Ed.*

16. Mario Mencía, op. cit., Vol. 1, 129-133.

17. Ibid., 151.

18. Military Intelligence Service. *Ed.*

19. Mario Mencía, op. cit., Vol. 1, 153-154.

20. See note 49. *Ed.*

21. Subparagraph in Law No. 7 of April 1943, which allowed for the creation of funds for teaching, used from the outset for the personal enrichment of government leaders. *Ed.*

22. The people's name for Decree-Law 2273, 1950, imposed by the Prío regime, because it silenced freedom of expression on the radio. *Ed.*

23. Mario Mencía, op. cit., Vol. 1, 153-156.

24. Aldo Isidrón del Valle, "La Generación del Centenario y sus primeras acciones" [The Centennial Generation and Its Initial Actions], in *Antes del Moncada*, ed. cit., 233-234.

25. Mario Mencía, *Tiempos precursores* [Presaging Times] (Havana: Editorial de Ciencias Sociales, 1986), 15.

26. The Accuser. *Ed.*

27. Paramilitary groups who thrived with Batista in power. *Ed.*

28. Aldo Isidrón del Valle, "La Generación del Centenario y sus primeras acciones," in *Antes del Moncada*, ed. cit., 236-238.

29. Ibid., 239.

30. An inter-urban transportation company. *Ed.*

31. Centro de Estudios de Historia Militar de las FAR, *Moncada; antecedentes y preparativos,* ed. cit., 204

32. Mario Mencía, *El grito del Moncada*, Vol. 1, ed. cit., 239-240.

33. Miguel Mariano Gómez, Cuba's president for only seven months in 1936. *Ed.*

34. José Martí's letter to his Mexican friend Manuel Mercado, May 18, 1895, considered as his literary testament. In Martí's *Obras completas* [Complete Works], Vol. 20 (Havana: Editorial de Ciencias Sociales, 1975), 161. *Ed.*

35. Mario Mencía, *El grito del Moncada,* Vol. 1, ed. cit., 244-247.

36. Ibid., 247-248.

37. Ibid., 248-250.

38. Fidel's qualifications in those examinations were one pass (60-69), eight good passes (70-79), five noteworthy (80-89) and eighteen outstanding (90-100 marks). Having studied those thirty-two subjects in one year he completed his doctorate in Law, a degree in Administrative Law and a degree in Diplomatic Law, and advanced in the completion of a doctorate in Social Sciences and a doctorate in Philosophy and Literature, which he abandoned to devote himself with fervor to social and political struggles.

39. Mario Mencía, *El grito del Moncada,* Vol. 1, ed. cit., 277-278.

40. Mario Mencía, *Tiempos precursores,* ed. cit., 99-100.

41. Santiago Cardosa Arias, "Presencia de Fidel en la finca Ácana, Matanzas" [Presence of Fidel in the Ácana Farm, Matanzas], in *Antes del Moncada*, ed. cit., 240.

42. *Mujalistas:* Followers of Eusebio Mujal, imposed by coercive means as leader of the Cuban Workers' Federation in order to implant a trade union policy against the workers' interests. *Ed.*

43. Santiago Candosa Arias, op. cit., 243-244.

44. Ibid., 244-245.

45. Ibid., 245.

46. Id.

47. Ibid., 246.

48. Ibid., 246-247.
49. Ibid., 249-250.
50. Ibid., 255.
51. Mario Mencía, *Tiempos precursores,* ed. cit., 129-130.
52. Centro de Estudios de Historia Militar de las FAR, *Moncada: antecedentes y preparativos,* ed. cit., 164.
53. Mario Mencía, *Tiempos precursores,* ed. cit., 131-132.
54. Ibid., 132.
55. Tomás Borges, op. cit., 293.
56. Mario Mencía, *Tiempos precursores,* ed. cit., 41.
57. Ibid., 42.
58. Ibid., 42-43.
59. Mario Mencía, *El grito del Moncada,* Vol. 1, ed. cit., 316-319.

TOWARD MONCADA

A MAN LIKE THAT IS BORN EVERY 500 YEARS

When Rubén Batista Rubio was dying dozens of people met every night at the Calixto García hospital for the latest news on his condition. All of them expected the fatal outcome at any moment. There, Renato Guitart met Fidel.

There is no testimony of what Renato and Fidel talked about that night, but the profound impression he left on the young man from eastern Cuba is recorded:

His father recalls that, on his return to Santiago de Cuba, Renato told him enthusiastically: "I went to the hospital to see Rubén and there I met a guy who is a phenomenon, what a mentality! How active! That man is indeed a revolutionary, dad! He has a forceful personality, and lives very much in the future. A man like that is only born every 500 years!" I asked who he was and he replied: "He's called Fidel Castro."[1]

THE EXACT POINT OF A TACTICAL CHANGE

On Friday, February 13, 1953 Rubén Batista died. People felt anger at the young man's murder. The next day, the funeral cortege that left the

University of Havana and accompanied him to Colón Cemetery consisted of more than 30,000 people.

However, the expression of the masses on that February 14 was to signal another really significant fact in immediate national events. It marked the exact point of a tactical change in the emerging revolutionary Movement headed by Fidel: that of avoiding situations mediating against the principal plan of confronting the dictatorship, which in those early months of 1953 was rapidly maturing.

Up until that moment, the Movement had taken advantage of any opportunity that presented itself to hit out at the regime in one way or another. Participation in mass activities had been one of its peculiarities from the outset. Even before joining the organization, its members had done so intuitively since March 10 itself, when many of them gathered at the University, out of a need to demonstrate their condemnation of the dictatorship.

March 16 and August 16, the dates of the Orthodoxy Party pilgrimages to Chibás' grave, and the silent May Day convergence at Carlos Rodríguez' tomb were mass activities in which many of the future *Moncadistas*[2] participated.

With the student body in ferment, the University had been an appropriate scenario throughout the whole of 1952. The campaign of swearing an oath of fidelity to the Constitution, followed by the symbolic acts of its wake and burial took place there. The May 8 march to Guiteras' grave started there. The popular commemoration of the 50th anniversary of the Republic on May 20 was held there. The remembrance event for the medical students shot down in 1871 was also staged there.

All the above demonstrations were attended by the men, who were prepared to give up their lives for their ideals. Having emerged from the very heart of the people it was natural that that revolutionary group should express its rebellion against despotism in mass protests by the people to whom they belonged.

Utilizing the press and clandestine radios were part of the same principle of forging links with the masses and preparing them for the combat.

Other considerations made this tactic a justifiable one. The mass protests expanded into political attacks on the regime, forcing it to reveal its repressive nature to the whole world. At the same time, mass action served to arouse and develop a state favorable to rebellion.

In terms of the Movement's external relations, these served to make contact with persons from the masses with the necessary conditions for entry into the organization. And internally, they were a determining method for forging awareness, readiness and discipline among the members, decisive factors at the time of selective evaluations.

The revolutionary agitator in Fidel grasped up until what time it was correct to employ this tactic, in accordance with the advances and adjustments at each phase of his revolutionary project.

An analysis of the agenda followed for participation in mass actions confirms that. Everything would seem to indicate that given the advance of the training program and, in general, the Movement's organizational level and training in military aspects, a conscious absence of this type of participation was notable towards the end of 1952. There was no action on October 10. The November 27 anniversary was commemorated, but on December 7—in the midst of combative military selection—the Movement did not make an appearance at any mass demonstration.

January 28, with its tremendous ideological and revolutionary significance, especially in the year 1953, was an essential date for those who, through their actions, were to earn the title of the Centennial Generation at the cost of their lives. Given this, the march of the torches and the parade to Central Park on the following day determined the end of the cycle of public participation by the Movement's cadres. Only an event that directly touched the conscience of the people and unanimously fired the masses on February 14 claimed the guiding presence of that dignified generation.

But, from that point on, the Movement as such stayed away from mass action. It was necessary to eliminate risks that could endanger the essential objective. It was being prepared in secret, but at a constant and rapid rate, to initiate the heroic achievement that would unleash in Cuba a revolutionary process that would transform our history.

The next time that Fidel and his followers would participate in a public demonstration, five months later, the cry of justice—moving call to the people's conscience and action—would be accompanied by the thunder of rifles outside the walls of the Moncada Garrison.[3]

WE STILL HADN'T MADE OUR OWN PLAN

In those months the National Revolutionary Movement (MNR), headed by Rafael García Bárcena, had thought up a plan to take the country's largest fortress with the help of a group of army officers. It is a fact that the MNR plan to take the Columbia fort was widely known in the so-called insurrectional sectors, many of which were infiltrated by enemy agents. Its postponement from March 8 to April 5 further increased chinks for infiltration by the repressive agencies, including the time signaled for its execution.

Like Fidel, who was in contact with García Bárcena in relation to his possible participation, there were more than a dozen similar cases. At one point García Bárcena met with Fidel, Abel and Montané in the apartment on 25th and O and explained all the details of the plan to them.

"He said that he was in contact with various military men, that the plan wasn't going to fail, that they were going to open the Columbia's doors," Montané related. "So we told him that we had heard about it from outside sources, that we were alerting him to that, because the plan was widely known. But Bárcena replied that that was good because it would throw the enemy off. It cannot be denied that there were many people of good faith in the MNR, but very ingenuous. Bárcena himself was a good man but totally ingenuous, his feet just weren't on the ground."

Many years later, Fidel clarified the nature of his relations with García Bárcena at that time:

"When García Bárcena came to talk to me, I told him: 'Don't look for anybody else.' I knew there was a whole pile of organizations that had twenty, twenty-five people, and that as soon as he began to talk everyone would get to hear of it, because there were so many of them in distinct organizations. I told him: 'If you have a plan let's discuss it and go out to get the weapons; we have enough people to carry it out, if there really is a chance of success.'

"At that time, in March 1953, we still hadn't made our own plan. In our efforts to cooperate with those who wanted to fight, we were still prepared to join anyone who took the first step forward, and he said that he had solid contacts. For that reason I said to him: 'Don't say anything more to anyone.' And, really, if he hadn't talked to anyone else, we

171

would have attacked Columbia and nobody would have known about it beforehand.

"But, a few days later, García Bárcena had talked to 200 different people in all the organizations, with everybody. That was the problem. It was the most publicized action in Cuban history. So we decided not to participate. Had he agreed with us, we would have made a plan and would have executed it although I didn't like the idea of taking Columbia. But I said to myself: 'Well, it could work out if he has military cadres prepared to rebel.'

"We still didn't have a plan of our own. At that moment we were still working in terms of coordination with the other groups. We didn't have any weapons, but we knew that they would turn up, that would be arms here. For that reason we infiltrated 360 men into the Triple A,[4] to collect arms which they said would be handed out for combat. But they never gave out anything. In that situation, what finally decided us to make our own plan was García Bárcena's failure."

Participation in the MNR project was discussed by the Movement's leadership. Despite everyone's anxiety to enter into action against the dictatorship, the reason why many wanted to participate in that attempt, Fidel expressed its deficiencies. Abel was the first to understand Fidel's reasons and in the end it was decided not to participate.

Convinced that the plan was going to fail, Fidel directed his closest collaborators not to be at home those days, so as to elude any repressive operation that could become widespread. Montané left for the Isle of Pines, and Abel, Haydée and Melba for Las Villas. Others made similar tracks. Fidel took advantage of the situation to travel to Palma Soriano and Santiago de Cuba, where he began to draw up practical measures for future operations that he was already planning.[5]

ORGANIZATION AND DISCIPLINE IN THE MOVEMENT

Many years later, addressing a group of students, Fidel Castro recalled:
We maintained our links with the University in all the preparations for the 26th of July, taking part in those demonstrations, because we had a force, one could say, we had proof of that. There were all sorts of

organizations and many and the same people in this, that and the other. We succeeded in having an organization of 1200 trained people. We made use of many points of law.

I forgot to say that everything concerning the 26th of July was organized under absolute legality. We used the Orthodoxy Party offices at 109 Prado, I met with each one of the cells there, we sent them there to train at the University and then in other places. It was a huge undertaking, and our support came basically from the youth of the Orthodoxy Party as it had a strong influence over the masses and much sympathy among young people. Of the comrades selected, 90% of them came out of the ranks of the Orthodoxy Party youth, rather than the youth leadership. Of course, that recruitment was achieved by working from below; thus some regions yielded many very good people, like Artemisa and, generally speaking, all of them.

We could only use around 160 of them in the Moncada action, but for every man we deployed in the Moncada and Bayamo attacks, eight were unable to participate. We could make a really good selection from the groups that had advanced to that point, but all completely legal.

There are many stories and interesting anecdotes of that period, all those months from March 10, 1952 to July 26, 1953. I will just give you one detail: I had traveled 50,000 kilometers in a little car that I had, a Chevrolet 50-315; I had bought it on credit and every now and then they took it off me; anyway, it burnt out two days before Moncada. But by that time we were hiring cars, we were already operating in another way, adapted to the conditions of course, as you can imagine.[6]

José Suárez Blanco, one of the assailants on Post 3 of the Moncada Garrison, relates:

Fidel's idea was to organize an insurrectional instrument that would channel the struggle into an armed one. Fidel put me in charge of that movement in Pinar del Río, an area that I know well as I'm from Artemisa.

Fidel's idea was to create a movement markedly social in nature, because our basis of action in power was sustained on eradicating the latifundia of that time, workers' participation in the capitalists' profits, educational reforms and the elimination of the professional army in the service of imperialism and reactionary forces.

Many members of the Movement were trained in the fields of Artemisa and Guanajay.

Fidel had asked me to find a location to give a group of comrades lightning training on commando operations. When I selected the place, he told me:

"Get hold of a pair of piglets to serve as a pretext in the case of being surprised."

The location selected was the Martín Mesa springs in Guanajay. When we were training, a lookout that we had placed warned us that General Rojas was coming with his entire staff. We quickly collected up all the weapons and brought out the pigs. When Rojas arrived with his henchmen, they waited until we had finished and then we left.[7]

Juan Almeida Bosque tells us:

The first weapons I ever saw in my life were those that Fidel gave us for firing practice in the University Martyrs' Hall: the famous M-1 which all the students of that period know, and the Springfield; the M-1 without a breech, which had a stick-on breech, and which passed through everybody's hands.

Those were the rudimentary arms with which we took our first steps, the first time of having contact with arms. At that time it wasn't like now, when here in this country everyone knows how to handle a gun and walks around with a gun.

Pedrito Miret was responsible for firing practice. . . .

I met Fidel there, he began to talk of revolution, what revolution was, the process, the setback implied by the coup d'état, that importance of youth—the living forces—uniting, and that he could count on persons without past complications.

That was my first contact with Fidel. He went about with a book by Lenin under his arm, a blue book, with the effigy of Lenin on the cover. That was the one that turned up at Moncada. Fidel had a gray suit, with a shirt collar that looked as if it had been much mended, his shirt a bit threadbare . . . and with that strength of character.[8]

In addition to the hundreds of men Fidel infiltrated into other organizations to see whether weapons could be acquired in that way, Abel Santamaría—acting on his instructions—, approached the Authentic action groups in order to make contact, penetrate them and sound out the possibility of obtaining arms.

As a result of these relations it was decided to mount a show of the Movement's strength and organization. With that aim, a former naval officer belonging to the Triple A was assigned the task of confirming those aspects. Ten houses were set up in different parts of Havana and hundred of perfectly disciplined comrades were brought together in them on the same day at the same time.

Gabriel Gil, head of the Lawton cell, recalled that he was given instructions to divide his group into two squads and order them to present themselves at intervals in two houses without arousing the neighbors' suspicions: one in Belascoaín Street and the other in San Rafael. There they met up with other persons. There was to be no talking or noise that might indicate the existence of those billets. "I didn't know what it was for," he told us on one occasion. "I was never told the objective of that order. After a couple of hours, during which nothing happened, we were informed that we could go until we were advised again." Gabriel Gil would learn of the reason for that strange mobilization during a collective interview in which he took part... fifteen years after the triumph of the Revolution.[9]

So what were the motives of that mobilization whose objectives were unknown to most of its participants? As Mario Mencía found out:

Apartment D on the third floor of 107 Jovellar Street, very close to the University, was second in importance as the center of activities for the Movement's leadership. Melba lived there with her parents, Manuel Hernández and Elena Rodríguez del Rey. "One night there was a review of the troops," is Melba's recollection of that demonstration. "That was one of the most audacious operations of those days. My house was very large. My parents and I were evacuated. When I returned later, I had a big surprise when I opened the door. It was full of young people from the front room to the back. And what was most surprising was the exceptional silence they maintained. Fidel had ordered an 'alarm' and the troops responded rapidly."

Abel picked up the Triple-A representative at the University of Havana in his car, and set about driving him to the various billets in his car. On entering the houses they found the men standing to attention. The ex-officer asked about the training they had received and, one by one, they replied with details of their physical training, and the types of weapons they knew.

"I was in the third house to be checked," explained Ernesto Tizol. "The man was pale and nervous. He said that we were crazy. 'How could you think of doing this within the City of Havana?' 'And where else are we going to do it?' we replied, 'didn't you want to see our Movement's organization and discipline? There were still seven more houses.' 'No, I'm not visiting any more. You're all crazy. They're going to take you all prisoner.' And he left.

"The talks continued afterwards. But they wanted the names and addresses of the Movement members and that, when the moment came, that we would join its ranks. Fidel said no, the men organized in our Movement would be led by us. That what they should do was to give us arms for our men and locate us in the most dangerous position for combat; that at the hour of battle we were prepared to occupy the riskiest position; that we knew what we should do at that point. At that point the talks with those people broke down."[10]

OUR OWN PLAN OF STRUGGLE

With the MNR's failure to take the Columbia camp, Fidel decided to carry out his own plan of struggle against the dictatorship with his Movement's scant forces and resources.

The limited resources (the Movement was overwhelmingly composed of young workers in very humble situations) determined the form that the insurrectional plan would take.

As there was no money to acquire good combat weapons, the plan involved snatching them from the enemy. "We were a handful of men," Fidel has said. "We didn't think that we would defeat the Batista dictatorship with a handful of men, or defeat its army, no. But we did think that that handful of men was enough, not to defeat that regime, but to unleash that force, that vast force, that immense energy of the people that was indeed capable of defeating that regime."[11]

In summary:

. . . During the first months that followed the March 10 coup Fidel's activities had three principal directions: agitation and propaganda aimed at denouncing the spurious and ambitious nature of the regime; the recruiting of people close to his belief of opposing a solution through revolutionary violence; and advocating the unity of everyone who was really ready to fight at any price against the dictatorship.

In advocating that unity of forces, Fidel was not aspiring to honor or a high position, he was simply offering himself as a foot soldier along with the growing contingent of men that followed him. These were his proposals to the Orthodoxy Party leadership. But that leadership had grown incapable of leading the people in that special situation of political institutional crisis. Fidel even established contact with other self-titled insurrectional organizations. However none of them would give him any weapons, and neither did any of them launch themselves into combat.

Given that situation and after twelve months without those with the resources to initiate the armed struggle against the dictatorship, doing so, in March 1953 Fidel decided to carry out his own plans of popular armed insurrection. And by that date the Movement was duly organized.[12]

Oscar Alcalde, one of the Moncada assailants, affirmed that Fidel's authority was never questioned, his leadership was accepted as a normal and spontaneous fact. "His relations with us were fraternal, and based on reasoning. He never imposed an order; he always sought our opinions, leading us to reality on the few occasions when we might not have agreed."

"Abel, who we admired and loved very deeply," added Melba, "also had an influence on our respect for Fidel. It was a respect and admiration that had nothing to do with standards imposed on us; it arose naturally from the acceptance and confidence that Fidel awoke in us through his conduct, optimism, capacity and revolutionary fervor, right from those early days."[13]

With great sacrifice money was collected to cover training costs and buy arms. They managed to collect over 20,000 pesos. How were those funds managed?

Pedro Trigo relates that one night, after a whole day spent collecting money, he went with Fidel to where he lived at that time. Fidel's little three-year-old son was ill. The apartment was dark... the electricity had been cut off. Fidel wrote a note to have the child seen by a doctor friend. He asked Pedro if he had any money on him. He left the five pesos that Trigo gave him in the house for medicine and food, and they continued their efforts until the early hours of the morning. When that incident happened, Fidel had more than 100 pesos in his pocket that had been collected that day.[14]

SECURITY MEASURES

. . . The Movement carefully maintained its rule of not admitting any soldiers. Teodulio Mitchell had been in the army in Palma Soriano, but no longer was; he drove a truck distributing soft drinks. Right at the beginning of the Movement an army corporal was enthusiastically introduced to Fidel by the Jaimanitas cell led by Tulio Martín and to which Generoso Llanes, Mario Grande, Ezequiel Barrios and Carlos Bustillo belonged. The man promised arms and explosives. Just one conversation sufficed. "He's no good," said Fidel. "Why do you say that, when the man is to be trusted?" asked Generoso in surprise. "He talks too much. He's no good," was Fidel's response.[15]

Fidel zealously attended to the finest details of the operation.

A new security measure; although Renato [Guitart] was from Santiago, it was decided that he would not take care of renting and preparing what would have to be the general headquarters for stashing the arms and assembling the men who would leave for Moncada. Renato would be responsible for renting and preparing various houses that would serve as transit points for a few hours, from their arrival from Havana to the final gathering at the headquarters. If those were insufficient, when the time came he would make hotel reservations until all the combatants had accomodation. He also had to acquire as many weapons and ammunition as he could, matching those the Movement was storing in Havana, rent an appropriate place in Bayamo to assemble the men in charge of the action in that city, and finally, draw a plan of the layout of the Moncada Garrison so as to better define the combat plan.

The group then devoted itself to localizing a place that would serve as a general headquarters on the outskirts of Santiago de Cuba. Tizol recalls that they first dove along the highway to Escandell Hill, "and, when we were descending we saw a campesino on a mule on a very sharp bend that the car had to negotiate very slowly. Seeing him, Fidel turned round and asked him:

"Hey, my friend, you going downtown?"

"Yes, I'm carrying a bit of coffee to sell."

"A lot?"

"No, about 100 kilograms of coffee?"

"You have much land?"

"No, a caró." [16]

"Is it yours?"

"No, rented."

"Don't worry, in a little while it's going to be yours."

Tizol commented: "I never forgot that. Fidel told him that as if it was the most natural thing in the world. Of course I related it to the attack, but at that time I didn't fully realize it would be through a great agrarian reform, and not just that campesino, but all of them who would be able to take possession of the land they worked.[17]

Tizol returned to Havana and Fidel and Raúl Martínez traveled on to Palma [Soriano]. The cell headed by Aguilera was located there. They arrived on Friday, April 3, two days before the capture of García Bárcena and the consequent failure of the Columbia assault.

Fidel met with Aguilera, Rafael Oliva and Nito Ortega at the latter's house. They went to lunch at the Topeca bar and Parmenio joined them there. The conversation covered various revolutionary themes. As instructed, the groups headed by Aguilera had suspended their acts of sabotage to avoid risking their security unnecessarily. The agrarian issue took up a good deal of time, with Fidel motivated by the presence of Parmenio, who knew a lot about land and the inhuman exploitation to which the coffee squatters were subjected. As always, in line with the standards of discretion established by the Movement, Fidel kept quiet about the instructions that he had given to Renato to rent a place in Bayamo. The central theme focussed on the Charco Redondo miners and it was very late when Fidel went to Nito's house to sleep.

"The next day, Saturday April 4, we went to the Charco Redondo mine," Aguilera recalls. "Fidel was very affected by the state of the miners.

It almost turned into a meeting, because the workers began to gather together and Fidel to ask them questions and inquire into their livelihood, what caused the work-related sickness affecting them and other problems. We practically had to dissolve a crowd of miners who gathered around him. Fidel saw the mines, saw the conditions in which they worked. At that moment I don't know why he had such an interest in that place. I never imagined that it was part of a study of the practical possibilities of the plan that was drawing nearer. Apart from really being interested in the workers' problems, he was also analyzing the revolutionary potential of that group of workers so close to Bayamo."[18]

FREEDOM MARCH

Shortly before the attack on the Moncada garrison, Fidel had learned that a member of one cell of the movement in Marianao sang and wrote songs, and he asked him to compose something of an epic nature.

Twenty-seven years later, Agustín Díaz Cartaya told us, "I began to work on that musical composition during target practice at the Los Palos farm, and I finished it two weeks later. It was originally called the "Freedom March." One day, when Fidel was visiting Mercedes Valdés, Hugo Camejo's mother, in Marianao, he asked me if I had managed to come up with anything, so I sang it to him. He liked and approved it."

The original words to the "Freedom March" consisted of four stanzas, the third one different from the one we know today.

Marching onward toward an ideal,
we're certain to carry the day;
in furtherance of peace and prosperity
we'll struggle so freedom will win.

Forward, all Cubans,
may Cuba ever prize our heroism,
we're soldiers united, fighting so our country may be free,
our weapons destroying the evil that has plagued our troubled
land

of errant, unwanted rulers and of cruel insatiable tyrants
who have dragged us down in the mire.

For us, death means victory and glory, too —
an epic that the future will know well.

Our flaming torch, through a clouded sky,
lights up a horizon of full liberty.

The people of Cuba,
bowed down by endless suffering and pain,
have decided to struggle until they find a real solution
to serve as an example for all who have no compassion,
and we are determined to risk even our lives for this cause.

Long live the Revolution!

While imprisoned in Boniato, the Moncada combatants received a message from Fidel suggesting that the words of the march reflect what had just taken place in Bayamo and Santiago de Cuba, and that the memory of the brothers who had died serve as a sacred force for unity in the ongoing struggle. Thus, a new stanza was written in the Boniato prison to complete the anthem:

Our comrades in Oriente[19] have died,
their sacrifice must not be in vain.
United we all must remain
to honor their memory and fight on to win.[20]

FIDEL WANTED TO MAKE ME A REVOLUTIONARY IN A COUPLE OF HOURS

Ramón Castro Ruz recalls:
Some months prior to the attack on the Moncada Garrison, I was in Marcané and Fidel rang me to tell me that he wanted to meet me the

next day and told me where: by a conduit located before reaching the entrance to the town Cueto, and that I should be there in the afternoon. I was waiting a while until he appeared accompanied by Abel Santamaría; Fidel wearing his unmistakable blue suit without a tie and Abel a *guayabera*. They were in an old car.

During our conversation, Fidel informed me that he was organizing a coup that would occasion Batista's army more than 4000 losses; he didn't tell me where, or with what weapons; he just wanted me to give him some money, which I really didn't have at the time. Fidel wanted to make me a revolutionary in a couple of hours and as he didn't tell me anything concrete about the action, I was skeptical.

We went to the Pintao's service station at the entrance of Cueto to fill up the car, and there Fidel saw Ernesto and Calixto Silva from Marcané; Roger Ricardo, the son of a truck driver; and Felito Couser, son of the chief security guard at the sugar mill; Fidel didn't want anyone to see him.

After we filled up with gasoline, we went over to Holguín. On the way we agreed that I would prepare a small group in the old Marcané sugar mill and in the Birán area and that we would buy all the arms we could. I did that, organizing a group of eleven comrades: Víctor Rodríguez Cabrera, Reynaldo Rodríguez, Manuel Méndez Mejías, Bermúdez, Juan Mustelier, Prende, Rogelio Quevedo, Ángel Rodríguez, Arsenio González, Anastasio Castillo and Carlos Cortiña.

Later, Ángel Rodríguez died in the war, fighting against Sosa Blanco near the electricity plant in Cueto; as did Rogelio Quevedo, who died in Barajagua on a reconnaissance.

That night in Holguín, Abel, Fidel, myself and Miguel Ángel, a rental car driver from Marcané, went to a cafeteria near the Dalama café (Dalama bar); we talked while waiting to be served with four milky coffees and sandwiches. A trio singing to the bar's clientele dedicated songs and boleros to us time and time again.

After a pause, the first voice extended his hat for a tip and chose Fidel for that gesture on account of his elegant bearing; Fidel put his hand in his pants pocket and placed three brown centavos or U.S. cents in the ballad singer's hat.

Shocked and indignant, the artist insulted us loudly. That was all we needed, him coming to clean us out at that time of night. The musician threw the cents out onto the street. An offended Fidel answered the angered musician: 'Listen guy, I gave you everything I had, but at the end of the day that's what your music's worth,' and at that point Troy began to burn.[21]

JULY 24 AND 25, 1953

Fidel didn't rest on the days leading up to the Moncada Garrison attack. He took care of all the details.

Friday, July 24, passed for Fidel in the same tone, moving between 25th and O Streets and 107 Jovellar, between the apartments of Abel and Melba and, in addition, made some special errands, always with Mitchell as his driver—first in the black Dodge and then in the blue Buick. He went to Calabazar with Alcalde. He picked up Pedro Trigo and Ernesto González and they went off to Boyeros. Filiberto Zamora, head of the local cell, wasn't there. They continued on to Santiago de las Vegas and it was the same with Celso Stakeman. Places and activities went by at whirlwind speed. At 25th and O, instructions, arms, ammunition, dispatching men. Dispatching arms, ammunition, uniforms, men and orders at 107 Jovellar. At 23d and 18th Streets, a meeting with Pepe Suárez and the Artemisa and Guanajay men. At dusk he went to Mario Dalmau's house in Cerro, there he had a sandwich and glass of milk, probably the only food in the whole of that turbulent day. Night came, and once again Rancho Boyeros highway. "On the highway there was an incident with a cop who fined us for disobeying a Stop sign," said Teodulio Mitchell. "Fidel told them we were in a rush to collect relatives arriving at the airport. When we left there he commented: 'Who could have told them that flights arrive at this time?'" They picked up Manuel Lorenzo, a civil aeronautics telegraphist, with whom Fidel talked of a job that he needed doing in Oriente Province. From Boyeros to Marianao. In Marianao to Raúl's café on 51st Street, a meeting with Aguilerita. A stop off at 303 Nicanor del Campo (now 4804, 39th Avenue, between 48 and 59), Fidel's apartment, good byes to his family. Luggage: a *guayabera* and a book by Lenin. From Marianao to Vedado, 910 11th Street between 6 and 8, Naty Revuelta's house, where he picked up a stencil and manuscript copy of the manifesto that he had handed over two days previously to be typed up, and to give her new instructions. From there to Güines Avenue, the central highway, to Jamaica, to Aguilerita's again; Nito Ortega got into Fidel's car. In Matanzas he bumped into Pedro Marrero. From Matanzas to Colón, to Mario Muñoz' house, instructions: wait at the fork for El Cobre; breakfast. Highway to Santa Clara. At López Opticians, 18 Cuba on the corner of Máximo Gómez, new glasses to replace those left behind at 107 Jovellar. Highway to Placetas, Cabaiguán, Sancti Spíritus, Ciego de Ávila, Florida. Camagüey for lunch. The highway to Sibanicú, Cascorro, Guáimaro, Tunas, Holguín, Cacocum, Cauto Cristo. . . .

As they neared Bayamo, Teodulio Mitchell was gaining on a green car. Up closer, he saw it was an Oldsmobile. He reduced speed. Yes, it was Ernesto Tizol. Overtaking him, Fidel made signs that he should follow. They entered Bayamo in convoy at around 6:00 P.M. on the Saturday afternoon. Both of them stopped in front of La Cubana bus office and talked for a while on the sidewalk. Fidel was thinking of leaving Tizol in Bayamo, but then he remembered that he had previously organized the mission to start out from Santiago to Bayamo, at the head of a column to reinforce this advance front to the Cauto when taking the Moncada, and decided to continue the journey. He sent word to Abel that he was already in Bayamo and would travel on to Santiago later. Tizol left in his car to cover the final stretch to Santiago de Cuba and Fidel headed for the meeting place of the men who would fight in Bayamo.[22]

When Fidel arrived at the Gran Casino hostel he met with squadron leaders Raúl Martínez Ararás—who would be chief of operations—and the squad heads Ñico López, Aguilera, Pérez Puelles and Orlando Castro, and detailed to each one of them the distinct steps for executing the attack on the garrison and the subsequent measures to be taken. He went through the plan time and time again and established the means and time of communicating the first part of the plan and distributing the uniforms and arms to the rest of the men.

Around 10:00 P.M. Fidel left Bayamo. "But just before reaching Palma Soriano," Teodulio Mitchell recalled, "we had to stop at an army control barrier. They were stopping all the cars and checking them. I stopped my car as well. A soldier approached me, but I recognized him. Like me, he was from Palma Soriano. 'Hello, Mora,' I said and saluted him. 'Is that you, Mitchell? Come on, you can go.' I started up the car and Fidel said to me out of the corner of his mouth: 'They don't have much time left.'"

It was gone midnight when, from the highway that snaked down the mountain the flickering of lights twinkling in the darkness came into view: Santiago de Cuba! It was night still, but it was already Sunday, July 26. Within five hours, breaking from the east with the sunrise, a new dawn.[23]

JULY 26, 1953: ZERO HOUR

Fidel entered the city and stopped for coffee in the central plaza bearing the name of the god of war [Marte Plaza].

The people of Santiago were in fiesta. The leader of the Centennial Generation had chosen the date for attacking the country's second-largest military fortress very well, having it coincide with the most famous and joyous of Cuban carnivals.

At Marte Plaza, Abel stopped the car. Getting out of the car with Pedro Trigo, Fidel directed him to find Dr. Muñoz in Melgarejo and return to that same spot. While Trigo waited in the midst of the din of carnival, Fidel disappeared from sight up a street, alone.[24]

By an extraordinary coincidence, in the midst of that wash of people, Gildo Fleitas came rolling along in a conga in the middle of the street. Fidel was overjoyed and called him over. He asked what had happened to him as the trio Benítez, Tápanes and González Seijas from the San Leopoldo cell joined them, as well as Gerardo Sosa and the taciturn Víctor Escalona. Weary and sweating but happy, Gildo explained the mechanic's delay in fixing the car. When they got to Santiago, they went in any case to the lodgings they were allocated, in the guesthouse in Victoriano Garzón Street. They didn't know anyone there and they decided to go out to see if they could reestablish contact. At that point Abel, Mario Muñoz and young bank employee Julio Reyes Cairo arrived. Effusively, Muñoz embraced Fidel:

"Fidel, has the zero hour arrived?" His question confirmed that this brave man, member of the command leadership of the Movement, whom Fidel had asked to come the previous dawn when they were passing through Colón, had traveled 600 kilometers in a disciplined fashion without knowing exactly what it was all about. And even so, he turned up. And waited for hours at a road fork until he was contacted.

"Yes, doctor," said Fidel, "it's zero hour."

"Congratulations!" exclaimed Muñoz, all the more enthusiastic, "What a day you've picked! I'm forty-one years old today, and I'm placing those years in your hands, a 26-year-old!"

And he embraced him again... It would be the last time.

The men organized themselves in three cars: Fidel in Mario Muñoz'. The presence of the doctor from Colón guaranteed another aspect of the plan's execution. In addition to his medical services, his knowledge as a radio ham would be of great technical usefulness in programming the call to the people. [25]

As Fidel had foreseen, things were not easy. By common consent with Montané and Guitart, Abel Santamaría had thought of offering himself as a volunteer in the vanguard group that had to neutralize the guards at Post 3, and enter the garrison first. But Fidel was not prepared to let him run so many risks. His designation at the head of the group that was to occupy the civilian hospital had the sole objective of guaranteeing him a greater chance of survival. Abel Santamaría was second in command of the Movement, he was animated by an exceptional enthusiasm, he had dedicated himself body and soul to his task, and of all the members, Fidel considered him the most capable of renewing and directing the struggle in the event of his own death. But Santamaría did not understand it in that way. He had too much admiration for Fidel to think that he could replace him. He was obsessed with a fear that they would kill Fidel and all hope of liberating Cuba would disappear along with him. And he ardently wished to fight at his side in the secret hope of protecting him, even at the cost of his own life. In that way, each one of them estimated the other's existence as so necessary to the Revolution that neither wanted to see the other exposed in an initial combat. This battle between two generous natures was played out between unbendable wills. Neither of the two was prepared to give in. The profound friendship that united them was based on discussion, but it is possible that things got confused with loftier reasons of an affectionate nature. Abel kept saying: "You're not going to do what Martí did, expose yourself unnecessarily." And Fidel replied: "My place is at the head of the combatants. It can't be anywhere else. But you, Abel, you have to live. If I die, you will replace me." The argument went back and forth on the same lines and turned into a vicious circle. The minutes went by. They were wasting time, and Fidel put an end to the argument by saying firmly: "No, no Abel. It's decided, you will go to the civilian hospital." Although he didn't raise his voice, there was no doubt whatsoever: it was an order. Abel recalled that a few hours before he had given a desperate order to Julio Trigo. "I'll go," he said. Fidel put an arm around him: "Come on, there are still some details to go over."[26]

Then Haydée and Melba approached him and communicated their intention of taking part in the attack. "No, no," said Fidel, "the two of you are to stay at the farm. You've done more than enough already." "Exactly," said one of them, "there's no reason to exclude us from the final phase because we're women." And they insisted with such vehemence that Fidel felt confused: He was a firm believer in gender equality and appeared to be adopting an attitude contrary to his principles. But, on the other hand, he felt so much affection for the two girls that he wanted to spare them the horrors of combat, if that should occur. "You're Abel's sister," he said finally, speaking to Haydée. "I leave Abel with the responsibility for that decision." "And me?" said Melba. "He'll decide for both of you." They immediately went off to confront Abel. He listened to them, more absorbed by their eloquence than convinced by their reasons. When they had finished, he began by with a categorical negative. But at that point Dr. Muñoz approached. He felt that the girls would be a great help to him as nurses in the civilian hospital. He said so to Abel and got his consent.[27]

Fidel addressed to the combatants:
Comrades:

187

In a few hours you can conquer or be conquered, but in any case, listen carefully, comrades!; in any case this Movement will triumph. If you win tomorrow, what Martí aspired to will be made sooner. If the opposite should occur, the gesture will serve as an example to the people of Cuba to take up the flag and continue onwards. The people in Oriente and throughout the island will be backing us. Youth from the Martí centennial, as in 1868 and 1895, here in Oriente we are giving the first shout of FREEDOM OR DEATH!

You already know the objective of the plan. Without any doubt it is dangerous and all of you who leave with me tonight must do so completely of your own free will. There is still time to decide. In any case, some of you will have to stay behind due to a shortage of weapons. Those of you who are determined to go please take a step forward. The orders are not to kill, only if it is unavoidable.[28]

Minutes before leaving for the Moncada Garrison, the leader of the Cuban Revolution stated the details:

"Comrades, listen," Fidel said. The low-voiced conversations stopped and everyone turned towards him, moving closer to him. When things were quiet, he told them:

"We're going to attack the Moncada Garrison. It will be a surprise attack. It shouldn't last more than ten minutes."

He went on to explain the plan.

Speed and surprise were the essential elements of the project. The combatants would travel in cars. The squad in the first car, taking advantage of the confusion that would be caused by their uniforms, would take the Post 3 soldiers prisoner and remove the chain between the two small pillboxes at the entrance. The cars would enter the camp, Fidel's in front. When it stopped, those following would stop as well. The combatants would get out, penetrate the buildings to their left, reach the dormitories, take captive those who gave themselves up and drive the rest back to the patio at the bottom of the camp.

A second group, comprising about twenty combatants, would take over the civilian hospital, whose back windows gave onto the Moncada area. Positioned at these windows, the hospital men would cut off from the rear any soldiers fleeing for the bottom.

The third group, composed of six men, would take the Palace of Justice. Its flat roof dominated the roofs of the camp buildings. If necessary, they would neutralize the machine guns sited there with their fire.

Fidel paused and stated: "You have joined the Movement on a voluntary basis. And today, you have to take part in the attack voluntarily. If anyone disagrees, now is the time to pull out." There was a silence, followed by murmurs.

A few seconds went by and Fidel saw Víctor Escalona advancing. He already knew about his attitude during the journey from Tizol, and before he opened his mouth Fidel knew what he was going to say to him. Escalona approached him looking very pale. Refusing to meet his eye, he said in a low and unsteady voice:

"We don't want to take part."

"We?" inquired Fidel.

"My group and I."

"All of your group?"

"No, Sosita will go with you."

"All right," said Fidel. "You and your group follow me."

"Where are you taking us?" said Escalona.

"To the kitchen."

Fidel wanted to isolate the group as quickly as possible to avoid contamination.

"Why?" said Fidel as soon as the door to the kitchen was shut. Escalona licked his lips and responded without looking at him.

"Because there aren't enough arms."

"Listen. They wouldn't be enough if it was an open field, but for fighting inside a building at short range, on the contrary they are very good. Especially the hunting rifles. The dispersal range of the lead is huge."

"The arms are inadequate," repeated Escalona without raising his eyes. Fidel looked at him more in pity than in anger and his regard halted on Escalona's three comrades.

"Do you agree with him?"

They nodded their heads affirmatively.

"All right, you're forbidden to leave the kitchen."

"What are you going to do with us?" exclaimed Escalona. Fidel looked at him:

189

"Calm down, nothing's going to happen to you."

He left the kitchen and closed the door behind him.

Abel was waiting for him.

"Another group's backing out," Abel informed him.

"Which one?"

"The student group. They said that they wouldn't fight with those arms. Of course, I isolated them in a bedroom. Montané has designated a sentry to look after them.

"I want to talk to you," said someone to Fidel's right.

"And what do you want?" asked Fidel turning on his heels.

"Do you recognize me? I'm Manuel Lorenzo, the radio telegraphist. I'd like to know what I should be doing in all this."

"Well, all right," said Fidel, "I'm counting on you to get the Moncada transmitter going when we've taken the garrison."

Manuel Lorenzo's eyes widened.

"But I'm not going!" he exclaimed in terror. "I don't want to do anything illegal."

Fidel looked at Abel. "Put him with the students," he said, with a movement of his hand as if he was swatting a fly.

"Is there anyone else who wants to pull out?," Fidel asked in a loud voice. The seconds ticked by. Nobody spoke.[29]

Jesús Montané and Generoso Llanes, both Moncada assailants, will never forget what Fidel said to them at Siboney farm a few minutes before leaving for combat:

"Before leaving Siboney farm," Montané recalled, "Fidel gave us the final instructions which were the same as he gave to the other groups participating in the action and in which he reminded us that we should be humane with the enemy and only shoot in the final instance, in the case of absolute necessity. "Someone asked Fidel what should be done with any prisoners that were taken, Llanes said, and Fidel replied: "Treat them humanely. Don't insult them. And remember that the life of an unarmed man has to be sacred."[30]

Already within the city of Santiago and in close proximity to the garrison:

For the second time Fidel stopped the black Buick he was driving along Garzón Avenue to allow the first car to enter the street leading to the Moncada Post 3 with a bit of distance. In any case, he had to give the vanguard group led by Renato time to neutralize the guards and to leave the entry clear so that Fidel's car, in second place, could enter the garrison, followed by the whole convoy.[31]

. . . The second car, driven by Fidel, followed the vanguard car at approximately thirty meters' distance and very slowly, to give them time to carry out their mission. At Fidel's side in the front seat were Reinaldo Benítez and Pedro Miret. In the back seat, from left to right, were Gustavo Arcos, Abelardo Crespo, Carlos González and Israel Tápanes.

On the left of the street, between the military hospital and the one-story house used by the deputy officers, there was a small avenue. When Fidel's drove past the military hospital, the attention of the combatants in the back seat was caught by an army sergeant who was walking quickly down that small avenue carrying a carton of food. While walking, he was looking suspiciously and fearfully at the second car—Fidel's—and at the third car, moving his hand to his revolver in a mechanical gesture.

Fidel wasn't looking at that sergeant. His sight was fixed further ahead, on the soldiers armed with submachine guns from the flying patrol standing with their backs to him at that point. Renato's shout ("Open the way, here comes the general!") had paralyzed them and they were gazing in surprise at the "sergeants" of the first car disarming the sentries.[32]

On July 26, 1963, ten years later, Fidel recalled:

At that moment I had two things in mind. Given that each sentry had a submachine gun, I was afraid that the flying patrol might open fire on our comrades who were busy disarming the sentries. Second, I wanted to avoid their shots alerting the rest of the garrison. Then I had the idea of surprising them and taking them prisoner.

That didn't seem to be too difficult, as they had their backs to me. . . .[33]

"We're going to arrest them," said Fidel. And with that he reduced speed. None of the occupants of the back seat paid any attention to that plural and nobody thought it referred to the flying patrol. They had their sights fixed on the sergeant with the carton who, still nervous and mistrustful, had come level with them. Gustavo Arcos grabbed at the car door and pulled out his revolver, ready to jump on the man and detain him as soon as the car stopped.

Everything happened then in a matter of two or three seconds. Fidel followed slowly alongside the sidewalk on the left, no more than three or four meters from the patrol, gently opened the door and drew out his Luger, more practical in this situation than the rifle he also carried. Having done this, he pulled up. Gustavo Arcos, behind him, opened the door and placed one foot on the sidewalk.

At that moment, the patrol soldiers turned round, as if moved by the same instinct, faced Fidel's car and pointed their submachine guns at it. Fidel accelerated and spinning the wheel to the left launched the car in their direction.[34]

The car door suddenly shot open. González fell onto the asphalt and Israel tumbled on top of him. When he got up, his weapon was in his hand. Without knowing how, he found himself between Fidel and Pedro Miret behind the car. He saw a soldier appear at the window of the military hospital. He shot at him, the barrel of his gun a few centimeters from Fidel's head. Fidel made a gesture, and placed the palm of his hand over his ear, as if the detonation had deafened him. At that precise moment, the alarm bell resounded in the garrison with strident force.[35]

The immobilization of Fidel's car had an even more disastrous consequence for the action. It should be recalled that the cars following him had received the order to stop when he did, at which moment the combatants were supposed to get out and assault the barracks to their left. If they had been able to follow Fidel's car inside the camp, he would have taken the general command and the others would have immobilized the troops in their dormitories by taking them out to the back patio. But seeing Fidel get out of his car and being unfamiliar with the location, the combatants jumped energetically out of their cars and invaded the buildings to their left, principally the military hospital, whose door was forced by Ciro Redondo and Guillermo Elizalde. They were still outside the camp!

Fidel desperately tried to regroup the combatants, to make them realize their error. But some of them failed to understand what he was shouting to them. Others didn't see him; they were already taking up positions in the houses on Trinidad Street, on both sides of Moncada Avenue that led to Post 3. "Move forwards, move forwards!" shouted Fidel, pointing to Post 3. He then ran toward the hospital and pulled out the men who had occupied it and ordered them back into the cars to move ahead into the garrison. He got into the Buick to lead them, but at that moment a car reversing from Post 3 crashed violently into the front of the Buick. Fidel got out of the car. The shooting was already intensifying. He saw a man arriving at 50-millimeter machine gun that could dominate their position with its power, and fired at him with his shotgun. The soldier threw himself to the ground; when he got up, Fidel shot at him again and once more the guard had to protect himself without being able to get the machine gun in action. That scene was repeated several times. The street was already being raked with gunfire. The comrades who were close yelled to him: "Get out! Get out!" But Fidel continued standing there, right in the middle of the street, firing and firing.[36]

The combat had already lasted for fifteen minutes. From the moment the alarm sounded there were no illusions as to the outcome of the fight. But their hatred of the dictatorship and their revolutionary impulse were so strong that nobody thought of abandoning the combat. A combat had been lost. There would be others. It was essential to preserve the Movement. The important thing was not to die gloriously and unnecessarily, but to win. And Fidel gave the order to retreat.[37]

When Fidel thought that all his men had left he got into the last car that was retreating under a hail of bullets. Shortly after, however, he got out again and gave his seat to a wounded combatant, remaining alone in the middle of the street. He began to retreat, walking backwards and shooting at the garrison, along Moncada Avenue to Garzón Street. He had already passed the military hospital when, unexpectedly, another car came towards him in reverse, almost from Trinidad Street, opposite Post 3; it was driven by Ricardo Santana from Artemisa. Fidel got in and before the car left that area three more comrades had gotten in.

Fidel ordered Santana to head for El Caney highway. At that point his basic concern was for the Bayamo comrades. If they had taken the city it was necessary to join up with them to continue the struggle; if they hadn't, the struggle would continue in the mountains. Hence his decision to head for El Caney, take the small garrison there, and seize its arms and munitions.

Instead of taking El Caney highway, Santana, who didn't know Santiago de Cuba beyond the tour he had made shortly before from the farm, took the road to Siboney. When they crossed the wooden bridge,

Fidel realized the error, but they had already gone too far in that direction and ahead was the car that Boris had abandoned to get in another and continue after he got a puncture. Fidel ordered Santana to stop. The men that had stayed there without being able to enter the combat emerged from the tall grass bordering the ditch and joined them.

A private car approached with two people traveling in it. Standing in the middle of the highway, Fidel forced them to stop. "One group with me and the rest of you follow me," he said, getting into the car that had just stopped, while ordering its driver to drive on to Siboney farm, where he got out with his comrades.[38]

At midday on that same Sunday, July 26, 1953, after a battered column of just twenty men had regrouped at the Siboney farm, Fidel began to scale the foothills of the Gran Piedra.[39]

TODAY IT WAS OUR LOT TO LOSE BUT WE WILL BE BACK

The Gran Piedra is climbed by a series of little steep hills leading to its peak. The sun was burning, the march exhausting. In certain parts the comrades disappeared up to their thighs in Guinea grass. The air was on fire, they experienced a burning thirst and had not eaten since the evening before. After some hours climbing, they reached a summit from which they could see the capital of Oriente Province, extending from the shore of its wide bay. They halted. With his hand resting on a tree, Fidel contemplated Santiago, and then his eyes returned to the small column around him. He regarded his comrades, the poor-quality hunting rifles with which they were armed, their faces hollowed and upset, and then said with a calm conviction: "Comrades, today it was our lot to lose, but we will be back.[40]

YOU HAVE CAPTURED US, BUT WE ARE NOT SURRENDERING

Surprised at 6:30 A.M. on the morning of August 1, while they were sleeping in a rustic palm-leaf hut, Fidel and two of his comrades were taken captive by Lieutenant Pedro Sarría Tartabull.

Years later, Lieutenant Sarría related how the capture of the leader of the Moncada Garrison assailants came about:
The first to emerge was Fidel, who halted in front of me, and behind came Oscar Alcalde and further back Pepe Suárez. But I counted the arms they had and there were eight Remingtons stacked almost together and then said: "Ah, five men are missing, where are they?" Fidel answered: "No, there's only three of us." I said: "And the five Remingtons left?" He said: "Well, there were another five but they went off." I said: "Where?" And Fidel: "Over there." I said: "No, because I've just come from the highway, it's not possible, at what time did they go off?" He said: "At about 4:30 or 5:00 A.M." I said: "At 5:00 A.M. I was already on my way here. It's not possible, they have to be around here." Then I said: "Boys, we're going to get ready for the return, facing the same way, in the same order, with about twenty meters between each man." And I said to them: "Well, boys, you've surrendered, now there's no problem..." "Surrendered no," Fidel said to me. "You captured us while we were sleeping and tired, but we have not surrendered." Then I asked sergeant Suárez if he had pen and paper. And I started to take down their details. I started with Fidel: "Well, you're all caught as you yourself said. Now, what's your name?" "Francisco González Calderín." "Age?" "26." "Native of?" "Marianao." "Occupation?" "Student." "Right, next. Come here. What's your name?" "Me, Oscar Alcalde." "Age?" "25 as well, or 21." "Occupation?" "Employee." "Native of?" "Havana." "Right, next. And what's your name?" "José Suárez." "Age?" "29 or 30." "Native of?" "Pinar del Río." Then it occurred to me that maybe he was the man already assumed dead, it could be the man that died on El Caney ridge seeking for the Alto de Villalón hill, en route for Ramón de las Yaguas. Fidel had been taken for dead since July 27; it had even come out in Salas Amaro's *Ataja* newspaper. Even the government was convinced that Fidel was already dead, but they had not as yet identified his body. That was the idea that came to me. Then I looked at him and said to myself: "Ah, this man's very dark, he looks mestizo," and to make sure, I turned my back on him without revealing my suspicions to my men, not to the others. I left him standing there in front of me, like you are, turned my back on him, took three steps back and then made a rapid half-turn and said to him: "What did you say your name was?" He replied

"Francisco González Calderín," and held my gaze. But I thought, let me check what I'm thinking. And I put my hand on his hair and it was very curly and hard, seemingly as a result of the sun and not wearing a hat for four or five days. Then I was half- convinced and said to myself: "No, there one who's been taken for dead, and another one; this notion of mine is unfounded because he's mestizo." You see, I knew Fidel here at the University when I was a student as well. He didn't know why I half turned and felt his hair, and neither did the others, and I said: "Right, to the highway, as I said before, facing the same way, twenty meters apart." As we approached the highway, about 500 meters away, I went behind with the arrested men—I already had them tied up—and I felt a pam... ping... pam... and said: "Hey, I want you alive." They said: "Yes, there's quite a few here." I said: "All right, but just the same." The shots continued and I said: "We're going to hit the ground in case some of them fly this way." Then Fidel said to me: "I want to die, I don't want you to take me anywhere." I said: "I'm the one in charge here, you're the prisoner. Get down." Lying down at my side, Fidel said to me: "I am the man you thought I was..." I'd already forgotten about that and said: "What?" He said: "I'm the chief as you thought there in the hut." And I said: "What man was I thinking about?" Then he said to me: "I'm Fidel Castro." And I replied: "Oh damn, yes I did think so but I discounted the idea, how you've changed boy, look how you are now, how much you've changed in such a short time." "So, now you can kill me, by killing me, it's all over and done with." Then I got angry and said to him: "But who's talking about killing here, don't you know what kind of a man I am, boy?"[41]

YOU CANNOT KILL IDEAS

Talking with students at a higher institute of education in Venezuela, almost forty-five years after Lieutenant Sarría took him prisoner, Fidel Castro recalled that incident.

Well we can reiterate what was said to me by a lieutenant who took me prisoner in a wood, at dawn, not far from Santiago de Cuba, a few days after that attack on the Moncada fortress. Exhausted from having to rest on stones and roots, we had committed the error—there's always an error—of sleeping in a little *varaentierra*[42] covered with palm leaves we'd come across. Without knowing whom we were, a lieutenant—a black lieutenant fortuitously—and some soldiers with swollen arteries thirsty for blood awoke us with guns pointing at our chests. We hadn't been identified. At first they didn't identify us, asked us our names and I said any old name: prudence, huh!, astuteness, no? Intuition perhaps, instinct. I can assure you that I wasn't afraid, because there are moments in life when it's like that, when you think you've had it and then you react more out of honor, pride or dignity.

If I'd given them my name, that would have been it: Bam, bam, bam! They would have finished off our little group immediately. A few minutes later they found various weapons left there by comrades who were not in any physical condition to carry on the struggle. Some of them were wounded and with everyone's agreement they were returning to the city to hand themselves over to the legal authorities. We were the only three armed comrades left, captured in the way I explained to you.

But that lieutenant was amazing! I have never told this story in detail before in public, he was calming the soldiers, and close to failing in that. When they were searching the surroundings and found the other comrades' arms, they were really mad. They had us bound and were pointing loaded guns at us; but no, that lieutenant moved from one side to another, calming them down and repeating in a low voice: "You cannot kill ideas, you cannot kill ideas." What made that man say something like that?

He was a mature man, he had studied at the University, some courses; but he had that idea in his head, and it occurred to him to express it in a low voice, as if talking to himself: "You cannot kill ideas." Well, observing that man and noting his attitude at such a critical moment when he could hardly prevent those furious soldiers shooting us, I got up and said: "Lieutenant"—just to him of course—"I am So and so, and the leader of the action." Seeing his gentlemanly conduct I couldn't deceive him, I wanted him to know who his prisoner was. And the man said to me: "Don't tell anyone! Don't tell anyone!" I applaud that man because he saved my life three times in a matter of hours.

Still under Lieutenant Sarría's custody, Fidel is interrogated by Colonel Del Río Chaviano in the Santiago de Cuba bivouac.

Some minutes later they took us away. The soldiers were still very wound up. Some shots rang out not so far away and put them in full combat gear. They told us: "Throw yourselves to the ground, throw yourselves to the ground!" I remained standing and said: "I won't hit the ground!" I thought it was a strategy to eliminate us, and refused. I said it to the lieutenant too, when he insisted that he was protecting us: "I won't hit the ground, if they want to shoot, let them." Then he told me—listen to what he said to me—"You are very brave boys." What an amazing reaction!

I don't mean to say that he saved my life at that point, but that he made that gesture at that moment. When we reached a highway, they put us into a truck. There was a commander nearby, a really bloodthirsty type, he had murdered many comrades and wanted the prisoners to be handed over to him. The lieutenant refused, saying that we were his prisoners and that he wouldn't hand us over. He put me in front in the cab. The commander wanted him to take us to the Moncada; but he didn't hand us over to the commander—here he saved our lives for the second time—nor did he take us to the Moncada; he took us to the prison in the middle of the city and saved my life for the third time. There you have it, and he was an officer in that army against which we were fighting. After the triumph of the Revolution, we raised his rank to captain, aide to the first president of the country after the triumph.[43]

WE HAVE COME TO REGENERATE CUBA

A journalist and commentator from the provincial CMKR radio station recalls:

On August 1, 1953, I arrived early at the radio station and heard that Fidel had been arrested and was in the Santiago bivouac. With that journalistic vocation that one carries inside, I grabbed a huge old tape recorder that was there and headed for the bivouac (the recorder weighed about thirty pounds).

There were many people on the sidewalk on the other side of the street facing the bivouac. Most of them were curious individuals who followed all these things. The people were expectant.

I joined that group and waited for an opportunity to get inside the bivouac. The morning went by. They were saying that Fidel was on the second floor and being interrogated. There was hardly any movement of people leaving the building.

I remember they wouldn't allow us on the street, only on the opposite sidewalk. Soldiers with shotguns were guarding the bivouac.

I remained attentive to any call for journalists or an opportunity to enter the building. Shortly after midday I heard a voice shout from inside: "Let the journalists in." They were going to bring Fidel before the press.

I said to myself: "This is my chance," and walked to the bivouac door. The guards stopped me, but I showed them my press card and they let me in. I took the stairs to the office. Various detainees were seated on a bench in an anteroom to the office. Later I learned that they were assailants as well.

Fidel was in the office. When I went to go in Commander Pérez Chaumont stepped in front of me and told me that I couldn't go in, there was no space for anybody else. I insisted and explained that I'd been waiting for hours and he couldn't leave me outside. In the end he let me in.

The office was relatively small. I think it was the bivouac chief's office. Colonel Del Río Chaviano was there with some other military men and journalists. So was Lieutenant Sarría, who arrested Fidel and brought him to the bivouac, having made the valiant decision to refuse to hand the prisoners over to that bloodthirsty commander, Pérez Chaumont.

That was my impression of the moment, but everything happened very fast. In the midst of the agitation and the rush I managed to find the tape recorder and prepare the equipment. I don't think that Fidel had begun to speak. I put the machine on the ground and started recording.

I raised my hand to ask a question. Maybe I formulated it in a somewhat timid tone given the circumstances surrounding the event and above all the arrested man. I inquired about the objectives that the assailants were pursuing with the July 26 action.

Fidel was standing erect in the middle of the room. If I remember correctly, he was wearing a light colored short-sleeved shirt and pants discolored at the knees, denim I think. You could see that his face, with a nascent beard, was sunburned.

In response to my question, and although I cannot remember his words exactly, Fidel—in a succinct and very concrete way—spoke of the revolutionaries' program in the event of their triumph.

He affirmed that the idea was to give back sovereignty to the people, to guarantee campesinos their permanence on the land, to liberate rural people from the threat of eviction and the dead time, to give workers participation in the fruits of their labor, to guarantee rights to small landholders, medical attention to the sick, education for children who lacked schools and teachers, to clean up public administration and make life in the country decent.

Fidel concluded his answer with a sentence that I have never forgotten. He said: "In short, we have come to regenerate Cuba."

Just one thing. While Fidel was saying all that, Chaviano—who was moving about restlessly and nervously—exclaimed half out loud: "This man is making politics." Nevertheless, he didn't dare interrupt.

That all took place in about fifteen or twenty minutes. The interview was very brief and I think there were only three or four questions. In response to another journalist, Fidel affirmed that he had heard Batista's Columbia speech on the events of July 26, and that "Batista had not told the truth."

My impression of Fidel at that moment is that he was serene. His words flowed firmly and unfalteringly. I don't think he gesticulated once.

In another part of his statement Fidel emphasized that elements of the old politics—in other words, the traditional politicians—had nothing to do with the organization of, preparations for and the action itself. He stressed that everything was done with the sacrifice, selflessness and patriotism of young men and women, and that the scant resources utilized in the assault were assembled in that way.

There was one moment when Fidel referred to the dictatorship soldiers who fell in the fighting and clarified that he respected the memory of those who had died fulfilling what "they considered to be their duty."

Meanwhile, Chaviano was becoming more exasperated by the minute. Fidel was very concrete, direct and concise in what he said. It was as if he knew that he didn't have much time and had to take advantage of every second.

At that moment, Fidel did not know in detail about the massacre being committed against the surviving revolutionaries. He was isolated in the mountains and his first contact with the city was that August 1.

Wanting to cut things short, Chaviano took advantage of the first opportunity to terminate the interview and vacate the room. I stayed behind for a few seconds to pick up the tape recorder and the auxiliary parts of the equipment. Chaviano told me that I had to go to the Military Intelligence Service (SIM) with the recorder and tape. His people insisted that I go with them. At the same time, Fidel asked me if it had recorded well, if it had come out well. I said "yes, yes..." It was a very awkward situation, virtually seconds. I felt a bit nervous.

But to be fair, I think that everybody there was nervous. I can tell you something, frankly, that the only serene person among all of us in that room—including Chaviano himself and the military men—was Fidel. Afterwards, at home and in a calmer state of mind, I reflected on the interview and came to the conclusion that that man was not any prisoner, that he was a distinct kind of prisoner.[44]

I BELIEVE IN THE PEOPLE

At his trial, Fidel serenely responded to the state attorney's questions:
"Did you participate in the attacks on the garrisons of Moncada in Santiago de Cuba, and Bayamo in Oriente Province, last July 26, in a physical or in an intellectual form?"

"Yes, I did participate."

"And those young men?"

"Those young men, like me, love the freedom of their homeland. They have not committed any crime unless it is considered a crime to want the best for our homeland; was that not taught us in school? Was...?"

"Confine yourself to answering the Public Ministry's questions."

"In what way did the accused expound the plan that was to be carried out to his followers? Did you explain to them the political baggage of it and the criminal action that they were to commit? Please answer that question, but restricting yourself to the question, I am asking you not to include a political harangue in your answer."

"I am not interested in making politics; my only aspiration is to let the truth be told."

"But tell the court how you convinced them."

"I definitely did not have to persuade them, they appeared before me at a stage when—all other possible routes being exhausted—they were convinced there was a danger of this generation being paralyzed and lost and that we had to take the road of armed struggle. Knowing how they felt I expounded my plan to them and they accepted it. I knew almost all of them as members of the Orthodoxy Party, I am not aware of the thinking and the plans of the leaders of that party, but I am sure that 99% of the youth, like these young people, understand that the only solution possible is warfare. Harmony could not be reached, although that was everyone's desire. I believe, Mr. Attorney, that I have answered your question."

"Yes, I see; but tell me, why did you not use the civil route to achieve your plan? After all, you are a lawyer."

"Very simple, because there was no freedom; after March 10, I could not talk any more."

"Do you mean to say that after March 10 it was not possible to make politics?"

"There were attempts, but the government showed itself hostile to any freedoms and we opportunely understood that any dialogue with the usurpers was useless. I personally lodged an appeal before the Emergency Court, declaring the regime that had seized power illegal. According to the law, Batista should have been sentenced to around 100 years' imprisonment, going by the crimes he had committed against Cuba. But the courts did not act as we hoped that they would."

"Can you tell the court where you obtained the money to buy weapons and organize the uprising? Was former president Prío your financier?"

"Just as José Martí did not accept the ill-gotten gains of Manuel García, known as King of the Cuban Countryside, we did not accept Carlos Prío's money. Neither Prío nor any other politician gave us money; our costs were covered by the effort and sacrifice of all the comrades, via generous donations from people that followed me to face death. I have a list of the names of every one of them and the amount that they contributed; almost all of them are dead, but I have confirmatory data that it was they who gave that money, amounting to a total of 16,480.00 pesos, spent to the last cent. On many occasions, that total was collected by doing without the most pressing necessities, like food and electricity and even work tools, which many people sold or pawned."

"Can you give more details of how you were able to collect that sum when your words imply that your friends had very scant resources?"

"Among those of us who are alive and those of us who were murdered, the following persons gave money: Jesús Montané—who is here—contributed the sum of 4000 pesos which was paid him as a bonus by his employers, General Motors when they wound up their operations in Cuba; Oscar Alcalde—likewise present—mortgaged his laboratory for the sum of 3600 pesos and liquidated an accounting office that he owned, making a further contribution in that way; Renato Guitart—who was murdered—gave 1000 pesos; and Ernesto Tizol placed a chicken farm that he owned at the disposition of the Movement; and Pedro Marrero sold the dining room dinner service, refrigerator and living room suite in his house, and the only reason he didn't sell the bedroom furniture was because I prevented him from doing so. Moreover, he asked a moneylender for 200 pesos to increase his contribution. Fernando Chenard—who appears among the dead 'in combat'—pawned personal effects and his photographic camera—his working equipment—the same one he used for the studio portrait of the sculptor Fidalgo, that was destroyed by the dictatorship police because he had sculpted a statue of Martí entitled 'For Cuba that is suffering.' Chenard's photos were published in Bohemia magazine on that occasion; Chenard gave 1000 pesos. Elpidio Sosa sold his position in the agency where he worked as treasurer for an important company; José Luis Tasende made a similar sacrifice, he was one of the comrades who made the greatest sacrifice. Abel Santamaría pawned his car, but that wasn't his only contribution: he gave much more, as if it was little, he gave his life, which will have no price when the Revolution triumphs. I could go on expanding the list, but it would seem to be a better idea to hand it over to the court, if you wish, in an orderly way, in writing, so that you can append it to the summary and investigate the veracity of everything."[45]

That was the reason for the Fidel's cutting response to the public prosecutor during the trial, when he asked if he had the help of a certain member of the government to successfully carry out his plan:

"We relied solely on our own efforts and with the help of all the people of Cuba, which we would have obtained if we had been able to communicate with them via radio. The possibility of some civilian or military person from the regime helping us is totally improbable."

"So, you just relied on the people?"

"Yes, on the people. I believe in the people."[46]

Immediately after the revolutionary triumph, in Santiago de Cuba's Céspedes Park, five years, five months and five days after the attack on the Moncada Garrison, Fidel reiterated this concept of his struggle to all Cubans:

"When I arrived on Cuba's beaches with eighty-two men and the people said that we were crazy and asked us why we believed that we were going to win the war, I said: 'because we have the people.' And when we were defeated the first time and were left with a handful of men and persisted in the struggle, we knew that it would be a reality, because we believed in the people. When we were dispersed five times in the space of forty-five days and met up again and renewed the struggle, it was because we had faith in the people, and today is the most palpable demonstration of that faith being justified. I have the total satisfaction of having profoundly believed in the Cuban people and of having inculcated that faith in my comrades. More than a faith, this faith is a complete security, and this faith that we have in you is the faith that we want you to have in us for ever."

This faith, this confidence in the people's revolutionary essence is a constant defining trait in Fidel; on December 12, 1953, he wrote from prison:

"What has weight at the hour of going into combat for freedom is not the number of enemy weapons, but the number of virtues in the people. Although one hundred valiant young men fell in Santiago de Cuba, that only means that in our country there are 100,000 other young people ready to fall as well. Look for them and you will find them, guide them and they will march forward, no matter how hard the way; the masses are ready, they only need to be shown the true route."[47]

TAKING THE SKIES BY SURPRISE

On the eighth anniversary of the attack on the Moncada Garrison, Raúl Castro affirmed:

The events of July 26, 1953 highlighted comrade Fidel Castro as the leader and organizer of the armed struggle and the radical political action of the people of Cuba...[48]

Fidel does not carry Cuba's national leadership just because he displayed valor and daring, firmness and decisiveness in the attack on the Moncada Garrison, but because, alongside that, he expounded the program of the homeland, the program of the people. And he not only expounded that program, but also demonstrated the will to realize it and pointed out the way of doing so.

When Karl Marx stated that the Paris communards "tried to take the skies by assault," it could be said of the Moncada attack that a few dozen young people armed with shotguns for shooting birds "tried to take the skies by surprise."[49]

HISTORY WILL ABSOLVE ME

Fidel's self-defense in the Moncada trial, resumed in the historical document known as History Will Absolve Me, *clearly expounded the program for which the youthful assailants of that military fortress were fighting.*

Fidel told a group of students about the difficulties he had to face during that trial:

At the trial, what I did was to assume my own defense. It's not that I regarded myself as a good lawyer, but I believed that I was the best person to defend myself at that time; I donned a gown and took my place alongside the lawyers. It was a political rather than a criminal trial. I wasn't attempting to get off, but to communicate ideas. I began to interrogate all those criminals who had murdered dozens and dozens of comrades and who were acting as witnesses; it was they who were on trial. Because of that, the next day they pulled me out of there, separated me, declared me sick. That was the last thing they did, because they wanted to do away with me for once and for all; but well, I knew very well why they acted with restraint. I knew and know those people's psychology, their mental state, the popular situation, the popular rejection of and great indignation over their murders, and I had a bit of luck as well: but the fact is that in the initial hours, while they were interrogating me, the book by Lenin appeared—someone pulled it out: "You had a book by Lenin!"

We explained what we were: followers of Martí, that was the truth, that we had nothing to do with that corrupt government that they had dislodged from power, that we proposed such and such objectives. Of Marxism-Leninism, we didn't utter a word. Nor did we have to say anything to them. We said what we had to say to them, but as the book came out into the open in the trial, I felt really annoyed at that point and said: "Yes, that book by Lenin is ours; we have read the works of Lenin and other socialists, and anyone who doesn't read them is an ignoramus;" that's what I affirmed to the judges and the rest of them.[50]

Then there was our program laid out when I defended myself at the trial. Those who didn't know we thought, didn't know because they didn't want to know. Perhaps they wanted to ignore that speech known as *History Will Absolve Me,* with which I defended myself there on my own, because, as I explained, they threw me out, they pronounced me sick, they tried all the others and sent me to a hospital to be tried in a small room. They didn't admit me into hospital exactly, but held me in

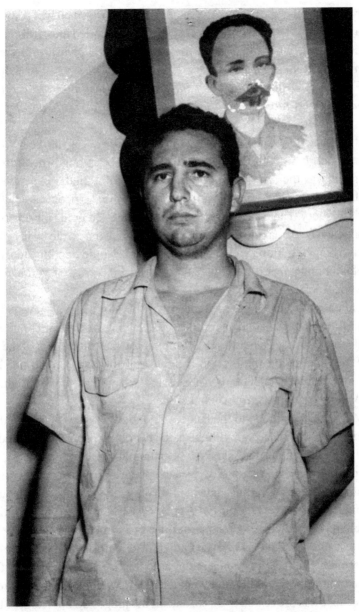

Symbolic photo of the Moncada trial. Behind Fidel is a portrait of José Martí, the intellectual author of that assault.

an isolation cell in the prison. The small room in the hospital was converted into a hearing with the court and a few people crammed into it, almost all military men, where they tried me and I had the pleasure of saying everything I thought, all of it, very defiantly.[51]

Fidel Castro Ruz concluded his historical testimony in the little room in Santiago de Cuba's Saturnino Lora hospital on October 16, 1953, by stating:

It seemed the Apostle [José Martí] would die on the year of his Centennial. It seemed that his memory would be extinguished forever. So great was the affront! But he lives; he has not died, his people are a rebellious people; his people are a worthy people; his people are faithful to his memory. There are Cubans who have fallen defending his doctrines; young men who, making unprecedented amends, came to die by his grave, to give him their blood and their lives so that he could continue to live in the fatherland's heart. Cuba, what would have become of you had you let your Apostle die!

I am about to close my plea, but I will not do it like all lawyers do, requesting that the defendant be released. I cannot ask freedom for myself while my comrades already suffer ignominious imprisonment at the Isle of Pines. Send me there to join them and to share their fate. It is understandable that honest men are either dead or in prison in a Republic whose President is a criminal and a thief.

My sincere gratitude to the Honorable Judges for having allowed me to express myself freely, without petty restrictions. I hold no grudges against you. I admit that you have been humane in certain aspects, and I know that this Court's Chief Judge, an impeccable man, cannot conceal his disgust at the prevailing state of affairs that obliges him to pronounce an unjust sentence. The Court of Appeals has yet to face a more serious problem: the indictments for the murder of 70 men, that is to say, the greatest massacre we have ever known. The culprits are still free and are armed. They are a permanent threat to the lives of all citizens. If the force of law does not fall upon them with all its weight due to cowardice or because it is prevented to do so, and all the judges do not resign, I take pity on your honor, and regret the unprecedented shame that will fall upon the Judicial Power.

I know that jail will be harder for me than it has ever been for anyone, filled with cowardly threats and hideous cruelty, but I do not fear it, nor do I fear the wrath of the miserable tyrant who took the lives of 70 of my brothers. Condemn me. It does not matter. History will absolve me.[52]

Minutes after Fidel concluded his testimony in the exercise of his right to self-defense, the court withdrew to deliberate and, on their reappearance, read out the sentence against the accused "as maximum author of a crime effected against state powers," dictating a fifteen-year prison term to be spent in La Cabaña Fortress in Havana.

However, in a resolution emitted that same October 16, Minister of the Interior Ramón O. Hermida ordered his transfer to the Men's National Penitentiary on the Isle of Pines.

ENDNOTES

1. Mario Mencía, *El grito del Moncada,* Vol. 1, ed. cit., 320.
2. Name by which the young men and women who assaulted the Moncada Garrison would be known. *Ed.*
3. Mario Mencía, *El grito del Moncada,* Vol. 1, ed. cit., 325-327.
4. Organization created by the Authentic Party after the March 10 coup d'état, to confront the Batista dictatorship with arms. Headed by Aureliano Sánchez Arango, the Triple A was weakened by politicking and phantom insurrections. *Ed.*
5. Mario Mencía, *El grito del Moncada,* Vol. 1, ed. cit., 339-342.
6. Fidel Castro, "Discurso pronunciado con motivo del inicio del curso escolar 1995-1996 en la enseñanza superior y sus 50 años de vida revolucionaria," ed. cit., 7.
7. Centro de Estudios de Historia Militar de las FAR, *Moncada; antecedentes y preparativos,* ed. cit., 224.
8. Ibid., 178-179.
9. Mario Mencía, *El grito del Moncada,* Vol. 2, ed. cit., 369.
10. Ibid., 370-371.
11. Mario Mencía, *Tiempos precursores,* ed. cit., 136.
12. Ibid., 121-122.
13. Mario Mencía, *El grito del Moncada,* Vol. 2, ed. cit., 406.
14. Mario Mencía, *Tiempos precursores,* ed. cit., 137.

15. Mario Mencía, *El grito del Moncada,* Vol. 2, ed. cit., 425-426.

16. Word used in the former province of Oriente for an agricultural measure equivalent to one tenth of a *caballería* (1.343 hectares). *Ed.*

17. Mario Mencía, *El grito del Moncada,* Vol. 2, ed. cit., 433-434.

18. Ibid., 436-437.

19. In the current version of "Freedom March" the word "Oriente," a province then, has been replaced with "Cuba." *Ed.*

20. Mario Mencía, *The Fertile Prison: Fidel Castro in Batista's Jails* (Melbourne: Ocean Press, 1993), 64-66.

21. Roberto Silva Pérez, "Cómplice y encubridor del ataque al Moncada" [Accomplice and Accessory to the Moncada Attack], *Ahora* newspaper, July 24, 1990.

22. Mario Mencía, *El grito del Moncada,* Vol. 2, ed. cit., 507-509.

23. Ibid., 510-511.

24. Ibid., 526.

25. Ibid., 526-527.

26. Ibid., 532-533.

27. Ibid., 534.

28. Centro de Estudios de Historia Militar de las FAR, *Moncada; antecedentes y preparativos,* ed. cit., 259.

29. Ibid., 536.

30. Mario Mencía, *El grito del Moncada,* Vol. 2, ed. cit., 537-539.

31. Ibid., 544-545.

32. Ibid., 547-548.

33. Ibid., 548.

34. Ibid., 548-549.

35. Ibid., 550.

36. Ibid., 553-554.

37. Ibid., 575.

38. Ibid., 576.

39. Ibid., 585.

40. Centro de Estudios de Historia Militar de las FAR, *Moncada: la acción,* ed. cit., 151-152.

41. Ibid., 198-199.

42. Type of small hut without a support or walls, with a leaky roof. *Ed.*

43. Fidel Castro, "Una Revolución solo puede ser hija de la cultura y las ideas," ed. cit., 57-58.

44. Centro de Estudios de Historia Militar de las FAR, *Moncada: la acción,* ed. cit., 360-362.

45. Centro de Estudios de Historia Militar de las FAR, *Moncada: antecedents y preparativos,* ed. cit., 289-291.

46. Mario Mencía, *Tiempos precursores,* ed. cit., 105.

47. Ibid., 105-106.

48. Raúl Castro Ruz, "Discurso pronunciado en el VIII Aniversario del Moncada" (Speech on the 8th Anniversary of the Attack on the Moncada Garrison), in *Moncada: la acción,* ed. cit., 405.

49. Id.

50. Fidel Castro, "Una Revolución solo puede ser hija de la cultura y las ideas," ed. cit., 51.

51. Id.

52. Fidel Castro, *History Will Absolve Me,* Annotated Edition (Havana: Editorial José Martí, 1998), 122-123.

PRISON BATTLES

INITIAL MEASURES DIRECTED FROM PRISON

*O*n *Saturday, October 17, 1953, the day after being sentenced, Fidel Castro was confined in Pavilion 1 of the misnamed Model Prison on the Isle of Pines.*

Those attempting to imprison his rebel spirit are mistaken; for the maximum leader of the Centennial Generation there was not a second of rest. He would devote all his time in prison to continue attacking the dictatorship and preparing the people for the struggle.

On December 12 the guidelines of the initial measures directed by Fidel from behind prison bars were definable:

1. To denounce "the atrocity of the torture and barbaric and insane mass murder" of nearly half of the young people involved in the July 26 actions.

2. On the other hand, to openly present to the people the "honorable and humane conduct of the assailants" as the district attorney himself proclaimed during the trial, in order to expose the false versions circulated and repeatedly used as propaganda by the regime.

3. To clarify the popular revolutionary nature—and not a putsch—of the July 26 actions and the political program we intended to put into practice in the event of its success, to the Directorate and the Orthodoxy masses.

In another context, he also directed a collection "to help the widows and families of the dead," but nothing for the prisoners, as "we do not want those who have lost their loved ones or household support to be evicted or to go hungry."[1]

QUEST FOR KNOWLEDGE

In prison, the Moncada assailants organized an academic program and a small library. Studying was very important and there was no time to lose.

Fidel himself detailed a normal day in a letter dated December 22, 1953: "At 5:00 A.M. sharp, when you think you've just shut your eyes, a voice yells: 'Line up!' accompanied by handclaps, and we remember —if we forgot it for a moment while we slept—that we're in prison. The lights, left on all night, glare more harshly than ever; our heads feel heavier than lead; and we have to get up! Naturally, I spend less than 30 seconds putting on my shoes, pants and shirt. I won't sleep again until 11:00 at night, when sleep catches me reading Marx or Rolland—or, as today, when I finish writing.

"To sum up: 5:30, breakfast; 8:00 to 10:30 A.M. classes; 10:45, lunch; 2:00 to 3:00 P.M., classes again; recreation until 4:00; 4:45, dinner; 7:00 to 8:15, classes in political economy and group reading; 9:30 P.M., silence.

"Every morning on alternate days from 9:30 to 10:00 I explain philosophy or world history. Cuban history, grammar, arithmetic, geography and English are taught by other compañeros. At night, I teach political economy and, twice a week, public speaking—that is, something like it.

"Method: instead of classes on political economy, I read to them for half an hour—descriptions of a battle, such as Napoleon Bonaparte's infantry attack on Hugomont, or an ideological topic such as Martí's plea to the Spanish republic or something similar. Immediately afterward, several fellows chosen at random or volunteers talk for three minutes on the topics in a contest with prizes, awarded by the judges we have chosen. On all patriotic dates, we have special talks on the topic.

"On the 26th of every month, a party; on the 27th, mourning —commemorative meetings with reflection and oral presentations on the subject. On the days of mourning, naturally, there is no recreation or diversion of any kind. Study days are from Monday through midday on Saturday."[2]

Photo taken for Fidel's trial for the Moncada attack.

Several of Fidel's letters during that period show the progress of his reading.

In November, it included several works by Shakespeare, A. J. Cronin's *The Keys of the Kingdom,* Axel Munthe's *The Story of San Michele,* Maurois' *Memoirs,* Rosie's *Memoirs,* Marías' *Philosophical Writings,*

García Lorente's *First Lessons in Philosophy,* Romain Rolland's *Jean Christophe,* and Victor Hugo's *Les Misérables,* of which he made the following criticism four months later:

"It's impossible to express how much Victor Hugo stimulated me with *Les Misérables.* Nevertheless, as time goes on, I grow a little tired of his excessive romanticism, his verbosity, and the sometimes tedious and exaggerated heaviness of his erudition. On the same topic of Napoleon III, Karl Marx wrote a formidable work entitled *The Eighteenth Brumaire of Louis Bonaparte.* Placing those two works side by side, you can appreciate the tremendous difference between a scientific, realistic view of history and a purely romantic interpretation. Where Hugo sees no more than a lucky adventurer, Marx sees the inevitable result of social contradictions and the conflict of the prevailing interests of the time. For one, history is luck; for the other, it is a process governed by laws."

How far did the eagerness for knowledge go—so that their time in prison would be fruitfully spent? On December 8, Fidel wrote:

"When I read the work of a famous author, the history of a people, the doctrine of a thinker, the theories of an economist, or the preachings of a social reformer, I am filled with the desire to know everything that all authors have written, the doctrines of all the philosophers, the treatises of all the economists, and the preachings of all the apostles. I want to know everything, and I even go through the bibliographies in each book, treasuring the hope of reading those books someday. Outside, I was restless because I did not have enough time; here, where there seems to be too much time, I am still restless."

On December 18, he mentioned William Thackeray's *Vanity Fair,* Ivan Turgenev's *A Nest of the Gentry,* Jorge Amado's *Luis Carlos Prestes: Champion of Hope,* the Dean of Canterbury's *The Secret of Soviet Strength,* Eric Knight's *Fugitives from Love,* Nikolai Ostrovsky's *How the Steel Was Tempered* ("a modern Russian novel that is a moving autobiography by a young man who participated in the revolution"), and A. J. Cronin's *The Citadel.* "I'm also studying Karl Marx's *Capital* in depth: five enormous volumes of economics, researched and set forth with the greatest scientific rigor. I have also begun studying Cuban authors: Félix Varela, Luz y Caballero, and so on."

Next, alternating with Lex Publishers' *Collected Works of José Martí* (his constant companion), he turned to Victor Hugo's *William Shakespeare;* Honoré de Balzac's *The Magic Skin;* Stefan Zweig's *Biography of Little Napoleon;* Rómulo Gallegos' *On Equal Footing;* A. J. Cronin's *The Stars Look Down,* Somerset Maughan's *The Razor's Edge;* four of the 18 volumes of the *Complete Works* of Sigmund Freud; and Dostoyevski's *The Brothers Karamazov, The Insulted and the Injured, Crime and Punishment, The Idiot, The House of the Dead, Poor Folk,* and the short story *Mr. Prokharchin.*

"My main attention, however, is on something else. I have rolled up my sleeves and taken on the study of world history and political doctrines," he wrote in a letter in March. Shortly afterward, when he had read Kant's *Critique of Pure Reason,* Mira y López' *Mass Psychology,* Cirilo Villaverde's *Cecilia Valdés,* and two biographies of *Bolívar* (Rourke's and Zweig's)," he wrote, in a letter dated April 4:

"It's 11:00 at night. Since 6:00, I have been reading one of Lenin's works nonstop—*The State and Revolution*—after having finished *The Eighteenth Brumaire of Louis Bonaparte* and *The Civil War in France,* both by Marx. All three of these books are interrelated and of immeasurable value."

He added,

"My ventures into the field of philosophy have served me well. After having knocked heads a good while with Kant, I find Marx easier than the "Pater nostrum." Both he and Lenin had a powerful polemical spirit, and I'm having a fine time with them, laughing and enjoying my reading. Implacable and formidable with the enemy, they were both truly model revolutionaries."[3]

I COMPLETE THE MEANING OF MY LIFE

In a letter dated December 19, 1953, Fidel described the value that prison would have for him and defined human being's attitude to life, stating:

What a tremendous school this prison is! Here, I have rounded out my view of the world and determined the meaning of my life. I don't know if it will be long or short, fruitful or in vain, but my dedication to sacrifice and struggle has been reaffirmed. I abhor being tied to petty trifles of comfort and self-interest. I think a man should not live beyond that moment when his life begins to decline and the flame that illuminated the brightest moment of his existence is snuffed out, when the force that guided his steps during his worthy period fades away.

Then you see dejection and repentance bearing that vile renegade off into the depths of degradation. He becomes ashamed of the only noble things in his life: his years of selflessness and generosity. This is the tendency of those who do the opposite of what they once preached. From then on, they look back on their own youth as a period of naiveté, rashness, inexperience and dreaming. They do not realize that in reality they are entering a period of impotence, frustration, deceit, and submissiveness; a miserable and ridiculous retreat; the sad spectacle of a man abandoning the path he has traveled, never to find it again.[4]

WE KEPT ON SINGING THE ANTHEM

Something unusual was happening in the Model Prison, increased security measures and the noise from outside alerted the Moncada combatants.

One of them, perched on the shoulders of another comrade, discovered that the dictator Fulgencio Batista was visiting the prison and they immediately decided to sing the "Freedom March" as loudly as they could. Fidel smiled while relating:

At first, Batista thought it was all part of the welcoming ceremony or that it was perhaps a chorus singing his praises. At first he was happy and he told the others who were with him to be quiet. Then he grew silent and began to get irritated when the words of our anthem spoke of the "insatiable tyrants who have plunged Cuba into evil." Almeida saw everything from the window. Then the police came but we kept on singing, even though a terrible thug, a killer called Pistolita [Little Pistol], was there. We were locked in, and besides that, I was isolated from the others until the end of our prison term. I'd been kept in solitary confinement in Santiago de Cuba until I was tried, so I must have spent nineteen of the

217

twenty-two months I was in prison in solitary. Near the end, my isolation was ended because they sent Raúl to the place where I was, several months before the amnesty.[5]

TOTAL SOLITARY CONFINEMENT

Fidel: total solitary confinement, alone. A cell to the left of the entrance to Pavilion 1.

He first referred to his new situation near the end of February, stating: "For the past two weeks I have been confined to a small solitary cell."

On March 1, the same day the other five were returned to the collective ward and before he learned how brutally they had been treated, Fidel gave a succinct and moving description of his own situation.

"I still have no light, after 17 days here, and they will not allow any candles. But last night, it was not just the darkness and solitude but also the rain. Darkness had just fallen when there was a rumble of thunder. Lightning flashed, cutting the darkness and illuminating the cell through the high windows, casting the shadows of the bars into the corners.

"Then came the storm, accompanied by a strong wind that blew the rain in, soaking everything. I did what I could to protect my books by putting them inside the suitcase and covering it with a blanket. Meanwhile, the bed got soaked; the floor was flooded; and the cold, wet air penetrated everywhere. Wet and chilled to the bone, I waited in a corner with infinite patience until the gale subsided. It was Sunday night!"[6]

There are some perspicacious notes on his incursions into the field of philosophy in these months, like this one in a letter of his dated March 18, 1954:

I fell asleep finishing *The Transcendental Aesthetics of Space and Time*. Of course, space and time disappeared for a good while from my mind. Kant made me think of Einstein, with his theory of relativity of space and time and his famous formula for energy: $E = MC^2$ (mass times the speed of light squared); of what relation there could be between their perhaps opposing concepts; and of Kant's conviction that he had found definitive criteria that saved philosophy from being buried, beaten down by the experimental sciences and the tremendous results of its discoveries.

Did Kant meet the same fate as Descartes, whose philosophy could not stand the test of events, because it went counter to the proven laws of Copernicus and Galileo? Kant, however, did not try to explain the nature of things—only the knowledge through which we arrived at it, whether or not it is possible to know the nature of things and, in line with this, when such knowledge is correct or erroneous. His was a philosophy of knowledge, not of the objects of knowledge. According to this, there should be no contradiction between him and Einstein. Yet there are his concepts of space and time, basic points for elaborating his philosophical system.

Is there a contradiction? Obviously it will not be difficult to find out. But while I consider this and the many other questions that constantly besiege me, I keep thinking how limited our knowledge is and how vast is the field that man has tackled with his intelligence and efforts throughout the centuries. Even the very relativity of this knowledge is saddening. How many theories and doctrines and beliefs, now outdated, used to be Bibles for science! How dearly man has had to pay for the progress of humanity![7]

On March 22, 1954, after six weeks incommunicado, Fidel wrote:
"Now I have light; I spent forty days without it and learnt to appreciate its value. I'll never forget it, like I will never forget the burning humiliation of the shadows; I fought against them, managing to beat them back for almost 200 hours with a pale and quivering little oil lamp, my eyes burning, my heart bleeding with indignation. Of all the human barbarities, the one I can least conceive of is the absurd."[8]

"I turn on the light at about 7:00 P.M. and then I begin to fight the mosquitoes. If I'm writing, I scare them by blowing cigarette smoke. Then I get under the mosquito net and start chasing one by one those that have managed to get in with me.

"But that's not all. As soon as I start to read, I realize that I've left my colored pencil outside. I go get it and open the book—and it turns out to be the wrong volume! I go out again to get the dictionary, or my glasses. What a problem! So now I've made a little pile to the right of the bed and another pile on the bed itself, of which I take very good care. I read as long as I can, usually 10, 12 or 14 hours a day.

"The cell is also inhabited by ants that eat everything: cheese, grease, bread. Strangely, the only thing they don't touch is the condensed milk. There's a constant battle among the animal life. The flies fight the mosquitoes; the frogs hunt the flies; and the ants, like tiny vultures, carry away whatever's left. The prison that I find so confining is a huge world for them.

"Every once in a while a small, bright bird flies up to one of the high windows, happy and free. Then I understand more clearly than ever what a crime it is to cage these birds, and I'm reminded of *The Story of San Michele*. In the late afternoon, the sun shines obliquely through the windows, and the shadows of the bars fall across the floor for several minutes."

Something new broadens the possibilities for amusement, at times ironically pointing to the bitterness of confinement.

On April 4, after reading Lenin's State and Revolution, *Fidel wrote:*

"Now I am allowed outside several hours every afternoon, as well as Tuesday, Thursday and Sunday mornings, in a big, empty enclosed yard with a gallery all around. I enjoy it very much, although I will come out mute. . . .

"I fixed up my cell Friday. I scrubbed the granite floor first with soap and water and then with scouring powder, then washed it down with detergent. Finally, I rinsed it with disinfectant, aromatic solution. I put everything in perfect order. The rooms at the Hotel Nacional are not as clean. . . .

"I'm going to dine on spaghetti with squid, Italian bonbons for dessert with fresh coffee, and then smoke a four-inch H. Upmann cigar. Aren't you jealous? They look after me and they take pretty good care of me. They pay no attention to what I say; I try to keep them from sending in things. When I go out in the morning in my shorts and breathe the sea air, I feel like I'm at the beach, and that there's a little restaurant here. They're going to make me think I'm on vacation. What would Karl Marx say about such revolutionaries?"

But these were fleeting moments. The harsh reality filtered through in other letters—along with the ever-present attitude of struggle. On April 11, he wrote:

"Some days ago, they took me to court. It had been a long time since I had seen fields and distant horizons. The landscape here is beautiful, full of light and radiant sun. I stood awhile talking to the employees in the trial court—very nice people—about national affairs. When I returned to my cell I felt strange, uncomfortable. I thought about what I had said to them. It was quick and precise, but I realized I had spoken mechanically. I had the feeling that the light, the landscape, the horizon—everything—had affected me, as if I had entered a strange, distant and forgotten world."[9]

The rest of the letter Fidel wrote on April 11, eight days after his first court hearing following the February incident, is more easily understood knowing this background. It reflects sadness but not discouragement. No matter how hard he was hit, his morale—based on what motivated him to fight—remained high:

"It has been only eight and a half months, but how much I have had to suffer in every way! I've spent most of the time alone; to a certain extent, that has been my fate. There's a law of inertia in the moral as well as the physical world, and both worlds also have their laws of gravitation; a thousand forces tend to slow you down, and sometimes you have to combat them with every ounce of psychic and spiritual energy.

"Your confidence in my determination to resist is not unfounded. It is true that I am bearing up firmly. But this is not a normal life I am leading; and it goes against the grain in every way. It's as if a body, which has its own shape, were being pressed into a different mold.

"The strange thing is that I have no personal ambitions; all my motives are moral ones—a sense of honor, dignity, and duty. The reasons others have for valuing life mean nothing to me. The greatest contradiction in my situation is that I am totally indifferent to physical and material punishment, to biological existence; I could mock all that with a smile. The only prison, chain, or force I recognize is that of duty. Physically, I feel powerful, confident that no force on earth can harm me—simply because I do not fear it. Nevertheless, the physical must submit to the moral, the innate rebel ever at war with calm, cold reason, which in turn is based on strong moral feelings."[10]

On April 5 he made a request:

"I have plenty of material for the study of the great contemporary political movements: socialism and fascism. I have nothing at all on Roosevelt's New Deal. I know of a one- or two-volume work in Spanish that contains a complete study of Roosevelt's program and what he did."

On April 15 he took up the same theme:

"Roosevelt. I mainly want information on him: his policy of raising agricultural prices, the promotion and conservation of soil fertility, credit facilities, the debt moratorium, and the extension of markets at home and abroad in agriculture; in the social field, how he provided more jobs, shortened the work-day, raised wages, and pushed through social assistance to the unemployed, the old, and the disabled; and, in the field of the general economy, his reorganization of industry, new tax systems, regulation of the trusts, and banking and monetary reforms."

In those months, he studied the most diverse authors and topics. His prison file contains some lists of the books that the censor received in his name and then passed onto him after checking them.

Along with a *Latin Grammar,* a *Dictionary of Idiomatic Expressions,* and Demosthenes's *Oratory,* his bed was surrounded with José Ortega y Gasset's *The Revolt of the Masses* and *New Horizons: Fundamentals of Politics;* Curzio Malaparte's *The Techniques of Coups d'état;* Gustave Le Bon's *Mass Psychology; Naked Fascism; The Age of Religious Revolution: Reformation and Counterreformation;* and Thomas More's *Utopia.*

Side by side with the *Complete Works* of Homer, *The Rubaiyat,* and works by Cicero and Mirabeau were Rafael Rodríguez Delgado's *Introduction to a Philosophy for the Atomic Age;* Jorge Mañach's *For a Philosophy of Life; This Human Peace;* Paul Schmidt's *Europe Behind the Scenes;* José Ingenieros' *The Mediocre Man;* and José Enrique Rodó's *Ariel* and *Motives of Proteus.*

He read Raimundo Cabrera's *Cuba and Its Judges; Contribution to the Draft Penal Reform;* Guizot's *On the Death Penalty in Political Terms;* and the *Constitution of the United States.* He read Engels's *The Origin of the Family, Private Property and the State* and *The Condition of the Working Class in England.* He also read *100 Best Poems;* Margarita Ferrer's *Seven Songs;* Oscar Wilde's *The Nightingale and the Rose;* Honoré de Balzac's *Eugénie Grandet, The Lily of the Valley,* and *Ursule Mirouët; The Martyrdom of a Genius; Don Juan;* Anatole France's *At the Sign of the Reine Pédauque* and *The Amethyst Ring; The Patriot;* Antonio Zambrana's *Francisco the Black;* Sinclair Lewis' *Main Street;* Leo Tolstoy's *Anna Karenina;* Cirilo Villaverde's *Cecilia Valdés;* and Carlos Loveira's *Juan Criollo.*

The historic theme was constant, however: *Miguel Servet and His Times; Morelos; The Losing of America;* Herminio Portell Vilá's *Lives of American Unity;* Raimundo Cabrera's *The Autonomy Campaign;* and the 10 large volumes edited by Ramiro Guerra, *A History of the Cuban Nation.* There were many works by Martí, and he also read a lot on Bolívar: *Bonaparte and Bolívar;* Emeterio Santiago Santovenia's *Bolívar and the Spanish Antilles;* and Emil Ludwig's *Bolívar, Knight of Glory.*

Nothing seemed to escape him in the field of politics; he read everything he had ever heard of. When informed, mistakenly, that the censor had held back two books that should have reached him, he wrote a brilliant letter defending his right to direct investigation. In passing, this letter lets us appreciate the great tact employed in his correspondence with that prison official, which enabled him to establish an incredible tie that was to be of great importance in the future:

"I have been informed that two books were confiscated. One of them is Trotsky's *Stalin.*

"I suppose this was done because it is called *Stalin,* because I cannot conceive of any other reason for such an action. Even if it had been written by a supporter of Stalin's and were a defense of him, I sincerely do not believe that should be a reason for confiscating it. But the fact is that in this case we are not dealing with an impartial critical study. This book was written against Stalin by Leon Trotsky, his most irreconcilable enemy; far from being a defense, it is an implacable attack on him. As you can see, the reason that might be adduced for confiscating it does not exist.

"I don't know what the other book is, but I suspect it is Curzio Malaparte's *The Techniques of Coups d'état,* because I seem to remember that somebody told me it was coming.

"I know this book well and it is nothing but a fanciful version of fascist, Nazi, Falangist, and other coups d'état, which does not stick to historical truth, since its author is more a novelist than a historian. It has no practical value. Sometimes I am sent books that I have already read. But all right: because it has such a suggestive title I admit that objections might be raised. In any case, I'm not interested in this book, if it is the other one that was confiscated. But I am interested in the first one—and I assure you that there is no reason at all for retaining it. It seems to me that a mistake has been made. Look into it and see for yourself.

"I am not bringing this up out of caprice. This is something that worries me very much. I have enough tact and sense of responsibility not to ask for any book that would go against the norms of healthy moral or disciplinary standards. You know full well that I am interested only in serious books. You will never see me obtaining pornographic or obscene books or reading matter of any kind that should not be admitted into a penal institution.

"It is a great source of concern for me that a book I requested, such as this one by Trotsky, should be confiscated simply because of its title, without examining its contents. This business of censorship should be handled with a sense of justice. Everybody reads in accordance with his education and culture.

"The study of economic, social or philosophical questions requires books and authors with the most diverse viewpoints so one can analyze, compare, etc. Without the freedom to read one cannot study either religion or sociopolitical doctrines.

"This problem arose once before, with other books, and Lieutenant Montesinos, to whom I explained the problem, settled it in a reasonable manner. I beg you to remember that I am a professional with more than one university degree—of which I do not like to speak often and which I mention in this case simply so you may understand that an incomprehensible limitation in this matter regarding books is quite humiliating and hard for me to take, because it interferes with something that is very personal to man: his desire for learning.

"Shut up in this building, I spend all my time studying. In doing so, I am not hurting or bothering anyone, nor does this damage the prison or the state. I am not asking for improvements of any kind or changes in the prison regulations.

"I have not asked for anything—only that no harm be done to me that is useless, senseless, and benefits no one. We have not had any difficulties for some time, and it may really be said that I am spending my days here as if I did not exist. I hardly ever write, so even the slightest difficulties with letters have completely disappeared, and I do not believe there is any intention to injure us without reason—at least, there shouldn't be.

"I have set forth my reasons. Look into them, and you will see they are well founded. If you consulted with your superiors regarding the seizure of these books, I beg you to set forth my reasons, confident that they will listen to them. I repeat that I am only interested in the book by Trotsky. The other, if it is Malaparte's, does not interest me. Above all, I would like an assurance that there will be no unnecessary difficulties concerning the question of books, which are cultural works authorized by the laws of the country. I await your response."

Fidel received not only a quick reply from the censor but also the books, which had just arrived at the prison. As a result, he immediately wrote the following note to the official:

"I am not to blame for the report that I received regarding the two missing books; Lieutenant Perico passed on the news to my guard.

"In any case, I am glad the mistake occurred, because I have had another opportunity to see how invariably kind you are; I am not sorry I sent you a reasoned, cordial letter, even though I was very annoyed by what I thought was an injustice, because I can write you only with the greatest consideration and courtesy.

"I know that if you do not solve a problem, it is simply because you cannot. I received the books with much joy, and this showed me once again that when people talk things over they understand each other, and that what men need is goodwill.

"In this case, you may rest assured I am very pleased and that all my concern has evaporated.

"Once more, I repeat my warmest thanks.

Fidel."[11]

HOW PLEASED I WOULD BE TO REVOLUTIONIZE THIS COUNTRY FROM TOP TO BOTTOM

Based on his knowledge of universal history and, above all, of revolutions that continued confirming his ideals, he wrote on April 6, 1954:

It is curious how similar all the great social reforms have been, from antiquity to the present. Many of the measures taken by the Paris

Commune in 1871 were similar to laws decreed by Julius Caesar. The problems of land, housing, debt and unemployment have arisen in all societies dating back to ancient history.

I am inspired by the grand spectacle of the great revolutions of history, because they have always signified the triumph of aims embodying the welfare and happiness of the vast majority as opposed to a tiny group of vested interests.

Do you know what episode really moves me? The revolution of the black slaves in Haiti. At a time when Napoleon was imitating Caesar and France resembled Rome, the soul of Spartacus was reborn in Toussaint L'Ouverture. How little importance is given to the fact that the African slaves who rebelled set up a free republic, defeating the greatest generals Napoleon had! It's true that Haiti has not progressed very much since then, but have other Latin American republics done any better?

I keep thinking about these things, because, frankly, how happy I would be to revolutionize this country from top to bottom! I am sure that all the people could be happy—and for them I would be ready to incur the hatred and ill will of a few thousand individuals, including some of my relatives, half of my acquaintances, two-thirds of my professional colleagues, and four-fifths of my former schoolmates."[12]

FIDEL COMPLEMENTS THE TACTICAL ORIENTATIONS

In a letter to Melba Hernández, on April 17, 1954, Fidel complemented the revolutionary movement's tactical orientations.

"First: The propaganda cannot be abandoned for a minute because it is the soul of any struggle. Ours should have its own style and be adjusted to circumstances. We have to go on constantly exposing the murders. . . . It is also essential to commemorate July 26 in a dignified way. In any case we have to have to organize an event on the University stairway: It will be a terrible blow to the government and one that has to be very intelligently prepared from now on; as well as other events in the Institutes, in Santiago de Cuba and abroad with the Orthodoxy Committees in New York, Mexico and Costa Rica. Gustavo Arcos should talk to the FEU leaders concerning the event on the stairway.

"Second: Work has to be coordinated between our people here and those abroad. To this end organize a trip to Mexico as soon as you can to meet with Raúl Martínez and Léster Rodríguez there and, after carefully studying the situation decide on the line to follow. . . . Don't allow any kind of underestimation; and make sure that you reach agreement only on a firm, clear basis with a probable successful outcome and positive benefit for Cuba. If not, it's better to go forward alone and keep the flag on high until these great guys in prison get out and get ready for the struggle with the greatest care. As Martí said: 'Knowing when to wait is the great secret of success.'"

Finally he recommended "continuing with the same tactic followed in the trial: defending our points of view without provoking irritation," and keeping up spirits in spite of everything and everyone "as we did in the difficult moments."[13]

FREEDOM CANNOT BE IMPRISONED

On June 18, nine days before two naval marines, likewise prisoners, were placed in his cell, which logically aroused his suspicions of a more direct and constant supervision of all his activities, he wrote:

"They have had me incarcerated in this solitary cell for four months and one week. They said at the beginning that it was for four months but really their intention is to keep me here indefinitely. I don't want to waste time expressing my opinion of these people: Castells[14] and his killer band were little angels compared to the gang of intransigent, soulless fools running this prison.

"To tell you the truth, this situation couldn't be much harder. I don't know how much that is due to the psychological torture and its unnatural effect, or realizing that they can do these things in Cuba with total impunity, accompanied by a shocking indifference on the part of the media."

In another letter six days previously he had reflected on the dramatic extent of his lack of communication:

"I only have company when they lay out a dead prisoner in the little funeral parlor in front of my cell—sometimes found hanged in mysterious circumstances—the strange murders of men whose health was liquidated by force of blows and torture. But I cannot see them because there is always a six-foot high screen facing the only entrance to my cell, so I cannot see any human being, alive or dead. It would be too magnanimous to allow me the company of a corpse!"

One visit slipped past the network: a brief conversation with Waldo Medina, the former Nueva Gerona judge, who was visiting the penitentiary. And the unexpected presence of Ramón Hermida, Minister of the Interior in Batista's regime, who had recently offended Fidel and had come to his cell to give him an explanation; Fidel accepted it "with the reservation of fully elucidating and solving this problem when I am released."

He was in solitary for 138 days. He would be there for 458 days. With the exception of his brother Raúl who shared the same cell with him some time later, he did not meet up with his fellow prisoners until he embraced them at the prison gates on the day they were released.[15]

Fidel managed to break the isolation imposed on him with resourcefulness and tenacity:

A little ball fell at their feet. It had come from the adjacent yard, tracing a parabola over the roof. Not a real ball, it was the kind the poorest children made, weaving strips of cardboard from packs of cigarettes over a central core of wadded paper.

Orlando Cortés Gallardo recalled that Miret picked up the ball in surprise and, not attaching any importance to it, kept on talking while he nonchalantly took it apart. When the stuffing came out, they saw it consisted of pages of paper covered with tiny handwriting—not the pieces of old newspaper usually used for this purpose. Curiosity led to surprise: the pages contained a message from Fidel.

This was how the first rudimentary yet effective means of communication was set up between Fidel and the rest of the Moncada prisoners on the Isle of Pines. Paper or rubber balls containing messages were thrown back and forth between the enclosed prison yards. It is said that sometimes an obliging guard helped out in this original form of correspondence, returning the balls when they fell short and landed on the roof.[16]

Even the ordinary mail was used, outwitting the prison censor. Between the lines of ordinary letters to relatives and friends, Fidel wrote with invisible ink—lemon juice, from lemons sent along with other foods, not arousing the slightest suspicion. Heat applied to the white paper brought forth the brown tracing of Fidel's precise instructions to compañeros along with damning denunciations. They ran rings around the regime during that period.

The first mention of this system appeared in a letter to Melba Hernández dated April 17, 1954, in which Fidel referred to "a means for you to get in touch with me every day if you want," but warned, "Keep this under your hat; only let Yeyé [Haydée Santamaría] know when she returns."[17]

INCREDIBLE TENACITY AND RESOURCEFULNESS

Reconstructed by Fidel, employing various ingenious methods, his defense speech, known as History Will Absolve Me, *was smuggled out of the model prison:*

Lidia Castro, Fidel's ever-active sister who was ready to run all kinds of risks, was to coordinate the work of producing the long document. Fidel reconstructed his defense speech in bits and pieces, written in ink or pencil or with lemon juice. Many letters which left the jail containing simple greetings to friends or acquaintances were immediately retrieved. Lidia, Melba, or Haydée ironed the letters, and the heat brought out the fragments of the defense speech that Fidel had written with lemon juice between the lines.

Several people were in charge of retrieving the letters, and four or five did the typing. All rules of secrecy and need-to-know were followed in this work. At 107 Jovellar Street, Melba's home, she and Manuel Hernández, her father, typed many of the fragments. All typewritten pages were delivered to Lidia Castro, who was responsible for keeping and hiding the manuscripts.

In June, the iron produced a paragraph containing a warning to the regime:

"I know that prison will be harder for me than it has ever been for anyone, filled with cowardly threats and hideous cruelty. But I do not fear prison, as I do not fear the fury of the miserable tyrant who took the lives of 70 of my comrades. Condemn me. It does not matter. History will absolve me."

With incredible tenacity and resourcefulness, the drafting of the document was completed. On June 18, 1954, in a letter to Haydée and Melba, Fidel issued instructions regarding aspects of the next phase of the plan:

"Meanwhile, I want you to pay special attention to the following:

"1. The speech. At least 100,000 copies should be distributed within a period of four months. This must be done following a well organized plan covering the whole island. Copies should be mailed to all journalists, lawyers' and doctors' offices, and teachers and other professional groups. . . . Precaution should be taken so the copies are not discovered and no one is arrested. The same care and discretion should be employed as if dealings with weapons. It must be printed in at least two different printshops, at the lowest price. A batch of 10,000 should not cost more than $300.00. . . . You must work on this strictly according to plan.

"The document is of decisive importance. It contains our program and our ideology—without which nothing of significance can be attained—and a denunciation of the dictatorship's crimes. These have not been publicized enough, and that is our first duty to those who died. It also tells of the role you two played, which should be made known to make your work easier. Having done this there are a series of organizational and propaganda tasks that I am working on now.

"2. Questions of finances should be handled according to a plan. . . . . This is one of the aspects to which you must give the greatest care, order, and coordination, as we did. Priority must now be given to publishing the defense. I'm sure many will help to defray the costs, for it is the most devastating attack that could possibly be published against the government.

Further on in this letter he expressed his view in the form of an axiom: "I believe that at this time propaganda is vital. Without propaganda, there can be no mass movement, and without a mass movement there can be no revolution."

The next day, June 19, he elaborated on this idea in another letter to Melba and Haydée:

"Our immediate task—and I want you to be fully convinced of this—is not to organize revolutionary cells to build our ranks. That would be a grievous error. Our task now is to mobilize public opinion in our favor, to spread our ideas and win the backing of the masses of the people. Our revolutionary program is the most complete, our line of action the clearest, and our history the most self-sacrificing. We have a right to the people's faith—without which, I repeat a thousand times, there can be no revolution."[18]

NOTHING AS FORMIDABLE AS THIS HAS EVER BEEN PREPARED IN CUBA

On discovering that agents from the Authentic Party were trying to capture exiles involved in the 26th of July actions, he advised Melba and Haydée on the attitude to adopt with elements alien to the Movement, detailed the tasks to be done at that time and once again outlined the principles of the revolution he was organizing. In one of those letters, dated June 18, 1954, he wrote:

What do you all think of the photocopy that M [Melba] brought from M [Mexico]? Isn't it just what I wrote to M before her trip? I want you all to preserve it carefully. I know you share my opinion of these people. It would be crazy to make a pact with them, following the road that has led so many Orthodoxy leaders to ruin.

Now more than ever I am convinced that we must keep the Movement independent, as we did in the most difficult moments, when no one wanted to pay any attention to us. I am aware of the great difficulties you face in your struggle, but do not despair. Always bear in mind what I have told you in each of my letters. Remember that nothing can be attempted until we are out and that it is always necessary to know how to wait for the right moment. Your mission is to prepare the way, keep together the courageous elements—of which there are never many—standing firm, and recruit all those who may be of use. Cuba is full of courageous men, but we must find them.[19]

The following day, June 19, he recalled in another of his letters:

"As members of the top leadership and as leading representatives of the Movement on the outside, you must strictly follow the decisions made here and do so with the zeal and discipline imposed on you by duty and the responsibilities your positions entail. You know that we have always taken a firm line on these matters, and I mean to do so again today.

"Any inclination to form a pact with the Authentic Party constitutes a serious ideological deviation. We did not form a pact with them in the past—when they had millions at their disposal and we were begging for pennies and suffering terrible hardships to purchase weapons because we believed they lacked the capacity, the morality and the ideology to lead the revolution. So how can we make such a pact today, over the bodies and the blood of those who gave their lives for their noble ideals?

"If in the past we weren't misled by their stories, fantasies, and braggadocio, why should we believe them now, when they have shown their true colors, in spite of their stolen millions? If all they did in the past was to hinder us, sabotage us, weaken our ranks, and decimate our cells with their lies and deceits—and then not even have the decency to denounce the regime's crimes—then what principle, idea, or argument could lead us to lower our noble banners before them?

"What did Prío do in the United States, where he had every opportunity to widely publicize the barbaric massacre committed in Santiago de Cuba? He kept miserably silent. Moreover, haven't they had more than enough time—just as they have had more than enough money—in the nearly two and a half years since then to fulfill 20 times over, the boast they've made 100 times: to make a revolution?

"The revolution cannot mean the return to power of men who have been morally and historically annihilated and who are totally responsible for the situation we now suffer. Always remember that our possibilities for success have been based on the certainty that the people would support the efforts made by honorable men who have upheld their revolutionary principles right from the start. Men who have deceived and betrayed the people can never aspire to that kind of support.

"I must warn you of several very important things so you will not let yourselves be impressed. At present, Aureliano[20] has not the slightest chance of leading an insurrection—Aureliano or anyone else—and anyone who claims it is possible is lying shamelessly. We should be the last to be fooled. Therefore, the Movement cannot be compromised by anyone or have anything to do with any insurrectional farce. We must give our consent to any agreement involving such matters. Beware also of those who thrive on intrigue, the petty politicians, and those who play at revolution!"

And Fidel later added:

"If we now have men in our ranks who only want to come out shooting and are willing to come to an agreement with the devil himself to get a gun, they must be expelled without any further thought, just as the cowards who back out when the time comes must be shot. The ones who brag the most generally do so out of desperation. We want no gangsters or adventurers, but only men who are aware of their historic destiny, who know how to wait and work patiently for the future of our homeland.

"This has been our main concern, and we have guided our steps in this direction, training our leaders through constant study and by building discipline and character. It doesn't matter whether we spend more or less time in prison, as long as we know we will fulfill our mission when the time comes. I assure you that nothing as formidable as this has ever been prepared in Cuba."[21]

AGAINST THE ELECTORAL FARCE

In an attempt to demonstrate that the country was returning to constitutionality, Batista convened supposed elections, where the opportunism of many of the so-called opposition parties was clearly revealed in their politicking. From prison, Fidel wrote:

"Politics is such a hoax! In my experience, even with the best men and the best parties, it is unbearable. Now, recalling all those meetings tirelessly and fanatically attended by so many idol worshippers who remained seated hour after hour, listening to twenty different speakers engaged in furious literary competition, in which all of them said the same thing, I believe that our people are infinitely patient and kind. Meditating in this solitary cell, I cannot understand how they applaud instead of grabbing their seats and throwing them at those charlatans. All these politicians are like actors in a theater—they play their roles, winning applause from the audience, and are damned if they are thinking of anything but election day, about which they're obsessed!"

233

Two months later, on June 12, he wrote:

"Decent people and the most politically aware have remained marginalized from electoral battles as a result of the coup that betrayed the election; we are witnessing a battle of thieves of yesterday and today; a fight among traitors; the traitors to the Constitution and the traitors to the suffering people; a battle between the creators of intimidatory violence and the founders of gangsterism, between tyranny and comedy, and a source of tragedy for the people. Anyone can win, but Cuba will lose in any case.

"What is important now is to safeguard principles: everything is saved if principles are safeguarded; from the depths of corruption the redeeming ideal will rise purer and cleaner."

And, a week later, in a letter dated June 19:

"It would be worth seeing what would happen if a third political front were to be formed; the number of hypocrites who would end up taking off the masks donned in search of becoming senators and representatives, ending up making a total game of government! The only thing missing, after that, would be Prío followers standing in any of those fronts and we would have the perfect takeoff point for our genuine struggle; on one side the criminals, thieves, politicians, apostates, traitors, corrupt individuals dividing up the Republic; and on the other, what remains of the honest, idealist and sincerely revolutionary in Cuba alongside the people. The sooner that happens the better."

In relation to the party of his extraction, in the first and only journalistic interview that was permitted during his imprisonment, Fidel advised:

"The Orthodoxy Party must unite; but unite to fight against the electoral farce and to keep on demanding a patriotic, democratic and dignified solution to the Cuban problem. A union made on the sole basis of presenting itself at elections would be very mean-spirited, opportunistic and lacking in heroism. The people would be right in believing that those who only come together for the easy conquest of collective posts not to make the sacrifice imposed by duty, are betraying the nation by basely compromising themselves with the conditions imposed by the de facto regime.[22]

Summing up the political events of 1954 several months later, journalist Enrique de la Osa commented in his *Bohemia* column "In Cuba:"

"There was the extraordinary case of the near crisis in Batista's cabinet over Fidel Castro. It so happened that on July 26, 1954, the first anniversary of the events in Oriente, Ramón Hermida, then minister of the interior, visited Fidel in his prison cell and had a long talk with him, details of which were never released. This enraged Rafael Díaz Balart, the undersecretary of his department, who, in an open letter, bitterly criticized his superior for that visit to 'the promoter of that criminal attack.' According to Díaz Balart, Hermida had offended the armed forces and the memory of the soldiers killed at the Moncada. Díaz Balart and the minister both resigned, and Batista had to step in to conciliate and overcome the crisis."[23]

AND NOW WE ARE MANY

Shortly after this, prison conditions were eased for Fidel, as he explained in a letter written in August:

"I continue to be isolated from the rest of my comrades. This is undoubtedly designed to hinder the intellectual training of the young men, whom they view as their most implacable adversaries of the future. They have even forbidden them to exchange books with me. Otherwise, I am better. They brought Raúl here. They connected my cell (which you saw in *Bohemia)* with another area four times as large and a big yard, which is open from 7:30 A.M. to 9:30 P.M. The prison personnel are in charge of cleaning it. We sleep with the lights out; we do not have to appear for line up or formations at any time during the day; and we get up at any hour we choose.

"Naturally, I had not requested any of these improvements. We have plenty of water, electric light, food, and clean clothes—all free. We don't even pay rent. Do you think it's better out there? We have visits twice a month. Utter peace reigns. I don't know, though, how much longer we'll be in this 'paradise.'"

In that same letter, he pointed out with the farsighted vision of an exceptional leader:

"Our time is approaching. Before, we were a handful; now, we must merge ourselves with the people. Our tactics will be different. Those who view us as a group will be sadly mistaken. We will never be characterized by a group mentality or group tactics. Now, moreover, I can dedicate myself body and soul to my cause. I will put all my time and energy into it. I will begin a new life. I am determined to overcome all obstacles and fight as many battles as may be necessary.

"Above all, I see our path and our goal more clearly than ever. I haven't wasted my time in prison, for I have been studying, observing, analyzing, planning and training the men. I know where the best of Cuba is and how to look for it. When I began I was alone; now we are many."[24]

IDEOLOGY, DISCIPLINE AND LEADERSHIP

In August 1954, journalist Luis Conte Agüero invited Fidel to be part of a civic movement. In a letter dated August 14, Fidel replied:
I fully agree with you on the need for it. You cannot imagine how many hours I have spent thinking about it and how many ideas I have, based on my experience over the past few years.

First of all, I think one of the biggest obstacles to establishing such a movement are the excessive personal interests and ambitions of groups and their chiefs; the difficulty of getting every man of worth and prestige to place himself at the service of a cause, a vehicle, an ideology, and a discipline, freeing himself from all vanity or ambition. . . . That is what I think, and I have repeatedly let you know that I haven't the slightest personal ambition, and neither do my comrades. Our only hope is to serve Cuba so that our comrades will not have died in vain.

Because of its importance, any step taken now would have to be discussed and agreed to by the majority—in the case of our group here, unanimously. It has become very difficult for me to discuss and to exchange opinions with my comrades, but we manage to keep in touch, and I will send them your letter.

Nevertheless, Luis, I have some doubts regarding how useful a contribution we can make now and whether it would not be broader and more meaningful if we were free—which I think is possible if an effective struggle is waged. . . .

The first task is to unite all our combatants, for it would be a shame to see our ranks depleted because of failure to carry out the initial task of convincing. On the basis of the experience gained prior to July 26, I can assure you that one tested and trustworthy young person is worth as much as a thousand others. Perhaps the hardest and most time-consuming task is to find those youth of quality and train them so that they can be a decisive force from the start.

On the basis of what we now have, we can greatly increase our forces. By that I mean incorporating other forces that are ready to unite in a firm and disciplined manner in order to create the movement necessary to defeat the ruling system. Those who believe that they alone have the required merits will be contributing to a greater scattering of the nation's moral and human forces, as well as helping to perpetuate petty and sterile habits of struggle—habits that are neither worthy of an intelligent and able people nor capable of crushing the opposition and the solidly united vested interests.

The following characteristics are vital to any genuine civic movement: ideology, discipline, and leadership. All three are essential, but leadership is fundamental. Was it Napoleon who said that one bad opposing general in battle was worth more than 20 good ones? You cannot organize a movement if everyone thinks he has the right to issue public statements without consulting anybody else. Nothing is to be expected from a movement made up of anarchists who at the first disagreement will go off on their own, disrupting and destroying the organization. The propaganda and organization apparatus must be so powerful that it will unmercifully destroy all who try to create tendencies, cliques, and splits, or who rise up against the movement.

The realities of politics must be taken into consideration; that is, we must have our feet solidly on the ground, without ever sacrificing the great reality of principles.

The program must comprehensively, concretely and courageously take up the serious economic and social issues confronting the country, so that a genuinely new and promising message can be brought to the masses.[25]

AN UNPRECEDENTED DEVELOPMENT

On October 29, three days before the elections, Fidel recounted in a letter to his sister Lidia what happened in the early hours of that morning in Santiago de Cuba:

Last night I was up until 1:30 A.M. listening to the last political campaign meeting in Oriente, on the Oriente Radio Network. Perhaps you heard it, too, or someone told you about it. I made a careful study of the psychology of the crowd, whose reaction is an unprecedented development. What a tremendous lesson for the high-and-mighties who were there![26]

Without any doubt, it was an unprecedented event: the people of Santiago at the meeting constantly interrupted the speakers by chorusing the name of Fidel Castro!

BINDING ALL COMBATANTS IN AN UNBREAKABLE SHEAF

"Elections" finally took place on November 1, 1954. With the last-minute withdrawal of the former president (1944-1948) and sole opposition candidate Ramón Grau San Martín, Batista was "elected" president with 1,262,587 votes. Logically, the highest vote gained by any aspirant in the whole history of the pseudo-republic in "popular elections" where, also logically, people only sporadically showed up at the voting booths. As in 1940, in gentlemanly compliance with demo-representative ethics, the "man" of September 4 proceeded to "legalize" March 10 with November 1.

For Fidel the panorama had been very clear, as was the historical necessity now:

"The similitude of the situations makes me recall Martí's efforts to bring together all honorable Cubans in the struggle for independence. Everyone had their history, glory, feats, everyone believed themselves to have more rights than the rest or at least as many; only the labor of love, comprehension and infinite patience of one man, with less glory than that held by others, could achieve that miracle. And I am sure that, without that magnificent effort, Cuba would still be a U.S. colony or dependency. Perhaps because of that the pages I most admire in Cuban history are not so much of feats on the battlefields, but that giant, heroic and silent undertaking to unite all Cubans for the battle."

What to do then, even in the unfavorable conditions of the prison?[27] Fidel *expounded that in his letter of August 14 when he wrote:*

"In the first place I have to organize the 26th of July men and unite in an unbreakable sheaf all the combatants, those in exile, in prison and on the streets, who together add up to more than eighty young men involved in the same turn of history and sacrifice. The importance of such a perfectly disciplined human cell constitutes an incalculable value in the aim of training fighting cadres for insurrectional or civic organization. Naturally a large civil-political movement has to have the necessary force to win power, by a peaceful or revolutionary route; if not, it runs the risk of being struck down, like the Orthodoxy [Party], just two months before the elections."[28]

WE WILL DRIVE THE GOVERNMENT CRAZY

In Mexico, two July 26 combatants, Ñico López and Calixto García, were planning to return to Cuba. In a letter written on January 1, 1955, Fidel instructed them as follows:

You should do so publicly and appear before the courts as Moncada combatants. I will explain the reasons to you. At this point you can do very little on the streets while we are prisoners. What I am proposing to you is something worthy of us and would move public opinion. The trial will be reopened and we could stir up the country right before Batista is sworn in on February 24. This would be a formidable psychological coup at a moment when everyone is clamoring for our amnesty. Once again, the legal hearing would be at the center of public opinion and would make a magnificent tribune for expounding our ideas, which would doubt-less have repercussions, given that the news is enjoying more freedom in the midst of the artificial climate of freedom the regime has concocted to make the electoral farce of November appear viable. Your arrival in

Cuba would be preceded by public statements that I have attached so that you can sign and send them on to CMQ, Miguel Quevedo, Conte Agüero, Pardo Llada, Unión Radio, Manuel Palacio Blanco, *Prensa Libre, El Mundo* and *Diario Naciona*l newspapers. There is a letter and a copy for each of them, which do not omit anything on account of greater or lesser sympathies. Those statements should be sent to Cuba by the same route via which you will receive this letter and should be handed over all together. As soon as they are made public I will let you know by cablegram. A few days later (pending your advice) the day, place and exact hour of your arrival will be announced in an equally wide-ranging form so that people will be there to meet you and maybe some journalists. People will be in charge of all that. This is discounting the possibility of your being immediately arrested and subsequently sent to Santiago de Cuba to be tried by the Emergency Court. I am against asking for any guarantee other than the backing of public opinion. In those circumstances, pending news from you, you will have the security of not being mistreated in any way. At this juncture they will try to avoid any scandal because there is a very favorable environment for political exiles and prisoners. On the other hand, the return of any exile is widely publicized, and in your case with much more reason.

You should make this plan known to the other comrades in exile as you see fit, but I will leave this up to you, as I do not want to put any moral pressure on them; I beg you not to forget this elemental discretion. If others decide to follow you before February 24, we will drive the government crazy at a time when it is caught up in creating the illusion of political normality at all costs, and could be a decisive factor for forcing it to dictate an amnesty.[29]

Fidel also foresaw another possibility and, in the same letter, instructed:

"If, by some chance, they do not want to arrest you when you arrive, to avoid exactly what we are aiming at, then present yourselves along with Baudillo Castellanos, who will be your counsel, before the Provisional Court in Santiago de Cuba. Tell them that you 'want to suffer the same fate as your imprisoned comrades,' and they will be forced to act."[30]

PREPARING FOR A LONG STRUGGLE

Fidel continued in his letter:

"There is no need to tell you that I don't think that we are wasting our time in prison. On the contrary, we are preparing the vanguard and the leaders of our Movement ideologically and intellectually. We are young and in no hurry. It would be wonderful to have 80 instead of 29 compañeros here! I have much more faith in those imprisoned here than in those scattered in exile, in terms of what they will be able to do for Cuba."[31]

"I am absolutely convinced that in present situation we must prepare for a long struggle, that will culminate in the fulfillment of the most cherished dreams of the Cuban people, who truly deserve a better fate. Day by day through our actions we have won their sympathy. Your action would win still greater admiration; and moreover, you would then join us in this workshop where we are forging the leaders of our generation, instilling in them the same thinking and the same doctrines and discipline. Under no circumstances will we have to remain here much longer, thanks to the strength of public pressure calling for our freedom. But even if we should, what does it matter? We have time on our side.

"I'm speaking to you frankly, with the bitter but instructive experience of 17 months' harsh imprisonment. For the last 10, I have been isolated from the rest of the compañeros, but the academy continues functioning rigorously and seriously, and the library is becoming more complete. You have no idea how much faith, morale and spirit of struggle and selfimprovement have reigned at all times.

"Our enthusiasm and fervor remain as great as ever, as does our readiness for sacrifice and our desire for struggle. While politicians who were never revolutionary—even though they tried to pass themselves off as such—try to use Cuba as a stepping-stone for their base ambitions, we are preparing ourselves for great revolutionary action on the very altar of sacrifice. For us, prison is our academy of struggle, and when the times comes, nothing will be able to stop us.

"Meanwhile, I sincerely believe that we can expect nothing from the political parties and pseudo-revolutionary groups, whose incapacity has been laid bare to all in the three years that have elapsed since March 10. With our blood, sweat, sacrifice, selflessness, and idealism, we are the only ones who have provided a ray of hope and faith in the disillusioned heart of the nation. Let us be worthy of this, knowing how to wait, knowing how to act, knowing how to grow stronger in adversity.

"We have lost a battle, but we have saved the honor of Cuba. We will return to the struggle. Only when not a drop of blood runs in our veins and the last of us dies—only then will they be able to say they have defeated us. We have lacked resources, but we have never been wrong.

"Do you remember how our ranks were decimated by the intrigues of political rogues and false revolutionaries of all stripes trying to make off with whole cells of our trained members, constantly sowing confusion and lies among them and throughout the country? I don't know if you know how much they slandered our Movement and how cowardly they hushed up the horrible murders of the prisoners within the Moncada garrison. We went to our deaths alone; we have been persecuted and imprisoned alone; and we will go on alone. So let us go forward. It would be a blind, crazy, and treacherous thing to join with those who have neither the authority nor the organization to be the vanguard of the Cuban revolution.

"I seek the unity of all Cubans—but worthy and noble Cubans, led by men who were never implicated in the shameful past. So what if we don't have any ill-begotten money? Did we, perchance, have any before July 26? That did not stop us—all the more reason for not stopping now, when we can count on the faith of the people, who saw us go empty-handed to our deaths for their freedom.

"You are one of the good ones, and I write you all this because I know you will understand me. I send a fraternal embrace to all those who, like you, remain loyal to the principles of those who died; the others, I believe, are not lost. I am firmly convinced that sooner or later they will see that I am right and that someday we will all march along the same road to glory that led us to the memorable dawn of July 26."[32]

I DO NOT ASK FOR AND WILL NEVER ASK FOR AMNESTY

The dictatorial government and certain political rogues interested in false leading roles were trying to take advantage of and manipulate a possible amnesty to include the Moncada assailants. Fidel alerted his sister Lidia to guard against any misrepresentation in relation to his principled stand:

Isle of Pines, March 13, 1955

Dear sister,

It has been a peaceful and placid Sunday, although the week has provided all sorts of details and concerns. Although it is already 11:00 P.M. I have regretfully laid down the book I was reading to write you these lines as I promised myself I would. For me the best time is when I forget about everything in the world and concentrate on the effort of learning something new and useful or that helps me to gain a better understanding of humanity.

Even though I always have so much to talk to you about, I prefer to wait for visiting days.

In the case of today I particularly want to tell you that on Saturday [March] 6 I sent a telegram to some guys who were organizing a radio meeting in favor of our release on the Onda Hispano-Cuba broadcasting program. Given that all my means of communication are likely to suffer changes en route, I am sending you a textual copy of it as written evidence. By chance, on the day of the radio program there was a power cut in this pavilion so I couldn't listen to it. It read:

"Our profound gratitude to you and your enthusiastic comrades who have spontaneously adopted the cause of our release. *It isn't* so much *the idea* that we most appreciate in this case, as we can endure imprisonment with our heads held high, but the gesture of support with which you encourage us. Today, serenely and firmly, we are enduring our fate patiently and without fear. Tomorrow, our first embrace will be for those who remembered us in this difficult hour.

Fraternally."

As you can see, delicately trying to avoid my response seeming like a snub, I explained that I wasn't expressing gratitude for their idea—in other words the amnesty—but the act, the gesture of thinking of us, more than often pretty much forgotten. I know many people are worthy of similar words, but I also have my gestures and, in this case, with my characteristic spontaneity it is for certain guys that have talked of us week after week and whom I barely know. I'm not interested in what group or tendency they belong to! I am fed up with all that intriguing and small-mindedness! Apart from that, I am not asking for and will never ask for amnesty. I have enough dignity to spend the next twenty years here or die of rage before that. But for now, I can at least be polite, and now and then tell half the world and that loud-mouthed lot who are always looking for a pretext to destroy your patience to go to hell.

Bring Fidelito to see me. Hugs from

Fidel

As by chance I ran out of paper just as I was getting into it, I am adding this PS to remind you (even though I don't have to) bring me the present of Fidelito if you can manage to come with him. . . .[33]

WE DO NOT WANT AMNESTY AT THE PRICE OF DISHONOR

The issue of political amnesty was one of the first points on the agenda after the announcement of the election date.

Bit by bit, the regime was dictating reprieves for its opponents until finally, it decreed what came to be known as a "false amnesty." Obviously those participating in the July 26 actions in Santiago de Cuba and Bayamo were expressly excluded.

Fidel immediately appreciated the tactical possibilities of taking advantage of this error. And what initially began as a persistent initiative by the most aware, enthusiastic and selfless family members of the imprisoned *Moncadistas,* would be transformed under Fidel's guidance into a forceful national campaign against the dictatorship.[34]

In March 1955, with Batista already the constitutional president in functions, popular pressure in favor of the amnesty mounted to the point of forcing fresh reprieves from government spokesmen. These were promoted situations that would be fully utilized. A meticulous document signed by Fidel was dispatched from the prison as a slap in the face to the dictatorship:

"There will be amnesty when there is peace. How could men who have spent three years preaching that they effected a coup d'état to bring peace to the Republic morally argue such a proposal? Well,

Fidel in the Isle of Pines prison holding his son.

there is no peace; the coup d'état did not bring peace: at least the government is acknowledging its lie after three years of dictatorship; it is finally admitting that peace has been lacking in Cuba since the very day that they assaulted its authority. . . ."

It was the moment to reiterate positions of principle:

"If we believed that a change of circumstances and a climate of positive constitutional guarantees demanded a change of tactics in the struggle we would do so only in deference to the interests and wishes of the nation, never in virtue of a compromise with the government, which would be cowardly and shameful. . . . And if our release should be tied to such a compromise our answer would be a round 'No!'

"No, we are not weary. After twenty months we feel as strong and whole as the first day. We do not want amnesty at the price of dishonor. We will not pass under the gallows of The Caudine Forks of ignoble oppressors. One thousand years of imprisonment before humiliation. One thousand years of jail before sacrificing our decency. We proclaim that serenely, without fear or hatred."[35]

ENDNOTES

1. Mario Mencía, *Tiempos precursores,* ed. cit., 184.
2. Mario Mencía, *The Fertile Prison: Fidel Castro in Batista's Jails,* ed. cit., 37-38.
3. Ibid., 40-42.
4. Ibid., 57.
5. Frei Betto, op cit, 135.
6. Mario Mencía, *The Fertile Prison: Fidel Castro in Batista's Jails,* ed. cit., 70.
7. Ibid., 42-43.
8. Mario Mencía, *Tiempos precursores,* ed. cit., 188.
9. Mario Mencía, *The Fertile Prison: Fidel Castro in Batista's Jails,* ed. cit., 71-73.
10. Ibid., 75-76.
11. Ibid., 46-51.
12. Ibid., 124.
13. Mario Mencía, *Tiempos precursores,* ed. cit., 184-185.
14. He is referring to Captain Pedro Abraham Castells, military supervisor of the prison during the Machado dictatorship, who earned an ill-fated notoriety for his crimes. *Ed.*
15. Mario Mencía, *Tiempos precursores,* ed. cit., 188-189.
16. Mario Mencía, *The Fertile Prison: Fidel Castro in Batista's Jails,* ed. cit., 104-105.
17. Ibid., 105.
18. Ibid., 107-109.
19. Ibid., 129.
20. He is referring to Aureliano Sánchez Arango, leader of the Triple A (AAA), an underground organization. *Ed.*
21. Mario Mencía, *The Fertile Prison: Fidel Castro in Batista's Jails,* ed. cit., 129-131.
22. Mario Mencía, *Tiempos precursores,* ed. cit., 190-192.
23. Mario Mencía, *The Fertile Prison: Fidel Castro in Batista's Jails,* ed. cit., 117.
24. Ibid., 117-118.
25. Ibid., 125-127.
26. Ibid., 140.
27. Mario Mencía, *Tiempos precursores,* ed. cit., 192-193.
28. Ibid., 193.
29. Ibid., 149-150.
30. Mario Mencía, *The Fertile Prison: Fidel Castro in Batista's Jails,* ed. cit., 151.
31. Id.
32. Ibid., 151-153.

33. Luis Conte Agüero, *Cartas de Presidio* [Letters from Prison] (Havana: Editorial Lex, 1959), 75-76.

34. Mario Mencía, *Tiempos precursores*, ed. cit., 194.

35. Ibid., 194-195.

THE 53-DAY BATTLE

THE MOST ELOQUENT PREACHING IS BY EXAMPLE

The amnesty of the Moncadistas *is about to become a reality. Raúl and Fidel should soon be leaving from prison and their sisters are preparing the conditions for receiving them. It is at this point that Fidel writes a long letter to Lidia whose text reflects his human sensitivity and that philosophy of austerity that makes him invincible.*

Isle of Pines, May 2, 1955

My dear sister,

Out of pure duty I sent you a telegram today explaining the convenience of renting the little apartment I mentioned in your visit. I did so because of seeing how excited you were with the one you found for 75 pesos and then felt remorseful thinking that my telegram would give you more accounting worries. Anyway, I'm happy to accept what you've been able to definitively sort out. I was in favor of the first for a number of reasons. I was thinking we could turn one of the two apartments into a sort of legal office where I could attend to my affairs and leave the other exclusively as a home for the four of us. Otherwise your home gets constantly invaded and any private life is impossible. As far as I'm concerned that's not important, but it is for Emmita and you as, like

248

all women, you both need a refuge, somewhere you can make a home, rearrange, order and disorder, change things around, without us men messing it all up. If not one day you'll end up being sick of the sight of people and the world. Given the number of years I've lived this kind of life and struggle I know how many little slips can lead to your home turning into an office. I could give you a thousand examples of that. I really regretted my office being in Old Havana when it was such an ordeal to get there! But when I shut myself away there to attend to matters or study I felt totally happy. It was the appropriate place to receive people properly, even if they came to give me stick or to bring me cases of unfortunate people with no lawyers or those in danger of being evicted, whom of course I never charged anything. I didn't feel the same when, ready to leave—not to go out of course—somebody arrived to babble on about trivialities. Then there were cases of very sensitive people who got upset when I couldn't give them the attention they wanted, although fortunately that hardly ever happened, because I'm a veritable stoic when it comes to putting up with impertinence. I know you can never totally avoid these little things, but you have to reduce them to the minimum, and that can only be done by creating habits and regulating your activities, even though in my case we're dealing with a naturally bohemian and somewhat disorganized temperament. Leaving that aside, there is nothing like having a place where you can throw your cigarette butts on the floor when you feel like it, without subconsciously worrying about a housewife on sentry duty to catch the ash in an ashtray; never mind terrifying others with the notion that you're sure to burn the sofa or the curtains. At the end of the day domestic peace and the agitation surrounding a fighter are two incompatible elements. Whenever possible, separating them is a sensible move.

As far as material comforts go, if it wasn't for the imperative of living with a minimum of material decency—believe me, I'd be happy living in a tenement and sleeping in a cot with a box to keep my clothes in. My diet would be a plate of yam or potato and to me that would be as delicious as manna for the Israelites. I could live sumptuously with forty cents well invested. I'm really not exaggerating, I'm being totally frank. If I start getting accustomed to needing more things in my life and forget that you can be deprived of everything and still be happy, I will be a less worthy person. I have learnt to live that way and that makes me much more to be fearsome as an impassioned defender of an ideal, reaffirmed and fortified by sacrifice. I can preach by example, always the most eloquent. The less I'm caught up in the demands of a materialistic lifestyle, the more independent and more useful I will be.

Why sacrifice yourself to buy me a *guayabera*, pants and the rest? I'm going to leave here in my gray wool suit, threadbare with use, even if it's full summer. Didn't I give you back the other suit that I never asked for or needed? Don't go thinking I'm an eccentric or have turned into one; the habit makes the monk, and I am poor, I have nothing, I haven't robbed a cent, I haven't begged from anybody, I've handed over my career to a cause. Why should I have to wear a linen *guayabera* as if I was rich or a civil servant or an embezzler? If I'm not earning anything at the moment, what I'll have is whatever they give me, and I can't, and shouldn't, and won't accept being the slightest burden on anyone. My greatest battle here has been insisting and insisting that I don't need anything. I have only needed books and I consider them as spiritual goods. So I can't help feeling worried about all the expenses in connection with our release. Even if they're strictly necessary I'm still very worried because I didn't think to ask you how you're managing to arrange everything. I'm not annoyed, but I do feel burdened by all this. You cannot rest easy if you don't demonstrate your concern and affection for us in some way, but we are as strong as oaks, insensible to privations, less needy than you who are making the sacrifices, than you whom we are sincerely reproaching. You don't need to demonstrate affection, we don't need proof of at every opportunity, certainly not with empty phrases. These are realities that have to be perceived. I'm really touched by your efforts to make us as happy as possible. But you can do that without material sacrifice! You want an example? Having my books all arranged and in order for when I get there would comfort me, make me really happy and give me more joy than anything else, and wouldn't make me feel sad or upset, or overburdened. I cannot allow myself weaknesses, if I indulge them today, however little they might be, tomorrow nothing can be expected of me.[1]

250

Fidel leaves the Isle of Pines Model Prison with others involved in the assaults on the Moncada and Carlos Manuel de Céspedes garrisons.

I'M THINKING OF STAYING IN CUBA

A few hours after leaving the prison, Fidel was questioned by a journalist:

"Are you thinking of staying in Cuba?"

"Yes, I'm thinking of staying in Cuba, fighting openly. To combat the government, pinpoint its errors, denounce its blots, and unmask gangsters, police thugs and thieves."

It was Friday, May 16, 1955. Day was dawning in the tiny fishing port of Batabanó in the south of Havana Province, which, in the children's literature of that time evoked images of salt-stained boats. . . .

There, it was still dark and the little *El Pinero* motorboat was moored alongside the quay. Every day since 1926, it had provided daily transportation between Nueva Gerona and Batabanó, and between last night and today, its placid routine was broken for this unusual group of passengers now disembarking from it.

Here, it is already light. And on the quay a growing contingent of people in a singular bustle, increased when a microphone on the quay was activated by a cable on *El Pinero,* along with a loudspeaker that somebody had brought. "Quiet, please!" A journalist started to ask questions that were answered and recorded for that day's Radio Cadena Habana transmission. Another question and another, and the man who had left the Isle of Pines Model Prison after twenty-two months in jail the afternoon before, replying and replying. The words were similar to those in the *Manifiesto al pueblo de Cuba* [Manifesto for the People of Cuba]—a mere glimpse of some rolled-up sheets of paper in the photos of the time—whose content was read out the afternoon before in the Isle of Pines hotel:

"When the regime was trying to convert the amnesty into an instrument of humiliation for its adversaries by making dishonorable demands, we clearly stated that as political prisoners we would not accept freedom on the basis of any imposed conditions. Having posed the issue in those terms, the regime was left with the option of negating the amnesty completely, or granting it without any conditions. The startling pressure of public opinion and the Cuban press finally opened the prison gates for us without any shameful conditions. This has been the great victory of the people in the last three years and is the only contribution to peace on the national horizon."[2]

And public peace (it was not for nothing that the *Moncadistas'* inclusion in the amnesty been hammered out for months and months between the principal press columnists and spokesmen for the regime and the diverse opposition) was likewise an obligatory reference for Fidel on the first day of his release. Only he did so using the method that had become his habit from the period prior to the March 10 coup, when he elected himself the highest judge of the Prío government: disorientating the enemy with surprisingly original ideas, stealing the initiative from it and forcing it onto the defensive. He referred to the much yearned-for peace in this way:

"It should never be forgotten that we Cubans love peace; but we love freedom even more. It is to be hoped that peace is not being used as a truce enabling the regime to consolidate its oppression and privilege through appeasement, thus allowing it to calmly enjoy the fruits of usurped power."

What he states in the *Manifiesto al pueblo de Cuba* in just forty-eight words—making mincemeat of the dictatorship's careful machinations over more than twelve months of verbal pugilism with the civil institutions and certain opposition voices—was reiterated by Radio Cadena Habana, *La Calle* newspaper and *Bohemia* magazine.

Having exposed the essence of the enemy's intention, he immediately goes onto the offensive:

"In order to attain a genuine peace in which the Republic is triumphant, the brutal attacks on the heroic student body and citizens in general have to end; the persona and rights of Cubans have to be respected as sacred; and democratic routes must be opened for the restoration of the people's sovereignty and the full realization of their great desire for justice and freedom. Those who oppose such legitimate and humane demands—the irrefutable rights of the Cuban people—by attempting to convert the island into the private fiefdom of an oppressive and rapacious clique; those who cannot keep their eyes or hands off the public treasury, the principal object and goal of their odious political hustling, will be criminally disturbing the peace of the Republic."[3]

FIDEL'S RECEPTION

The press of that time doesn't say anything, but the photos are there. More than a hundred people invaded the platforms and waiting rooms of Havana Central Railroad Station from dawn onwards on Monday, May 16, 1955.

"At 7:45 A.M. the Batabanó train entered on one of the tracks in the left section. The train was still moving when it was virtually assaulted. Fidel Castro was dragged out of a window and set on someone's shoulders. A group of mothers who had also lost their sons in the bloody incident unfurled a Cuban flag and began to sing the national anthem. Hundreds of voices accompanied them."

They don't appear in the photos of the time, but the press noted it: the FEU was out in full force in the midst of the excited crowd. And given that the FEU was out there in force, so was José Antonio Echeverría, displaying the plaster cast on his left arm, the credential of his most recent confrontation with the police, this time in Matanzas Park when he was returning from El Morrillo on the night of May 8 after honoring the memory of Guiteras on the 20th anniversary of his death. José Antonio was released four days before Fidel left the model prison, and immediately announced:

"The student body is on a battle footing and on May 20 will demonstrate under the slogan: 'For the Republic of Martí' on the University stairway, also a fitting venue for the Cuban people to welcome home the political prisoners and exiles. We are calling on all the people to mobilize and attend this demonstration, at which political prisoners, exiles and student leaders will speak. Doctor Fidel Castro has been invited to close this unparalleled patriotic event."[4]

THEY ARE PERSECUTING US WITH UNDISGUISED FURY

"Now that we are free (as Fidel stated the same day of his release) and are not disturbers of the peace, we openly ratify that if a change of circumstances and a regime of positive guarantees should demand a change of tactics in the struggle, we would make such changes in deference to nation's supreme interests, but never in virtue of any commitment to those who are unlawfully in power over and above the people's sovereign will. It now behooves the men of that regime to demonstrate that those guarantees are real and not, as to date, lying promises."

The regime's response can be seen from the point of view of Fidel himself:

"Last Thursday night, at the end of a fully legal radio meeting in which I was invited to speak, the police violently entered the studio, reproaching the station administrator and taking away all the documents.

"Yesterday, May 20, state police agents entered without a warrant the residence of comrade Pedro Miret, who left prison with us, and carried out a thorough search, to the concern and distress of his family.

"More symptomatic is the fact that on approaching the University of Havana that same night as a FEU-invited speaker, a heavy police cordon prevented me from entering the precinct. Many citizens were brutally attacked and the meeting was suspended without any justification whatsoever, despite its orderly, peaceful and civic nature.

"Those who commit these kind of provocative actions cannot be interested in peaceful coexistence at a time when the country urgently needs calm.

"Given these circumstances, how can the exiles return to Cuba, if the men released from jail barely five days ago are already being persecuted with undisguised fury?"

He was well aware of the nature of the dictatorship and hence its reactions. He could calculate its movements. He knew the result of the game beforehand without precipitating it, because he was more interested in the united force of the people than a quick political victory over the regime. Thus, he insisted:

"We are confirming with deep regret that the regime is not prepared to give guarantees to its adversaries; but in any case and despite the risks involved we shall remain on national territory, because we are aware that a forced exit from Cuba would ruin any chance of a civic solution. Although the government is clearly determined to block all routes to peace, we shall persist in our plans to unite all the country's moral forces and demand a decorous and peaceful way out of the tragic situation of Cuba with the unanimous backing of the people."[5]

LA CALLE: HIS BASIC JOURNALISTIC TRENCH

In the afternoon of June 7, 1955 in Vedado, Jorge Agostini Villafaña was assassinated. Four days later, Fidel published an article in La Calle *newspaper under the heading "Facing Terror and Crime," where he not only exposed the horrendous incident but also demonstrated the regime's responsibility:*

"Jorge Agostini was assassinated, there is absolutely no doubt of that. Even admitting the police version as correct, everybody knows what happened.

255

"Textually the report states: 'He was found to be carrying a doctor's bag containing a pistol and two cartridge clips.' So, Agostini did not shoot, he did not use the weapon, he didn't even try to use it. And unless they had powers of divination, his killers couldn't have known that there was a pistol and two cartridge clips in that doctor's bag.

"Moreover, as opposed to one bullet wound, Agostini's body was riddled with shots, turning it into a human sieve. You don't have to fire so many · shots at a man to prevent him from escaping; those marks on the victim's body only occur when there is cruelty, when someone is shot when already on the ground."

This knowledgeable criminological analysis was followed by Fidel's unmasking of the essential political element.

"Why that hunting down of a human being who was not wanted by any court? Agostini was one of the beneficiaries of the recent amnesty. . . .

"Over and above party and tactical affiliations the death of Jorge Agostini hurts all of us Cubans. There is no justification for it, nor will there ever be. These are the first fruits of the Mr. Batista's speech in 'Batista Boulevard' when he said that 'his men had their ways.'"[6]

Fidel lashed out at those alleged pacifists who played the dictatorship's game by insisting on solutions through legal channels, and challenged the fallacy of the independence of the judicial powers.

With the perspective of time, the multifaceted objectives in the final paragraph of Fidel's article denouncing Agostini's murder, still ring out clear today.

"Will this savagery go unpunished? Is there perchance a group of men that have the right to snuff out the lives of their fellow humans with greater impunity than the hardest gangsters ever had? . . . Let us put the virtue of our judges and courts to the test. No more crimes without punishment. Justice, justice, justice!"[7]

Although various newspapers offered him regular columns, when he left the penitentiary Fidel selflessly chose La Calle *as his basic· political-journalistic trench for combating the regime.*

By doing so, Fidel gave up economic benefits such as the 200 pesos per month offered him by Raúl Rivero, the editor of *Diario Nacional.*

Fidel's decision is all the more impressive recalling the material hardships that constantly beset him.

Apart from Sundays, when Luis Orlando Rodríguez' evening paper wasn't published, Fidel went to *La Calle* office every afternoon, entered the small office assigned to him—the location of the typewriter that he used to strike and strike again at the dictatorship—and stayed on to personally revise the pages until he left at night with a bunch of the first editions—the ink still fresh—in his hands.

Because of that, Fidel wrote in an appeal: "*La Calle* newspaper cannot collapse, it mustn't collapse due to a lack of resources. That would be shameful! If the dictatorship closes it down, that's one thing, but don't let it perish for lack of help! The people have a duty to help it, and the people will help it!"

In *La Calle,* Fidel wrote what he couldn't say on radio concerning "the valiant battle being waged by Ferrocarriles Consolidados [a railroad company] in the provinces of Oriente, Camagüey and Las Villas, which deserves the support of all the people. "They are defending the interests of all sectors of the national economy by combating a despicable measure, that of withdrawing millions of pesos from circulation for the benefit of a foreign company which, having spent fabulous sums on plant and accumulating juicy profits year after year, is now claiming to be on the verge of bankruptcy. The destitution doesn't lie in the company but in the morals and the shamelessness of such rulers."

And as a clear class reaffirmation:

"When the servile pens of the created interests write editorials in favor of the foreign company, our words have to come from the heart together with the workers. There is a hunger for bread and a hunger for freedom. For them, our sympathies as the revolutionary combatants that we are and always will be together with all just causes, with the poor of this world."[8]

The history of this period in *La Calle* exemplified Fidel's maximum utilization of the mass media at a certain political juncture of the dictatorship, overcoming numerous obstacles whose most notorious expressions can be seen in the following incidents:

- Thursday, May 19: warrant, seizure of documents and arrest of the administrator of the radio station where he was to speak.

- Friday, May 20: police cordon blocking public attendance, a power cut and repeated shooting at the tribune in which he would close a meeting called by the FEU for the University of Havana.

- Monday, June 6: closure of the "Hora Ortodoxa" [Orthodoxy Hour] a radio program on which he was spoken, by order of the Minister of Communications.

- Thursday, June 9: due to appear before the television cameras, Fidel himself related the unprecedented events:

"For all those reasons it was no surprise to me that when I arrived at Channel 11 at 8:00 P.M. last Thursday for our regular weekly televised space, I discovered another resolution, closing it down for seven weeks."

- And, On Monday, June 13, the completely unheard of: the Minister of Communications prohibited any participation by Fidel Castro in any kind of Unión Radio and TV Channel 11 programming in telegram No. 142, R-OV-OF Urgent.

Things had gone past censoring or temporarily closing a newspaper edition or a radio or television program: a person was being closed down![9]

26TH OF JULY REVOLUTIONARY MOVEMENT

In terms of the changes taking place in the Movement in order to adapt to everything that had occurred from July 26, 1953 to May 1955, the name of the Movement itself was highlighted.

Having retained the concept of a Movement, the events of July 26, 1953 conditioned the extension of the organization's name to the 26th of July Revolutionary Movement. Fidel had already proposed this idea during his imprisonment. Various letters from that period attest to that.

It is no coincidence that the first issues Fidel discussed with his comrades in Nueva Gerona after leaving the penitentiary on that May 15 included the completion of his organization's name. During the crossing to Batabanó on *El Pinero,* the night of May 15-16, he posed the question again. He asked his comrades for their views, and listened to suggestions. And he expressed his idea and it was accepted: the 26th of July Revolutionary Movement. When the Movement's national directorate was restructured several weeks later and revolutionary comrades who had not belonged to the organization up to that point were incorporated, Fidel once again promoted discussion on this issue and it was definitively registered for history at that moment.[10]

FIDEL'S HISTORICAL LINE

The best cadres of the Revolutionary National Movement (MNR) joined Fidel after his meeting with Rafael García Bárcena, as is recalled by one of those men:

"Yes, it was in Bárcena's house," Faustino Pérez stated, "but something was immediately apparent in the conversation: two distinct strategic focuses, not in terms of ideological issues, which weren't covered, but in the forms and methods of how to focus the problems of the struggle. The difference was immediately apparent: Bárcena tended towards a military conspiracy, supported by civilians, by groups of civilians rather than an organization. And Fidel had more faith in organizing the struggle starting with the masses in a popular movement that would take up arms against the dictatorship. So there was no agreement.

"But Fidel didn't let things come to a split. He said: 'We don't see any contradiction. For example, you can work in that context and organize soldiers who want to fight against the regime. And then I can organize the popular forces, the people. And at a given moment we can bring both factors together.'

"But there and then, as some of the comrades in the Bárcena Movement, we decided that we would join Fidel."

When Hart, Faustino and various members of the MNR left that meeting together with Fidel, they also left with Fidel's historical line.[11]

ASPHYXIATING VIGILANCE

Meanwhile, Fidel's exile from media communication with the masses to which he was condemned by the dictatorship was complemented with the sudden absence of his name in any statements by the regime's spokesmen. However, the overt vigilance exercised over him by the repressive agencies was becoming steadily more asphyxiating.

Divining faculties were not needed to deduce the hidden trap beneath that coincidence. Fidel only evaded the safe bet of a provocation with unforeseen results by being very patient and highly mobile. With the early days of July passing by one after the other, time was pressing. Fidel had already speeded up steps for the action that would culminate the 53-day political battle.

Silently, discretely, moves had been made to obtain a passport for him. Silently, discreetly, a tourist visa was negotiated with the Mexican ambassador. And he began to draw up what could have been the final part of his political testament but which turned into the death sentence of March 10... and against March 9.

Very soon, the little apartment containing nothing more than a bookcase, a desk, a chair, two armchairs and a fold-up bed would be dismantled forever. They had only been able to pay the 60-peso monthly rental once. But many people would remember the very-handy rice and fish for six people that could be stretched to twelve portions if more comrades arrived, which Lidia cooked when Cheíto, the door-to-door salesman, had the luck to catch something on his line the night before from the wall of Havana's Malecón.

For her part, Lidia had already had to sell the refrigerator for the second time in her life due to an urgent need for money. Both those occasions were related to Fidel's leaving the country. The first was seven years previously in 1948, when the then university student leader left Cuba for Central America and Bogotá, Colombia.

The last forty-eight hours that Fidel spent in Cuba up until the afternoon of July 7 were just like all the hours of every day since May 15. Dozens of people. Numerous places. Appearing anywhere. Dropping in on *Bohemia* magazine. Journalist Agustín Alles was working on a survey of Prío's comeback. Fidel left him a statement, words he had just written. His farewell. Alles would publish them, but in the form of interview replies. But Miguel Ángel Quevedo was to mutilate them. He suppressed the part that was like a declaration of war, and where Fidel talked of coming back. And about the dictatorship. About a beheaded dictatorship. A Bolivarian evocation by Martí. That part would never be printed, but it would be heard on the radio. Montané was to have distributed it in many places although it would only be broadcast in its entirety on radio after

Fidel had left. Twice by the Onda Hispano-Cubana station, and once by COCO.

The night before was extremely agitated. July 6. Lidia was packing his suitcase. More books than clothes. Once again dozens of people came to the apartment. Or he went out to see them. Once again showing up all over the place, asking to use the phone. One call. Others. To how many people?

"I-62-68?"

"Yes."

"Pepín, Alejandro here..."

That could have been the start of any one of the telephone calls that Pepín Sánchez received after the March 10 coup in his house at 6, Patrocinio, a few meters from the former tram stop in the Víbora barrio.

Pepín Sánchez, Chibás' "best and most faithful collaborator," didn't know that Alejandro was Fidel's second name, nor did he know then that it was the pseudonym Fidel used to sign his writings in *El Acusador* before the Moncada attack. Fidel would also use it later in some of his letters from exile in Mexico and, afterwards, in many notes during the war in the Sierra Maestra.

But he knew that was the name that Fidel used to call him, like now, wanting to know if he'd be home that night so he could come and see him. Yes, he would be. He would wait for him then.

However, before nightfall, Fidel would be seen in other places. Once again in Carmen Castro Porta's apartment on Paseo and 25th, where at other times he had talked with the pro-Martí women's group. He arrived there and "read us out a statement that had to come out in the press," wrote Neneína. "He was simultaneously saying goodbye and asking for opinions on the future general strike that was part of his plans. Amazing. Two pro-Martí women were to see him off when he left." And from there he went to ask the Cadena Oriental de Radio station to give the women the space reserved for him that he couldn't use because of the censorship to which he was subjected.

In Las Delicias de Medina café on L and 21st, he was seen talking animatedly with José Antonio Echeverría and Fructuoso Rodríguez. Ñico López and students Osmel Francis and Pedro Azze were also there.

261

More than two hours went by before Pastorita Núñez came to pick him up in a battered car. Just fourteen months later Fidel and José Antonio were to meet again, outside of Cuba, when they signed together the pact of revolutionary unity known as the Letter from Mexico.

He would see be seen with and seen many other people that day. And make call after call. And eat that night with lawyer Jorge Azpiazo, his old co-disciple at the University and office colleague, who was with him at various times during those final days. And he would arrive late at the house of Pepín Sánchez, who was very happy to see him, as he knew the dangers Fidel was exposed to in that battle against the dictatorship.

With that memory acknowledged by everyone who knew the former member of the Orthodoxy Party's National Directorate, Sánchez would relate many years later how that night Fidel talked to him in general terms concerning his plans while pacing incessantly about the ample lounge. And how he asked him for a lemon and an electric iron to demonstrate how to write invisibly on paper with the juice and afterwards reveal what was written with the heat of an iron. That was the method he used to insert secret messages within innocent letters written from abroad.

He recalls him sitting: "Right there. And right there, at that table, he wrote the dedication." Pepín was referring to the words with which Fidel autographed the first underground edition of *La historia me absolverá*, which he left him as a memento that night. The dedication ended with some of the words that would be suppressed in his farewell statement in *Bohemia* magazine.

It was also his goodbye to Pepín. He was going to Mexico in a few hours.

The 53-day battle with the police was over. Or almost over.

A few hours later various cars left simultaneously from different points of Havana in the direction of Rancho Boyeros Avenue. Two left from 23d and 18th in Vedado. Fidel traveled in the first with his son Fidelito, his sisters Lidia and Emma, and Concepción Cheda, the young pro-Martí lawyer. Gustavo Ameijeiras, Ángel Pla and María Laborde got in the second car. Halfway there they stopped and Fidel transferred into the car driven by Gustavo.

At the airport, while going through the boarding procedures to leave on Flight 566 of the Mexican Aviation Company, Fidel talked with those who had accompanied him at such a crucial moment. In addition to those that left from his house, radio commentator Guido García Inclán, student leaders René Anillo and Juan Nuiry and, significantly, four notable Orthodoxy lawyers: José Manuel Gutiérrez, Francisco Carone, Rubén Acosta and Gerardo Marín, were all there.

Maybe yet another precaution? None of his comrades from the national leadership of the Movement were at the airport.

A brief conversation apart with Nuiry and Anillo to remind them of the possible political significance of the upcoming commemoration of the second anniversary of the attack on the Moncada Garrison nineteen days later at the University of Havana. And finally, the close handshakes and embraces..., the last—as if he wanted it to last forever—with his little son, whom he hugged tightly in his arms.

Using the same departure gate as his brother Raúl fourteen days earlier, Fidel now followed him. It was Friday, July 7, 1955, and during his flight to Mexico the final action of the political battle against the regime gained with singular mastery was commencing: *Bohemia* magazine was reproducing 265,000 copies of the statement he made before leaving and which had to get to all the people by that means:

"Carlos Prío cannot return to Cuba unless he is sent to Castillo del Príncipe where various Cubans falsely charged with terrorism are being held, in a case that includes Prío as the man most responsible for the terrible scheme. Thus it is inconceivable that Batista and his minister Santiago Rey could publicly state that Prío would not be molested, when there are three orders out for his arrest, dictated by the Emergency Court. For Prío to return to Cuba without difficulty, they would have to pass a new political amnesty, or admit that the courts do exactly what they are ordered to do by the Minister of the Interior and Dictator Batista.

"If Carlos Prío is able to return to Cuba and comfortably install himself in his La Chata residence, why are Juan Pedro Carbó, Manuel Carbonell Duque, José Machado and others facing charges in the same case as that of Prío, at the time of making these statements? Why have Pascasio Lineras, Manuel Alfonso and Evelio Duque been detained for over two weeks?

"My own brother had to take the road to exile, having been charged in the same case with having placed a bomb in a Havana cinema when he was 1000 kilometers away with my sick father in Oriente Province. Thus I do not know if Prío's words announcing his peaceful return to Cuba are sincere.

"Will they let him speak; let him appear on some television program; let him write; give him the opportunity to engage in public activities? If so, he would indeed be a lucky man because, according to the Constitution supposedly in force, as a citizen like any other and with the same rights, I am absolutely banned from engaging in any of those licit activities, being cloistered on account of an unheard-of personal file, opened for an indefinite period in the Ministry of Communications, as confirmed by telegram 142, R-OV-OF Urgent, dated June 12, 1955, sent to Unión Radio and Canal 11. And all this before the drastic closure of *La Calle* daily.

"Prío could accept returning under those conditions and maybe that would please Batista; but I am not prepared to do any favors for this outrageous regime. I am already packing my bags to leave Cuba, even though I had to borrow the money for a passport, because it isn't any millionaire that's leaving, just a Cuban who has given everything and will give everything for Cuba. We will come back when we can bring to our people freedom and the right to live decorously, without despotism and without hunger.

"After six weeks out of jail and having seen the intentions of the ruling clique, ready to stay in power for twenty years, as requested by flatterers and unscrupulous individuals, I no longer believe in general elections. With all the doors of civic struggle closed to the people, there is no other solution than that of 1868 and 1895. The outrage signified by this regime for all those who have fallen for Cuba's dignity, from Joaquín de Agüero to Jorge Agostini, has to be redressed.

"As I stated before the Santiago de Cuba Emergency Court when I was on trial for the July 26 actions, we are Cubans and being Cuban implies a duty: failing to fulfill it is a crime and a betrayal. We live with pride in our homeland's history; we learnt it in school and have grown up hearing talk of freedom, justice and rights. From an early age, we were taught to venerate the glorious example of our heroes and martyrs.

Céspedes, Agramonte, Maceo, Gómez and Martí were the first names engraved on our brains. We were taught that the Titan [Antonio Maceo] affirmed that freedom was not something begged but conquered with machete blades. We were taught that for the education of citizens in a free homeland, José Martí, our national hero, wrote in his Libro de Oro:[12] 'When there are many men without decorum, there are always others that have within them the decorum of many men, and those are the ones who rebel with a terrible force against those who rob the peoples of their liberty.' We were taught that October 10 and February 24 are glorious anniversaries to be patriotically welcomed, because they mark the dates when the Cubans rebelled against the infamous yoke of tyranny. We were taught to love and defend the beautiful flag with the solitary star and daily sing an anthem whose verses say that 'to live in chains is to live submerged in insult and ignominy,' and 'that to die for the homeland is to live.' "[13]

ENDNOTES

1. Luis Conte Agüero, op. cit., 90-92.
2. Mario Mencía, *Tiempos precursores*, ed. cit., 200-201.
3. Ibid., 202-203.
4. Ibid., 207-208.
5. Ibid., 209-201.
6. Ibid., 219-220.
7. Ibid., 221.
8. Ibid., 223-224.
9. Ibid., 224-225.
10. Ibid., 234-235.
11. Ibid., 244.
12. He is referring to José Martí's *La Edad de Oro* (*The Golden Age*). Ed.
13. Ibid., 246-253.

EXILE IN MEXICO

I ALMOST WEPT ON TAKING THE PLANE

In the afternoon of July 7, 1955 Mexicana de Aviación Flight 566 touched down at Mérida airport from Havana. The days in exile were beginning for the tall man in a well-worn gray winter suit, twenty-eight in a month's time, who was descending the steps with a firm step and a searching regard, and who only had to wait in the baggage hall for a run-of-the-mill suitcase with more books than clothes in it.

"It's hard to explain how bitter the necessary and useful step of leaving Cuba has been for me. I almost wept on taking the plane," Fidel wrote seven days later to the comrades on the directorate of the 26th of July Revolutionary Movement, in a letter to Faustino Pérez, dated July 14, 1955, Mexico City.

The stopover in Mérida was a brief one. Just the time necessary to board the next plane that would take him to Veracruz, in a southwestern flight over the Gulf of Campeche.

His state of mind—where the individual never predominated social obligations—didn't stop him from embracing Cuban sculptor José Fidalgo in Veracruz and directing him to establish contact by correspondence with the Tampa and New York émigrés "so as to win those Cuban cells over to our cause."

On Mexican soil, shortly after arriving.

On July 8 Fidel arrived by bus in Mexico City. "The first night I met with Raúl and two or three Cubans of confidence at the house of a Cuban woman resident there for a number of years, who has been a real mother to the Moncada people in the days of cold and hunger," he wrote in that same letter, in which he highlighted what María Antonia González' help meant to the Cuban revolutionaries.

"We drew up a little working plan ranging from a quick way to get general news on Cuba to reaching influential figures in this country, whose friendship and sympathy could be useful," he continued, adding:

"We are making contact little by little with the rest of the Cubans from various political affiliations—that are few—, receiving a magnificent welcome from all of them. There are other Cubans who have lived here for a long time whose sympathies we are aware of, who have relations and resources and whom we will approach later on."[1]

"How can the rest of them imagine this life?" Fidel wrote two weeks later in a letter agitating for news from his comrades in the leadership of the movement, having heard nothing to that point. "It is sad, solitary and hard. It feels like being destroyed in a thousand pieces when you are estranged from the homeland to which you can only return in an honorable way, or never. You would have to comprehend all the firmness of this decision to judge our spirit. I am still going about recovering all the pieces of my personal sentiments, which are those of a man who has renounced everything in this life, out of a sense of dignity, ideals and duty."

In a letter dated July 14, he offered more details on his early days in the Mexican capital.

"I'm living in a little room and devoting my free time to reading and studying. Now I am informing myself on the Mexican revolutionary process under the direction of Lázaro Cárdenas. Later on I'm thinking of drafting the complete revolutionary program that we're going to present to the country in the form of a pamphlet that can be printed here and introduced clandestinely into Cuba. I will send it first to you so that you can discuss it although I hope that by then some of you will be here.

"The basic norm of my moves here is and always will be supreme caution and absolute discretion; just as if we were in Cuba. I have managed to make myself as inconspicuous as possible. As you make advances over there we will be advancing over here. I think that everything is perfectly realizable as we conceived it in general terms."[2]

On July 16 Fidel wrote to a friend:

"I spent the initial days trying to find a place to stay and adapting to the new environment. I'm gradually organizing myself and stepping out strongly.

"As far as resources are concerned, I'm already living on the last of the funds. My personal expenses are very modest but also involve feeding two or three good Cubans here. We cook in the house of a Cuban woman, and get by on more or less anything. I'm maintaining a strict budget with the few cents I brought and hope that with this system nobody will go hungry now or later. Everyone has got lodgings more or less resolved in their own way."[3]

IF WE'RE LEFT ON OUR OWN, I'LL BE THERE GUN IN HAND

With tenacity and immutable faith, Fidel worked incessantly in great penury. One demonstration of that is the excerpt from this letter:

Here I really need collaborators; we need a group of the best comrades on both sides. You will find a terrain that I am cautiously getting to know, and for each of you the days will be less bitter than those I've had get through, making my way in a completely new scenario, full of anxiety about what was left to be done there. However, nothing disheartens me, as nothing should dishearten you. On the contrary, with every day that passes, I discover a new detail, a way of getting round barriers that seemed insurmountable, of fulfilling our word to Cuba at all cost. I am gradually confirming how reality can be adjusted to our dreams, full of faith that however long and broad the way, our struggle will culminate in total success. For me, the days in this city and this land will soon be like those in the months preceding July 26.

However, it should be borne in mind that I am working with tremendous obstacles because of a lack of resources. We might even have to go hungry in these initial months. I have already arranged to take my overcoat to a pawnshop to get out the first manifesto; here those places are state run and charge an insignificant interest. If the rest of my clothes have to follow the overcoat, I shan't hesitate for a second. Contrary to those miserable individuals who abandon their principles, sell themselves, surrender themselves, who betray Cuba by vilely groveling for the electoral crumbs tossed at them by the dictatorship, this is our time! The hour of Cubans like us with pride and faith, those of us who know how to persevere to the end, to win or to die for our cause.

Maybe if the way was easy, I wouldn't feel so happy and animated. In that case, how could we compare ourselves to those who in other times forged Cuban independence in the face of obstacles one hundred times greater?[4]

The second anniversary of the Moncada attack was commemorated with two activities in the Mexican capital on Tuesday, July 26, 1955. In the first one, in the morning, Fidel laid a wreath at the Monument to the Child Heroes of Chapultepec; and in the second, that night, he spoke at a meeting sponsored by Latin American exiles in the Spanish Athenaeum. That gathering "was a veritable communion of spirits and the promise of an American future; the greatest homage lay in its simplicity, because it wasn't just a Cuban tribute to our fallen. The event was very heartening as it was spontaneously organized by young Americans from different countries currently suffering the rigors of despotism. Everyone had July 26 as their own date. Seated next to us on the platform was Doña Laura Meneses, wife of the Puerto Rican nationalist leader Albizu Campos, that incomparable model of selflessness and sacrifice whom somebody called the apostle of the Americas, and whom I compared to a Christ nailed to the cross for thirty-eight years."

On August 1, 1955, Fidel received the first letter sent to him by the leadership of the Movement in Cuba. His reply dated August 2 includes this paragraph, which gives a more general picture of his situation:

"Although it's already 4:05 A.M. here, I'm still writing. I don't know how many pages it will come to in total! I have to give them to the messenger at 8:00 A.M. I don't have an alarm clock, so if I go to sleep I'll miss the post; so I won't go to sleep. Right now I'm going to sit down to write the rest of the documents that are coming out at the end of the week. I've got catarrh and a cough and my whole body aches. I don't have any Cuban cigars and I really need them. This is the picture in brief."

And the closing paragraph, in which as always, Fidel's optimism and vision of the future make him forget the many contretemps, a dazzling song to hope emerges in their place:

"Look: I have great faith, not a religious faith, rather a rational and logical one, because at this hour of tremendous confusion we are the only ones who have a line, a program and a goal. And the determination to attain it or die in the attempt! I am thinking of devoting myself to drafting our complete program soon and submitting it for your consideration. It will be a message of hope for a better world to the people of Cuba and the commitment to seek for it with our lives and our blood."[5]

Nevertheless, Fidel would not break down into impotent grief under the harsh personal conditions and that bitter distance from his subjugated homeland. He confirmed that himself—words upon deeds—three months after his leaving, in an anti-imperialist speech on October 9, 1955 in Chapultepec Park, repeating what he affirmed just one week after leaving Cuba:

"For that reason I absolutely abstained from making public statements on my arrival. Moreover, decency prevented me. One has no right to weep in any place in the world for Cuba's tribulations while there is just one Cuban prepared to take up a rifle to remedy them. If we talked of our shameful political situation, the Mexicans could well ask: 'And what are the Cubans doing?' It's not as if they didn't have any problems of their own! In the most unfortunate of cases, it could be said of us tomorrow that we were prepared to die facing an impossible situation, but never that we were seen weeping from impotence."[6]

Long before returning, he would anticipate it again in a letter to his comrades in the Movement's leadership in Cuba. I have here a beautiful extract from that letter, which encloses the simple secret that led our people toward the Revolution:

"I am thinking of carrying my task in this out fully. In this case I am not referring to writing letters and manifestos from this lonely little room, but to the other that is no less important. I am optimistic that I will carry it out, simply and discreetly. I consider things so important and delicate here that I will endure with resignation the bitterness of this absence and convert all my distress into momentum, into the burning desire to see myself fighting on Cuban soil as soon as possible. I am going to reiterate my promise that if what we desire is not possible, if we should be left on our own, you'll see me arriving on some beach in a boat with a gun in my hand.[7]

LET'S BREAK THE CURTAIN OF SILENCE

Fidel spent the initial months in exile drafting a series of documents to send to Cuba, as he explains in one of his letters:

Now we shall enter the scenario with thousands and thousands of clandestine manifestos every two weeks at least.

The first manifesto to the people should arrive in your hands by Sunday at the latest, via a person of total confidence. At least 50,000 have to be printed. You should have everything ready so that as soon as the lead[8] is made, printing can start. They should be on the streets on August 16, the fourth anniversary of Chibás' death, so that a few thousand can be distributed in the cemetery.

You will also find a 'message to Orthodoxy members' for that anniversary which should be mimeographed, and which I will make one of you responsible for in a separate letter.

If I have enough time, I am thinking of drafting another message to be distributed on the 15th at the Orthodoxy Party convention in the Martí theater, which will be attended by people from all over the Island. This work in the heart of the Orthodoxy movement is extremely important in terms of halting the electioneering trend and to prepare people's spirits for an economic contribution. Above all, masses of men and women from all parts of Cuba will be meeting over those days, and they will be the messengers of our revolutionary slogans. Make sure you take advantage of that members' congress, that you have a presence there, send our most enthusiastic men to give cheer to the revolutionary line, to ask for a one-minute silence for the fallen in battle and to proselytize as widely as possible among the masses attending. Let's make ourselves felt there and on the following day at the cemetery. We have to give faith of life and incessant activity. You'll see how we shall break the curtain of silence and open the way to the new strategy.

The second manifesto will be a criticism of earlier tactics and a vehicle for launching the first slogans of insurrection and a general strike.

The third manifesto, which will come out in early September, will be a call for an economic contribution, although I will make reference to that point in the preceding ones. By that date all the ends must be sewn up so that the contribution can be made effective, so the appeal can't be launched before then. It is vital that at least 100,000 copies of that manifesto are run off.

The fourth will be directed to the Armed Forces, and so on successively."[9]

I WON'T ABANDON YOU

Ernesto Guevara de la Serna and Fidel Castro Ruz met for the first time in María Antonia's house and a close affinity between the two quickly became apparent.

Already the legendary Che, Ernesto Guevara wrote about that moment:

I met him on one of those cold Mexican nights, and I remember that our first conversation was about international politics. A few hours later —around dawn—I was one of the future expeditionaries. . . ."[10]

Fidel Castro, aided by a small team of close friends, devoted all his vocation and extraordinary spirit of work to the task of organizing the armed group that would leave for Cuba. He hardly ever gave classes in tactics because time was too short for that.[11]

Life was very difficult for the Granma *expeditionaries. Many of them were detained. Che recalls:*

Some of us were jailed for fifty-six days, counted one by one, with the perennial threat of extradition over our heads (Commander Calixto García and I are witness to that). But at no point did we lose our personal confidence in Fidel Castro. And it's a fact that Fidel made some gestures that you could almost say compromised his revolutionary activity in the cause of friendship. I recall that I specifically put my case to him: a foreigner illegally in Mexico, with a whole series of charges against me.

I told him that on no account should he stop the revolution for me, and that he could leave me; that I understood the situation and that I'd try to go and fight from wherever they sent me. The only effort that should be made would be to try and have me sent me to a nearby country and not back to Argentina. I also remember Fidel's incisive reply: "I won't abandon you." And so it was, because he had to divert precious time and money to get us out of the Mexican jail. Those personal attitudes in Fidel toward people he appreciates are key to the fanaticism that he creates around him, where there is a personal adhesion in addition to the adhesion of principles. . . .[12]

IN CHAPULTEPEC WOODS

October 10 passed by silently in Cuba while a third member of the national leadership of the MR-26-7 [26th of July Movement], Melba Hernández, arrived in Mexico to stay there with Fidel. Apart from the student activities where children and young people recalled the date with patriotic fervor, the political situation in the country denied the essence of that glorious anniversary.

A recorded speech pronounced the day before (Sunday morning) in Chapultepec woods, Mexico City, would save for posterity the testimony that—at least outside of national territory—both Cubans and peoples of all the Americas honored the date by expressing the rebelliousness of the entire continent.

That eminent man's first words on that intensely cold morning were: "When coming here to address you, a Martí phrase likewise commemorating October 10, the eve of Cuban independence, came to my mind. Martí said that there was an element of shame in oratory, in these times of an excess of words and a lack of deeds."

A few minutes before, after the band of the Secretariat of Defense had played the national anthems of Mexico and Cuba, a group of Cubans headed by Fidel Castro had placed a wreath at the bust of José Martí; on the ribbon, the Martí inscription was both a synthesis and a reminder: "I am the son of America and I owe myself to her."[13]

WE SHALL BE FREE OR WE SHALL BE MARTYRS

Like Martí in the past [19th] century, Fidel planned a tour of the United States with the idea of linking to the 26th of July Movement all those Cubans who wanted to collaborate and, at the same time, of bringing together the dispersed Cuban émigré community in that country in order to structure a fundraising base. Everything collected in the United States, plus the contributions sent from Cuba by the Movement, would be needed to cover the essential costs of starting to equip and train the group of men who were to enter Cuban territory and continue the struggle.[14]

In the first half of September, Juan Manuel Márquez had traveled to Mexico to inform Fidel of the magnificent prospects existing in the Cuban émigré community in the United States for transforming it into a great support force in the struggle against the dictatorship. Returning to the United States, Juan Manuel determinedly devoted himself to planning Fidel's tour of locations in that country with the largest concentration of Cubans.

On October 20, Fidel arrived in Philadelphia. On Sunday 23 he reached New York by train where, a week later, there was a big rally in the Palm Garden. The bases had already been established for setting up patriotic 26th of July clubs in Union City, New Jersey; Bridgeport, Connecticut; Elizabeth, Long Island and other locations.[15]

Addressing a large audience of émigrés in New York's Palm Garden on October 30, Fidel stated for the first time:

"With all responsibility, I can inform you that in the year 1956 we shall be free or we shall be martyrs. This struggle commenced for us on March 10, has lasted almost four years to date, and will end with the last day of the dictatorship or our last day."[16]

As a reaffirmation of the truly revolutionary objectives of his project, Fidel also pronounced the following words:

"The Cuban people desire more than a simple change of leader. Cuba is yearning for a radical change in all spheres of public and social life. The people have to be given something more than liberty and democracy in abstract terms, we have to provide a decorous existence for all Cubans; the state cannot ignore the fate of any citizen born and raised within it."[17]

WE BASE OUR POSITION ON MARTÍ

The following week Juan Manuel Márquez and Fidel left for Florida. Their arrival in Miami produced similar scenes of enthusiasm as those in New York. However, they had to call a halt in the intensive campaign to respond to an attack by Bohemia *magazine under the paternalistic title "Fidel; Don't Do Batista a Service."*

In his response, Fidel reaffirmed his well-known points of view on the solution to the Cuban political situation, and rejected any similitude between that situation and the one of 1933. At the same time, it was another example of his ideological coherence with the finest of our revolutionary wealth.

"We base our position firmly on Martí's democratic and revolutionary philosophy; the guerrillas[18] of today will have to argue against him, because we propose to follow his work. We are faithful to his philosophy of actions rather than words, because we are disposed to transform into a reality the Cuba he dreamed of, which was frustrated by political merchants, ambitious and bad governments, who in fifty years of republic have only served to enrich hundreds of rogues, none of whom have spent a single night behind prison bars."

At the same time he again demonstrated his acute comprehension of the dialectical development of our concrete reality, while re-identifying himself with the humble classes of the people:

"With the shattering of the nation's constitutional rhythm and an intensification of all the evils of our political life, on March 10 a new revolutionary cycle opened, much to the shame and misfortune of the nation. That has probably been its only positive outcome. I am interpreting the sentiments of the majority of my fellow-citizens by affirming that the people, tired of dictatorship and politicians incapable of redeeming it, are turning his eyes to revolution.

"We are not missing the eternal detractors, those who, by appealing to the most selfish sentiments of the human species, are accusing the revolution of bringing mourning into their homes in an attempt to conceal the real and unanswerable fact that every year hunger, parasites, epidemics and governmental neglect leave ten times more victims than those resulting from the bloodiest of revolutions. And as political intriguing has not been able to do away with those evils, political intriguing is bloodier than revolution.

"To those who say that it is upsetting the country's economy, my response is: for the rural peoples who have no land the economy does not exist, for the million of Cubans without work the economy does not exist, for the railroad, port, sugar, textile, and bus workers and those in many sectors who have had their wages mercilessly cut by Batista, the economy does not exist, and only revolution can offer them the certain hope of an economy that does not exist for them today."

And with another Martí invocation, Fidel ended his speech in a memorable style:

"For a young person in Cuba today the only honorable way left is to join the revolution. I am serving Cuba, and 'those who do not have the valor to sacrifice themselves, should at least have the sense to remain silent in the face of those who are sacrificing themselves.'"[19]

I HAVE NEVER FELT MORE CONTENT

In a letter sent to the comrades remaining in Mexico, Juan Manuel Márquez described the U.S. tour and in particular, the results of the labor that they had concluded in New York. Fidel only had time to add a brief postscript. The text of the letter read:

Miami, November 14, 1955

My brothers:

In New York the welcome given to Fidel was an emotional one, given the crowds and their sincerity. And the Palm Garden meeting went far beyond our hopes. The unity of groups that had been irreconcilable was quickly obtained around the 26th of July [Movement]. We had 5500 pamphlets printed with a preamble signed by all the organizations.[20]

All the organizations affiliated with the 26th of July, a hall was found to hold dances every Saturday to collect funds; moreover the hall has a bar as well, all absolutely free.

In the Palm Garden men and women wept like children, possibly more because of sad memories of the enslaved homeland than the eloquence of the speakers. We also held meetings and events in various towns close to New York where there are groups of Cubans, but all this activity was a prelude to the grand meeting in the Garden.

In Union City in New Jersey the comrades who invited us to a meeting forgot to ask permission and the cops were soon surrounding the place. Fidel and I left by a side door while the comrades entertained the police; two blocks away a car picked us up and for a moment felt happy, for the cause of Cuba was giving us a new emotion.

When the heat was really on and the Cuban consul was trying to complicate things for us we slipped away to Miami, but we left the seeds of insurrection firmly planted in New York.

As you know, we got into *Bohemia* through the event at the Garden and I think that this door will be open for ever. Just today Fidel sent with one of our people his reply to the article that appeared in the last number signed by a gentleman whose origin, nationality and occupation we do not know.

We have a meeting in that city's Flager Theater on Sunday 20, at 11:00 A.M. and without exaggerating or falling into silly illusions we are expecting it to be superior to the one in New York. This will be another motive for perforating the harsh attitude of the Cuban press to our Movement.

Today, the 14th, I arrived at 5:00 A.M. from a tour of Tampa that Fidel considered opportune for the meeting we're thinking of organizing there on November 27, also the anniversary of the [murdered medical] students and the anniversary of a beautiful speech pronounced by José Martí on that same date, with the same motive.

In Tampa we were joined by *La Gaceta* newspaper editor, a great admirer of Fidel and a man of important relations and prestige. Doctors Blanco and Trelles also came, as did a workers' leader of much weight in Tampa.

The plan for there is to hold a meeting for which we were lucky enough to immediately find a venue with a capacity for 2000 people. Previously, Fidel is to visit the cigar factories and the leaf-stripping plants to speak to the workers there before the meeting.

On the 7th, anniversary of the fall of the Titan [Antonio Maceo], there will be a meeting of Cubans in Key West—where this pilgrimage ends for the time being—so then we'll be able to see and embrace each other again.

We miss mom María Antonia very much. We miss her stew, her attention and concern for us, her affection—a selfless and sincere affection—as well as her "heavy-caliber" words that always make one laugh and never wound. We also miss the good Alicia, Carlos, Aldama, and Quelo, who we think of every day, especially those times when his audacious hair creeps over his ears.

We've worked very hard and suffered a bit; in the battle with men there are always a certain number of difficulties; but it's great to be able to affirm that the stimwittedness or selfishness of useless people has been diluted in the encircling wave of good people.

Fidel is happy, he's met many old friends here, and I could tell you many good things, but I'll leave it to him when we get back. Personally I have worked with him in everything and can tell you that we have made a huge leap forward.

My wife popped over here and we spent a week together, she couldn't even see the dove park, because we went from meeting to meeting, and were all happy, but as happiness in the homes of the poor is short-lived, it occurred to us to call and see how our daughter was and they told us she had acute appendicitis with the prospect of an immediate operation. Given that situation she left immediately.

All these setbacks get absorbed though, because the struggle, the desire to be useful and the hope of seeing a free Cuba compensate the combatant for the pain of a father. As Fidel said, I know that in '56 we shall be free or we shall be martyrs and am yearning for the moment to give the portion of sacrifice that befalls me to my homeland.

The note about my residence is not true, but it wouldn't affect me in any way if it were correct. I came with a 15-day permit they gave me in San Antonio and Fidel has one month. In New York Fidel and I went to the consulate or the immigration department and they gave us a few days more. Fidel's lasts until the 20th and mine until the 5th; if we go over that date we'll have to ask for another permit. We won't forget about the presents and errands. We've received all the letters and information. That's all for now and hope to see you very soon. An embrace for everyone from your brother who remembers and loves you.

Juan Manuel Márquez.[21]
Fidel added the following note:
O.K.

There's not a lot I can add on how exceptional this journey has been. All our calculations on the enthusiasm and fervor of the people fell well short. It will have extraordinary significance in the propaganda order. I've launched the fundraising appeals in all the written material. The piece to come out in *Bohemia* will have more repercussions than the letter on the amnesty or "Chaviano, you lie."

On money we have still not a favorable balance. The printing of 5500 pamphlets cost $500.00 plus other costs like sending information for *Bohemia*, etc. which amounted to $700.00. A further 5000 pamphlets are being printed.

That second print run will be paid for in New York. All the pamphlets will be on sale at $1.00. People will buy them like hot cakes. That will leave an outgoing of $9000.00 but by the beginning of December I hope to have a few thousand pesos. Those are the reasons why I haven't sent you money. I never felt more content.

Fidel[22]

26TH OF JULY VERSUS MARCH 10

On April 1 Bohemia *magazine published Fidel's article "The 26th of July Movement," in which he expressed the principles and ideals that inspired the organization as opposed to the opportunistic opposing parties hopeful of a solution through dialogue with the dictatorship's representatives. Fidel stated:*

Now it is the struggle of the people. And the 26th of July Movement was organized and strengthened to help the people in their heroic struggle to recover the liberties and rights snatched from them.

26th of July versus March 10.

For the pro-Chibás masses the 26th of July Movement is something distinct from the Orthodoxy thought: it is the Orthodoxy movement without its leadership of landowners in the style of Fico Fernández Casas, without sugarcane latifundistas in the style of Gerardo Vázquez, without stock market speculators, without magnates of industry and trade, without lawyers and their large interests, without provincial capos, and without political intriguers of any kind. The best of the Orthodoxy movement is waging this beautiful struggle with us, and to Eduardo Chibás we offer the sole tribute worthy of his life and his holocaust: the freedom of his people, which those who solely wept crocodile tears over his grave can never offer him.

The 26th of July Movement is the revolutionary organization of the humble, by the humble and for the humble.

The 26th of July Movement is the hope of redemption for the Cuban working class, which the political camarillas can never offer them; it is the hope of land for campesinos who live like pariahs in the homeland that their grandparents liberated; it is the hope of return for émigrés who had to leave their land because they were unable to work or live in it; it is the hope of bread for the hungry and justice for the forgotten ones.

The 26th of July Movement makes its own the cause of all those who have fallen in this harsh struggle since March 10, 1952 and serenely proclaims before the nation, their wives, their children and their brothers and sisters that the Revolution will never compromise with their persecutors.

The 26th of July Movement is a warm invitation to close ranks extended with open arms to all Cuban revolutionaries without petty party differences and whatever their former differences might have been.

The 26th of July Movement is the healthy and equitable future of the homeland; it is honor undertaken before the people, the promise that will be fulfilled.[23]

A CALL FOR REVOLUTIONARY UNITY

On July 16, 1956, the 24th birthday of José Antonio,[24] who was preparing to leave Havana for Chile, Fidel locked up with twenty-six comrades in the Miguel Shultz 26 Migratory Station in Mexico City. Something plotted for a long time by the dictatorship, which included an assassination attempt, seemed to be at the point of realization. Its distorted reflection fanned public speculation in Cuba, and Fidel himself took charge of clarifying matters in a detailed piece published by *Bohemia* on July 15. Never defeated, Fidel ended "Enough of lies!" with his customary confidence and constant optimism, while reiterating a call for revolutionary unity as an indispensable condition for accelerating victory:

"The 26th of July Movement, which has conserved intact all its forces and its spirit of struggle, proclaims the need to unite all people, all arms and all resources against a dictatorship that is dividing us, hunting us down and murdering us separately. A dispersal of forces spells the death of the Revolution, but the unity of all revolutionaries spells death for the dictatorship."

José Antonio, who had immediately leapt to Fidel's defense when the news of both the latter's arrest and the loss of an arms cache acquired cent by cent with great sacrifice reached Cuba on June 21, took up the charge in his characteristic tone of energetic defense and attack in a polemic against Jorge Quintana in an article published by *Bohemia* on July 22.

Jose Antonio's confidence in the revolutionary Mexico of Lázaro Cárdenas for asylum rights was confirmed when, after an intensive campaign by workers, students and academics, the extradition claim for Fidel and his comrades was dropped and they were released.

When Fidel, already released, celebrated his 29th birthday in Mexico City on August 13, 1956, José Antonio was to be found in Santiago de Chile for a continental student congress, which was subsequently suspended. So he traveled north, stopped over in Costa Rica and, in the last week of August, slipped across the Mexican border.[25]

PRINCIPLES ARE WORTH MORE THAN CANNONS

The August 19 [1956] edition of *Bohemia* contained an excerpt of the summons brought against Fidel by Rafael Salas Cañizares, chief of Batista's police, in which he accused him of accepting aid in the form of cash and arms from the dictator Trujillo. Taking advantage of the enmity between Batista and Trujillo, the former's spokesmen spread all kinds of information about an alleged Dominican military invasion of Cuba.

The idea was to create an atmosphere of fear and confusion among the people by accusing the approaching revolutionary explosion of having Trujillo's backing and thus to deter popular support for the rebels.

In its following number *Bohemia* published a letter of response from Fidel that clearly stated the falsity of the charge brought by the notorious Batista killing machine and spelled out his real motivation. In one part of his letter Fidel noted:

"I am one of those who believe that in a revolution principles are worth more than cannons. We went into combat at Moncada with caliber 22 guns. We have never counted the number of weapons that the enemy has; as Martí said, what counts is the number of stars on ones forehead.

"We wouldn't exchange even one of our principles for the arms of all the dictators put together. The most dignified response that we can give to the dictatorship's spokesmen is the attitude of men like us, disposed to fight and die against forces incomparably superior in resources without accepting foreign aid.

"On the other hand Batista will never say no to the tanks, cannons and planes sent him by the United States, not to defend democracy but to massacre our defenseless people. The habit of speaking the truth in Cuba is already being lost.

"One day, not so far away now, that campaign of infamy and lies will have its fitting response in the fulfillment of the promise we made that in 1956 we would either be free or martyrs. I serenely ratify that here in the full awareness of what it implies four months and six days prior to December 31.

"No setback will prevent us from fulfilling our pledged word. One cannot speak in any other terms to a people grown skeptical through deceit and betrayal.

"When that time comes, Cuba will know that those of us giving our blood and our lives are its most loyal sons, and that the arms with which we are going to win its liberty were not paid for by Trujillo, but by the people, cent by cent and peso by peso. And if we should fall, as Martí said to the illustrious Dominican Federico Henríquez y Carvajal, we shall also die for the freedom of the Dominican people. . . ."[25]

THE INSURRECTION WILL BE INVINCIBLE

Fidel and José Antonio met on Thursday, August 29 in the apartment on Pachuca Street on the corner of Márquez, Mexico City. They talked all that afternoon and through the night until 5:00 A.M. on Friday 30, with only one other person present, René Anillo, who had arrived in Mexico two days previously.

Melba Hernández, Jesús Montané and Cándido González also lived in that apartment and the four shared domestic tasks. Once a week they alternated kitchen duties, washing up and cleaning in an egalitarian lifestyle whose budget was eight USD cents per head per day for food. While Juan Manuel Márquez was attending to émigrés in the United States, living in that country or in Mexico, other MR-26-7 leaders like Ñico López, Pedro Miret and finally, Faustino Pérez, arrived over the following months to work alongside Fidel.[27]

The two leaders who met in the Pachuca Street apartment on August 29-30, 1956 in practice were fused by a cardinal objective. Thus tactical differences between the two organizations had no place in that meeting, their definition being set aside for a future extended meeting.

On that first opportunity, in addition to discussing the situation and the diverse factors that could contribute to unity, the conversation focussed on details of the document to be drafted and the urgency of the commitment by the MR-26-7 to the people to reinitiate the armed insurrection.

In the afternoon of Friday 30, Fidel and José Antonio finally signed a document which would come to be known historically as the Letter from Mexico, in which the two organizations decided to "concretely unite their efforts to overthrow the dictatorship and carry out the Cuban Revolution."

The most general explanation for the achievement of that objective was recorded in point four of the accords, in a reiteration of Fidel's strategic plan: "We consider the social and political conditions of the country to be propitious and preparations sufficiently advanced to offer the people their liberation in 1956. Seconded by a general island-wide strike, the insurrection will be invincible."

Forty days later, in the second week of October, José Antonio returned to Mexico to implement the accords in concrete measures.[28]

THE PROMISE TO THE PEOPLE CARRIES MORE WEIGHT

In Mexico City, on October 16, Fidel bade farewell to José Antonio Echeverría who was leaving for the United States on a stopover en route to Cuba. They would never see each other again.

A week later, on October 24, on the same day that José Antonio arrived at José Martí airport in Havana after a three-month absence, Frank País arrived in the Mexican capital for the second time to meet with Fidel over five days.

Frank had made his first trip to that country in August, when he met with Fidel personally and gained his authorization for all rather than part of the funds collected by the Movement in his province to be handed over to the Action Front, as had previously been the case. This led to a method of collection within the action body itself. That new direction allowed the groups more autonomy and rapidity of movement, and more chance of acquiring weapons with greater secrecy.[29]

In addition to the final adjustments to details of the support for the landing plan, focussed on the rebel uprising of November 30 . . . on his second visit to Mexico Frank asked Fidel to postpone the expedition's arrival in Cuba, so as allow more time to acquire weapons and better preparation. However, Fidel's determination to fulfill the promise to the people to re-start the war in 1956 carried more weight.[30]

THE *GRANMA* ENTERS THE HISTORY OF THE REVOLUTION

From mid-1956, Fidel had been looking for a boat to make the expedition to the Cuban coast. Antonio Conde, El Cuate, helped him in this.

Some time later, in September, Fidel and El Cuate met up touring the area of the Tuxpan River, very close to the little town of the same name, with the aim of finding a suitable place for testing weapons. Fidel stopped to observe a white recreational yacht anchored in the river and wanted to find out more about it. When he discovered it was for sale, he decided that this was the vessel that would take them to Cuba. Euphoric at the discovery, he returned to Mexico City to immediately arrange to buy it. The *Granma* had entered the history of the Revolution.[31]

Without losing time, they started to repair the cabin cruiser. It was in a very bad state, due to being shipwrecked in a cyclone in 1953 and left under water for some time. Chuchú Reyes, who only had a rudimentary knowledge of mechanics, received the mission of getting the *Granma* in a condition to make the crossing. To that end he contracted various workers who immediately started work on the vessel. With exceptional tenacity, Reyes completed the task assigned to him as best he could.

They changed the yacht's engines, took out all its useless ballast, and gave it a new generator and a new lighting system. The deck was remodeled and water and fuel tanks fitted. A new keel and other minor repairs made her seaworthy enough to be taken out and tested.

Despite the love and dedication with which they worked, pressure of time made it impossible to do all the repairs necessary, including some really important ones. Repaired with urgency, the little boat was to leave on its historical mission in a defective and unsafe state.[32]

REVOLUTIONARY STRUGGLE: THE ONLY WAY POSSIBLE

On November 19, the press published two statements from the "president of the republic" and the chief of the armed forces, in an evident pejorative emulation. Batista said: "The public order will not be changed in any way by those attempts at disturbance, nor will there be what they have decided to call an invasion. Neither the organization that they possess—of which we are aware—nor the pseudo-military offensive they propose is capable of giving rise to the merest skirmish." Meanwhile, Tabernilla essayed a point of view expressed in more martial language: "Any possibility of a landing as Fidel Castro has announced is impossible. From the technical point of view, any prospect of a landing on the part of exalted groups, lacking in discipline and military knowledge and without combat elements to that end, will be a failure."

However, the real state of mind of the regime's personnel was made clear by a series of secret orders imparted to all military commands starting November 5, which included watching out for certain vessels (the *Granma* appears on the list) and intensive air and naval maritime patrols of both coasts of Oriente Province.

Surprisingly, on the same day, the *Alerta* newspaper, whose proprietor and editor Ramón Vasconcelos was Communications Minister for the regime, published a full-page special interview with the maximum leader of the MR-26-7, illustrated with various photos, by an *Alerta* correspondent in Mexico. In the interview, Fidel focused on four main points:

First.- The Movement would be prepared to waive its position on the following bases: the assumption of the presidency of the Republic by an impartial figure who has the confidence of all Cubans, the holding of general elections in a space of ninety days, an amnesty for all political and social prisoners and the restitution of all military men court-martialed on account of the events of April 4.

Second.- Given the regime's charge of alleged threats of aggression by Dominican despot Rafael Leónidas Trujillo: the breaking off of diplomatic relations with that regime, a documented exposé to the Organization of American States (OAS) and the mobilization of the country for national defense.

Third.- In what constituted a formal declaration of war, Fidel stated and reaffirmed: "If there is no national solution within a space of two weeks from the publication of this interview, the 26th of July Movement is at liberty to initiate the revolutionary struggle at any point, as the only way possible for salvation. We fully ratify the promise of 1956."

Fourth.- And, in a convincing denial of the governmental infamy of linking the MR-26-7 with Trujillo's alleged aggression plans, he echoed Antonio Maceo's position in the 19th century (when he stated that only the possibility of a U.S. intervention in Cuba would prompt him to fight on the side of Spain). And Fidel nobly proclaimed: "But even in these circumstances we declare that if pro-Trujillo elements should invade Cuba in the midst of the war, we would be prepared to call a truce and turn our arms against the nation's enemies.[33]

THERE'S NO ALTERNATIVE, I WILL GO TO CUBA
ON THE DATE SPECIFIED

The treason of a deserter from one of the Cuban revolutionaries' training camps led to the loss of arms and shells and the capture of two combatants.

In this situation the communist leader Flavio Bravo arrived in Mexico, fulfilling an agreement by the Popular Socialist Party (PSP) Executive. His aim was to meet with Fidel to try and coordinate actions against the Batista dictatorship. A few weeks previously, Osvaldo Sánchez Cabrera had discussed similar proposals with Fidel.

The PSP considered such a meeting necessary because, in its opinion, the country's internal situation was unsuited to military action before December 31. It felt that an action of that type was not appropriate at that time and could condemn it to failure, and wanted the expedition to be postponed.[34]

In the PSP's assessment, the economic situation had temporarily improved on account of the latest sugar harvest, but prospects indicated an open slump. The opposition was very disunited; the Party line of a single united front and mass struggle had not advanced sufficiently.

The PSP had proposed a tactic of united mass action to young revolutionaries in other parties until the insurrection happened; and that they should work together, as divided they would be unable to lead the masses.

Thus the meeting was intended to explain to Fidel the idea of working within a united front based on those concepts; to ask him to postpone his return to Cuba; and in concrete terms, to prepare a brief document denouncing the situation, calling on the opposition for unity, demanding a general election with guarantees for all parties and opposition groups, and the facilities to organize it.

In the PSP view, it was necessary to defeat Batista's compromise plan (built on partial elections and an alleged party reorganization), given that it wouldn't solve the country's problems.

The document to be proposed to Fidel would be an open letter to all the parties and would call on workers, students, campesinos, youth and civil institutions to unite in struggle. Fidel would thus head an urgent and final call for a peaceful solution. Batista's certain rejection of this proposal would justify armed action against the dictatorship in terms of public opinion and the people.

The PSP view was that if the expeditionary landing could be made to coincide with a powerful sugarcane strike, the success of the operation would be fully guaranteed. However, the strike could only take place after the start of harvesting in January, and thus it was recommending delaying the date of the expedition from December 1956 to January 1957.

Fidel explained to Flavio that he understood the arguments put forward by the PSP, that the reasoning was solid, but that he had no other alternative, he had to come to Cuba on the specified date, as he had promised the people. At the same time, comrades were being detained. Pedro Miret was already a prisoner, the rest had gone underground, and a house containing arms had been seized.

Fidel also explained that they were under intense persecution and that if their leaving was postponed, he would lose everything, men and arms.[35]

ENDNOTES

1. Mario Mencía, *Tiempos precursores,* ed. cit., 257-258.
2. Ibid., 258-259.
3. Ibid., 259.
4. Ibid., 261-262.
5. Ibid., 262-263.
6. Ibid., 264.
7. Ibid., 264-265.
8. In reference to the typographic composition of the text. *Ed.*
9. Mario Mencía, *Tiempos precursores, ed. cit.,* 268-269.
10. Ernesto Che Guevara, "Una revolución que comienza" [A Starting Revolution], in *Obras 1957-1967,* Vol. 1 (Havana: Casa de las Américas, 1970), 267.
11. Ibid., 192-193.
12. Ibid., 193-194.
13. Mario Mencía, *Tiempos precursores,* ed. cit., 274-275.
14. Centro de Estudios de Historia Militar en las FAR, *De Tuxpan a La Plata* [From Tuxpan to La Plata] (Havana: Editora Política, 1985), 15.
15. Mario Mencía, *Tiempos precursores,* ed. cit., 280.

16. Ibid., 279.

17. Id.

18. Before the triumph of the Revolution, the term "guerrilla" defined traitors to the country. It was the name given to those born in Cuba who made up the ranks of the Spanish colonial army in the 19th century to fight against the Cuban patriots battling for our independence.

19. Mario Mencía, *Tiempos precursores,* ed. cit., 280-282.

20. The pamphlet that Juan Manuel is referring to is the second edition of *La historia me absolverá,* which was printed in the United States and was distributed among the Cuban émigrés at the cost of one dollar.

21. Centro de Estudios de Historia Militar de las FAR, *De Tuxpan a La Plata,* ed. cit., 17-20.

22. Ibid., 20.

23. Fidel Castro Ruz, "El Movimiento 26 de Julio" [26th of July Movement], *Bohemia* magazine, no. 14 (April 1, 1956).

24. That same day, José Antonio Echeverría had just been reelected president of the Federation of University Students and was general secretary of the Revolutionary Directorate, an organization advocating armed struggle as a solution for the Cuban situation. *Ed.*

25. Mario Mencía, *Tiempos precursores,* ed. cit., 303-304.

26. Centro de Estudios de Historia Militar de las FAR, *De Tuxpan a La Plata,* ed. cit., 77-78.

27. Mario Mencía, *Tiempos precursores,* ed. cit., 304.

28. Ibid., 305.

29. Ibid., 308.

30. Ibid., 309-310.

31. Centro de Estudios de Historia Militar de las FAR, *De Tuxpan a La Plata,* ed. cit., 79-80.

32. Ibid., 80-81.

33. Mario Mencía, *Tiempos precursores,* ed. cit., 312-313.

34. Ibid., 314.

35. Ibid., 314-316.

RETURN TO THE HOMELAND

WORK REQUESTED RUN OUT

Shortly before leaving for Cuba aboard the Granma *cabin cruiser, Fidel informed Frank País of his departure via a code sent in a cable in the name of Duque de Estrada. Talking of that event, Fidel affirmed:*

Our idea was to land there quickly, commandeer some trucks and seize Niquero at dawn, as well as the highway, or rather road, leading from Niquero to Pilón; but the way we had to land made that plan impossible. We would have been able to take the Niquero Garrison without any problem, in spite of the forces there being on the alert because the Santiago uprising on December 30 had taken plase and they had to mobilize forces for Oriente Province.

There were tactical questions of how to organize that (the uprising) —two criteria. The Santiago people were in favor of it being simultaneous with the landing. As we perceived ourselves as being stronger in terms of arms and training, we thought it was better for us to arrive, and for the people in Santiago de Cuba to mount the insurrection when the enemy forces moved towards the landing location. But they strongly defended the idea of a simultaneous action.

Surrounded by helpers and some of the men who accompanied him on the *Granma* cabin cruiser, including Ernesto Che Guevara, seated first on the right.

I sent them a cable telling them when we were going to land. Sometimes I've said jokingly that it was the first time in my life that I gave notice of something, because in all these things the surprise factor is decisive. But, acting heroically and out of solidarity in a desire to help us in the operation, the Santiago de Cuba comrades calculated five days starting from the coded cable, taking that for our departure date, because I'd said: "When we leave, we'll send you a cable: 'Work requested run out.' That was the code that we were leaving for Cuba".[1]

SONG TO FIDEL

Before embarking in the Granma, *Ernesto Guevara de la Serna wrote a beautiful poem dedicated to the expedition's leader, entitled: "Canto a Fidel" [Song to Fidel].*

Let us go,
burning prophet of the dawn,
by remote unlit paths
to liberate the green crocodile you love so much.

Let us go,
defeating outrages with our foreheads
covered in Martí rebel stars,
let us swear to attain triumph or meet death.

When the first shot sounds and the entire
brushwood is aroused in virgin wonder,
you will have us there, serene
combatants, at your side.

When your voice spills to the four winds
agrarian reform, justice, bread, freedom,
you will have us there, with identical
accents, at your side.

And when the cleansing operation
against the tyrant arrives in the end,
you will have us there, awaiting
the last battle, at your side.

The day that the beast licks the wounded flank
where the nationalizing dart has struck it,
you will have us there, with proud
hearts, at your side.

Do not think that decorated bugs armed with gifts
can diminish our integrity;
we ask for a gun, its bullets and a crag.
Nothing more.

And if the iron intervenes in our way,
we ask for a shroud of Cuban tears

to cover the guerrilla bones
in the passing into American history.
Nothing more.

Mexico, 1956.[2]

ON BOARD THE *GRANMA*

It rained the whole night of November 24. Rain fell abundantly in Santiago de Las Peñas and in Tuxpan, on both sides of the river. Bad weather. Vessels to remain in port. It will have to leave in any case. It is the only and desperate chance.

A well-built man, over six foot in height, covered with a black cape on which the rain was beating, supervised the passing of men and bundles toward the wooden quay. It was the same man who had left Cuba seventeen months previously on "a voyage from which he would not return or return with the dictatorship beheaded and at his feet." He was returning!

He watched the figures descending the muddy path in single file to the white silhouette of a small cabin cruiser, which nobody knew could swallow up so many men until the eighty-second boarded.

The engines purred. The moorings were loosened. The cabin cruiser separated itself from the dock. Its lights were turned off.

Half an hour later, escaping the vigilance of the maritime post, the prow broke against the first waves in the Gulf of Mexico and, with them, the national anthem of their homeland in the breasts of the men. The far-distant motherland, but so close that they carried it in their hearts.

Half an hour before, on the quay, four people watched the cabin cruiser melt into the distance. Standing beside Cuate Conde and Piedad Solís, seeing the white silhouette shrinking as if it was rapidly becoming one with the night and the rain, Melba Hernández asked: "What's the time?" It was Alfonso Gutiérrez who answered: "12:20 A.M."

Midnight. A new day was beginning. A new date for history began twenty minutes ago: November 25, 1956, the day the *Granma* left Mexico. . . .[3]

When the cabin cruiser reached a suitable distance from land, the lights were switched on. Intensely moved, all the expeditionaries sang the national anthem and the "26th of July March." When they were over, the cries of "Long live the Revolution!" and "Down with the Batista dictatorship!" fused with the roaring of the wind.[4]

During the crossing, Fidel utilized the yacht's port side as a firing range for adjusting the gun sights. He placed a dartboard in the prow and fired at it from the stern. As always, the leader of the 26th of July Movement took care of any detail that could influence the success of the revolutionary undertaking.[5]

During the day of November 30, the *Granma* maintained its course headed for the Grand Cayman. Early in a sunny morning with good visibility, the cabin cruiser crossed paths with a merchant ship. In the end it didn't arouse suspicions, as all the combatants hid and only the crew was visible. At midday the *Granma* radio began to pick up information on an uprising in Santiago de Cuba. With that news and visibly put out at the length of the crossing, Fidel commented to Faustino Pérez: "I wish I had the faculty of flying."[6]

While the forces of the dictatorship were dispatching orders to localize and capture the cabin cruiser, *Granma* was navigating to the south of Little Cayman and Brac Cayman, about five to six miles from the coast. In the afternoon of December 1, the maximum leader of the 26th of July Movement addressed all the expeditionaries to inform them that the landing would be at a point close to the town of Niquero, in southern Oriente Province. At the same time he outlined the military organization and structure of the expeditionary contingent.[7]

Having informed them of the troop structure, Fidel himself proceeded to hand out weapons to the combatants. The best, almost all automatic weapons, he gave to the vanguard detachment. . . . The radio equipment consisted of a receptor plant and a portable Walkie-talkie. The campaign wear, distributed some days previously, consisted of a backpack, a pair of boots, two olive-green uniforms and a beret for each combatant.

All of them put on their uniforms and threw the clothes they had been wearing up until then overboard.

On leaving Brac Cayman behind, the *Granma* was set on course for Cruz Cape. That night at sea was rough, and large waves covered the prow of the cabin cruiser, which advanced slowly. As landing was imminent, nobody slept on board. Roque the pilot and Mejías at the wheel constantly went up to and down from the cabin roof in an attempt to locate the Cruz Cape lighthouse on the horizon. They knew that the coast was close, and were navigating in the dark to avoid any encounter with naval patrol units.

At around 1:00 A.M. on December 2, pilot Roberto Roque fell overboard. He was scanning the horizon from the command cabin roof when the vessel was tossed by a powerful wave. At the cry of "Man overboard!" Fidel gave orders to stop the cabin cruiser and maneuver until the comrade was rescued. For almost an hour the boat turned time and time again on its course, but bad weather and the total darkness made it impossible to find Roque. He was already given up for lost when Fidel ordered a final effort: the yacht turned again and, with the help of a lantern, everybody scrutinized the waves in search of their lost comrade. Shortly afterwards a distant voice was heard responding to the expeditionaries' shouts. The weak cries of pilot Roque guided the vessel to him. His comrades threw him a line and, with much effort, they managed to get him on board, provoking jubilation among all the combatants. While Che Guevara and Faustino Pérez attended to the nearly drowned Roque, in their joy at the rescue some of the others shouted out: "Long live free Cuba!"[8]

IN THAT DIRECTION, UNTIL WE RUN AGROUND

Years later, answering a journalist's questions, Fidel confided:
You can't imagine the joy on board when we rescued that man, but it must have taken us about forty-five minutes, apart from the fuel which was down to about two inches. That lost time prevented us from making a more exact effort to find the little dock of Las Coloradas, about one kilometer ahead.

The journalist asked Fidel if that was in Los Cayuelos, and he answered:
Yes, they did a good job in calling it Cayuelo (Little Cay).

When he said that we had to make a third circle, I said: "No." I asked him a formal question—it was formal because I more or less knew where we were: "Is that the island of Cuba? Are you sure that's the island of Cuba?" I knew it was, of course—we had passed through the Grand Cayman and all that—but I almost wanted him to say that it wasn't a cay, if you understand me, because it would have been awful to land in a cay. But I asked him that question with some irritation and even a certain sarcasm, because we could already see the mountains, elevations and all that. So I said: "Right, point the boat at full speed in that direction until we run aground." So he went in that direction.

Those were the conditions that took us there. We didn't know what terrain it was, but we were unlucky, because we found ourselves on terra that was not firma and our coasts are usually firm, even if they do have cays.

With all the weight I was carrying on my shoulder, I asked René, who still didn't have a backpack: "René, explore," to René Rodríguez, and René, quick, slim, lightweight and always very ready, said: "No, it's all right, it's firm." So I followed, but with that great weight I began to sink, it was a great effort just to move my feet. The rest of them more or less jumped into the water; a boat was launched, a shot escaped; but our little boat was a little aluminum one on board the *Granma,* it wasn't made for swamps; so, with a huge, tremendous, terrible effort we managed to land the group. A few comrades were left until last and Raúl was on board unloading things: arms, munitions, everything that could be taken from the boat.

At first we advanced along a piece of firm bank that suddenly turned into water; but there was so much that we suddenly had the impression —at least I did—of having fallen into a cay. It was already daylight, Batista's planes were searching for us, his boats, and even a boat that passed by saw that maneuver; that was the one that advised them in Niquero, and that's why the planes arrived so quickly.

We were approximately two hours crossing those small lakes before reaching terra firma; you don't know what a joy it was to know that we were finally on terra firma! But we didn't have all the comrades with us, some were missing. There was a group of eight who got lost on that trek.[9]

As the men emerged from the swamp, we noticed the absence of Juan Manuel Márquez and another seven comrades. During the march this group had strayed from the route followed by the bulk of the column and managed to come out at a point further to the north.

While waiting for all the combatants to arrive, Fidel ordered Crespo to go and reconnoiter a house he had seen. When Crespo reached it, he found campesino Ángel Pérez Rosabal, whom he took to the leader of the expedition. When Fidel explained who they were and what they proposed to do, Pérez Rosabal offered to take them to his house and make them something to eat.

In the campesino's house, they heard firing from the coastguard gunboat 106 and the FAE[10] on Las Coloradas mangrove swamps. As they didn't know exactly what type of forces were firing, Fidel ordered them to head for a little thicket nearby to hide and wait for Juan Manuel Márquez and the remaining comrades to arrive. After spending some time there, the order came to reinitiate the march. With Pérez Rosabal as guide the column headed for the Sierra Maestra.[11]

ALEGRÍA DE PÍO

In the early hours of the morning of December 5, the *Granma* men reached a small thicket, very close to the Alegría de Pío sugar cane plantation.

The rebels were exhausted and long days of marching lay ahead of them. For that reason the decision was taken to make camp and everyone quickly made themselves comfortable. Many of them removed their boots and dumped the heavy backpacks to lie down on the grass; other headed for the cane field to eat sugar cane. Not far away, was a dense forest, and a sentry was posted at the entrance to advise of any danger. In reality it was a very insecure place to disband a column, but weariness and the need to restore energy won over safety.[12]

In the early afternoon, the encamped expeditionaries noticed that aircraft had intensified activities in the area. However, already accustomed to the presence of light aircraft, they didn't pay much attention and continued resting and preparing food.

At 4:15 P.M. while the rebels were lunching on crackers and sausages, an isolated shot was heard, but many of them thought that a comrade cleaning his weapon had let it off. The reality was otherwise, the sentry hadn't noticed the dictatorship's soldiers approaching and that shot was the signal to open fire on the revolutionary combatants.[13]

The surprise attack disconcerted the expeditionaries. Many of them returned fire, but the conditions of the terrain and the general state of confusion conspired against any attempt at organized resistance.

Half an hour after the initial encounter, the forces of the dictadorship set fire to the cane field to force the rebels out. Aircraft from the FAE joined in the attack and began strafing the brushwood and its surroundings.

While that was going on Fidel tried to regroup the men in another cane field close by, but there was such a degree of confusion that his efforts were in vain. At that point Universo Sánchez came up to him and they both withdrew to a little thicket at a short distance from the first group. On the way Juan Manuel Márquez passed close by them but was unable to join them. Fidel and his comrade got as close as they could to the little thicket and waited there for nightfall to cross it. At dusk they saw a silhouette coming towards them and were about to open fire when they recognized Faustino Pérez, who was approaching unarmed. Shortly afterwards the three of them crossed the space separating them from the thicket and buried themselves in the undergrowth.[14]

The result of the encounter in Alegría de Pío was terrible; the expeditionary force was dispersed and its offensive and defensive capacities destroyed.[15]

At the end of that tragic day of December 5, the members of the rebel column tried to orient themselves in the direction of the Sierra Maestra, despite their ignorance of the area and the difficulties they were experiencing. With no idea as to what had befallen the leader of the 26th of July Movement, the decision to continue the struggle prevailed.

In Alegría de Pío fate reunited many combatants in irregular groups, while others remained on their own. All of them took different routes that naturally led them to distinct fates.[16]

Fidel, Faustino and Universo spent the night of December 5 hiding out in the little thicket close to the dispersal area, from which they clearly heard all the soldiers' movements. At dawn they decided to bury themselves in the cane fields again and hide among the leaves and straw of the new cane. Around midday a FAE plane reconnoitering the area discovered them and opened fire. After every circuit of the aircraft they moved rapidly; thus they were able to change hiding place various times, literally burying themselves in the chaff and calling out to each other to check that they were all still alive. After the attack they stayed in the cane field until dusk.

When night fell they began to walk in Indian file between the sugarcane rows in an easterly direction; they crossed field boundaries with extreme caution, as they frequently heard shots and bursts of machine-gun fire indicating the presence of soldiers in the area. Slowly, they advanced at night and hid out during the day, little by little gaining ground until, on December 10, they left the cane fields behind and emerged at a place called Río Frío, where they crossed between two points occupied by soldiers.[17]

Twelve days after the Granma *landing, on December 14, 1956, the dictatorship's chief army command decided that the expeditionaries had been crushed, and ordered the gradual retreat of its operational troops.*

At 8:00 P.M. on December 15, Fidel, Faustino, Universo and the other three took advantage of the siege and military patrols being lifted and set out again. They crossed the Pilón road without any mishap and, in a nonstop journey of eleven hours, covered forty kilometers of hills, streams, and meadows. At 7:00 A.M. on December 16 they reached Ramón "Mongo" Pérez' farm in Purial de Vicana. The leader of the revolution was safe.[18]

Raúl Castro's group didn't stop either, and continued its advance toward the distant blue mountains of the Sierra Maestra.

At dawn on December 15, Raúl, Efigenio [Ameijeiras], René Rodríguez, Ciro [Redondo] and Armando Rodríguez reached the home of campesino Julián Morales, who was willing to help them. On his instructions they continued to Luis Cedeño's store, acquired some food and returned to Morales' house. After a while, after giving both campesinos letters of thanks, the combatants set off again.[19]

At night on December 17 they reached the house of Joel Hidalgo, Mongo Pérez' son-in-law, who told them how to advance to Purial de

Vicana. Further on, in La Aguadita, they had a brief rest in Santiago Guerra's house, to whom Raúl also gave a written testimony of their thanks.

Finally, in the early hours of December 18, they came across Hermes Cardero's house and once again introduced themselves as dictatorship soldiers. After talking for a while, the revolutionaries and the campesino established a mutual confidence and the former revealed their real identity. Cardero was willing to cooperate; he prepared food for everybody and then led them to a coffee plantation close to his home. Raúl decided to give him his driving license as a means of identification, after which Cardero left to advise Mongo Pérez, on whose farm Fidel was located. After easily confirming that Raúl really was the brother of the 26th of July Movement leader, they left to communicate the news with the promise of returning that night to get the whole group.

Around 9:00 P.M. Raúl and his four comrades set out to cover the short distance separating them from Mongo Pérez' farm, located at a place known as Cinco Palmas, in Purial de Vicana.[20]

NOW WE'LL DEFINITELY WIN THE WAR!

Finally, at midnight, they sensed people approaching. Under the palms in Mongo Pérez' sugarcane plantation the two brothers hugged each other in an emotional embrace, and then ensued the historical dialogue.

"How many guns have you brought?" Fidel asked Raúl.

"Five."

"And my two make seven! Now we'll definitely win the war!"[21]

In the early hours of December 21 Juan Almeida, Ernesto Guevara, Camilo Cienfuegos, Ramiro Valdés, Reinaldo Benítez, Rafael Chao and Francisco González reached Purial de Vicana. On December 23 Faustino Pérez was given the mission of heading for Manzanillo to make contact with the MR-26-7 in that city. Then Calixto Morales reached Purial de Vicana. Two days later, headed by Fidel, the group of fifteen combatants initiated the march for the Sierra Maestra.[22]

Reflecting on those times, Ernesto Guevara recalled:

301

"Some fifteen physically and even morally destroyed men came together and we were only able to carry on because of Fidel's great confidence at those decisive moments, which came from his strong character as a revolutionary leader and his unbreakable faith in the people.[23]

ENDNOTES

1. Fidel Castro, interview by Martha Moreno, *Granma* daily (December 5, 1996).
2 Ernesto Che Guevara, "Canto a Fidel," *Tricontinental* magazine, no.83 (May 1982), 75.
3. Mario Mencía, *Tiempos precursores,* ed. cit., 316-317.
4. Centro de Estudios de Historia de las FAR: *De Tuxpan a La Plata,* ed. cit., 93.
5 Ibid., 95.
6. Ibid., 97.
7. Ibid., 100
8. Ibid., 103-104.
9. Fidel Castro, interview by Martha Moreno, *Granma* daily (December 5, 1996).
10. Army Air Force. *Ed.*
11. Centro de Estudios de Historia Militar de las FAR, *De Tuxpan a La Plata,* ed. cit., 109.
12. Ibid., 115.
13. Ibid., 116.
14. Ibid., 117.
15. Ibid., 118.
16. Ibid., 119.
17. Ibid., 139-140.
18. Ibid., 142.
19. Ibid., 143-144.
20. Ibid., 144-145.
21. Oficina de Publicaciones del Consejo de Estado (Publication Office of the Council of State), *Diario de la Guerra* [War Diary] (Havana, 1991), 89.
22. Centro de Estudios Militares de las FAR, *De Tuxpan a La Plata,* ed. cit., 238.
23. Ernesto Che Guevara, "Proyecciones sociales del Ejército Rebelde" [Social Projections of the Rebel Army], in *Obras 1957-1967,* Vol. 2, (Havana: Casa de las Américas, 1970), ed. cit, 12.

Este libro se terminó de imprimir en los talleres gráficos
de Quebecor World Bogotá S.A., Bogotá, Colombia.